Reading the Mate

READING THE MATERIAL THEATRE develops and demonstrates a method of theatrical performance analysis that takes into account the entire theatre experience, from production to reception. Beginning with semiotic and cultural materialist theory, the author quickly moves into detailed politicized analysis of the ways in which specific aspects of theatrical production, and specific contexts of reception, shape the audience's understanding of what they experience in the theatre. It concludes with five case-studies of the cultural work performed by a major Shakespearean repertory theatre, a small nationalist theatre devoted to new play development, a major New York-based avant-garde touring theatre company, a British socialist company dedicated to the work of Shakespeare, and a range of international festivals. This accessible volume provides a first-step introduction to key terms and areas of performance theory, including reception history, performance analysis, and production analysis.

RIC KNOWLES is Professor of Drama at the School of English and Theatre Studies, University of Guelph, Ontario. He is author of *Shakespeare and Canada: Essays on Production, Translation, and Adaptation* (2004) and *The Theatre of Form and the Production of Meaning: Contemporary Canadian Dramaturgies* (1999), editor of *Theatre in Atlantic Canada* (1988), and co-editor of *Modern Drama: Defining the Field* (2003) and *Staging Coyote's Dream: An Anthology of First Nations Drama in English* (2003).

Theatre and Performance Theory

Series editor
Tracy C. Davis, *Northwestern University*

Each volume in the Theatre and Performance Theory series introduces a key issue about theatre's role in culture. Specially written for students and a wide readership, each book uses case studies to guide readers into today's pressing debates in theatre and performance studies. Topics include contemporary theatrical practices; historiography; interdisciplinary approaches to making theatre; and the choices and consequences of how theatre is studied; among other areas of investigation.

Books in the series

Reading the Material Theatre

Ric Knowles

CAMBRIDGE
UNIVERSITY PRESS

PUBLISHED BY THE PRESS SYNDICATE OF THE UNIVERSITY OF CAMBRIDGE
The Pitt Building, Trumpington Street, Cambridge, United Kingdom

CAMBRIDGE UNIVERSITY PRESS
The Edinburgh Building, Cambridge CB2 2RU, UK
40 West 20th Street, New York, NY 10011-4211, USA
477 Williamstown Road, Port Melbourne, VIC 3207, Australia
Ruiz de Alarcón 13, 28014 Madrid, Spain
Dock House, The Waterfront, Cape Town 8001, South Africa

http://www.cambridge.org

First published 2004

Printed in the United Kingdom at the University Press, Cambridge

Typeface Plantin 10/12 pt   *System* LATEX 2$_\varepsilon$ [TB]

A catalogue record for this book is available from the British Library

Library of Congress Cataloguing in Publication data

Knowles, Richard Paul, 1950–
Reading the Material Theatre / Ric Knowles.
    p.   cm. – (Theatre and Performance Theory)
Includes bibliographical references and index.
ISBN 0 521 64331 7 – ISBN 0 521 64416 X (pbk.)
1. Theater – Semiotics. 2. Theater – Philosophy. 3. Theater
audiences – Psychology. 4. Theater and society. I. Title. II. Series.

PN2041.S45K58   2004
792′.014 – dc22   2003064048

ISBN 0 521 64331 7 hardback
ISBN 0 521 64416 X paperback

The publisher has used its best endeavours to ensure that the URLs for
external websites referred to in this book are correct and active at the
time of going to press. However, the publisher has no responsibility for
the websites and can make no guarantee that a site will remain live or
that the content is or will remain appropriate.

Contents

Illustrations

Acknowledgments

Like all scholarly books, this one is in effect a collaboration with all those other scholars working in the field, past and present, on whose insights I have consciously and unconsciously drawn. My own particular and most direct debts, beyond those acknowledged in the text itself and its apparatus, are to four groups: members of the Shakespeare Association of America, who have always been challenging and inspirational, and who heard and responded helpfully to an early version of Chapter Six; members of the Association for Canadian Theatre Research, without whose consistent support and encouragement I would not have even entered the field; members of the editorial team and board at *Modern Drama* (especially my co-editors Joanne Tompkins and Bill Worthen); and finally members (faculty, students, and former students) of the School of English and Theatre Studies at the University of Guelph, where I teach – and most especially there to my friend and colleague Harry Lane.

More specifically, I would like to thank my singularly reliable research assistants Nicole Aplevitch, Christopher Tracy, Sheena Albanese, and Patricia Tersigni, as I would like to thank those at various theatre companies around the world who have directly supported my research, including: Neil Murray at the Tron Theatre, Glasgow; Jan McTaggart at the Traverse Theatre, Edinburgh; Diane Garant and Nathalie Beaulieu at Ex Machina in Quebec City; Maria Fleming, Ciara Ní Shuilleabhain, and Ciarán Walsh at the Druid Theatre, Galway; Dyane Hanrahan at Corcadorca, Cork; Matthew F. Gordon, Chloe Veltman, and Barbara Matthews at Cheek by Jowl, London; Polly Stokes at Theatre de Complicite, London; Nick Marsden at Curtis Brown, London; Tim Chapman at Tarragon Theatre, Toronto; Jane Edmonds and Ellen Charendoff at the Stratford Festival

Archives; Kim Whitener, Richard Kimmel, and Clay Hapaz at the Wooster Group, New York; Ana Alvarado at El Perférico de Objetos, Buenos Aires; Emma Forbes at the Edinburgh International Festival; Annie Gascon at the Theatre Festival of the Americas; and Laurel Ryshpan at the DuMaurier World Stage. For permission to publish the illustrations I am indebted to photographers Guillermo Arengo (via Ana Alvarado at El Perférico de Objetos), Laurence Burns, Michael Cooper, Paula Court, Kevin Low (via the Traverse Theatre), Terry Manzo (via The Stratford Festival), Joan Marcus (via Theatre de Complicite) Joe Phillips, and Cylla von Tiedemann; and to Canadian Actors' Equity Association, Tarragon Theatre, and actors Martha Henry and Michael McManus.

I am deeply and directly indebted for their specific and ongoing help and support in this work to Hélène Beauchamp (for her intelligence, hospitality, and friendship), Susan Bennett, Mayte Gomez (for sending me materials on Robert Lepage), Barbara Hodgdon (for lending me her massive files on the ESC, and many other things), Michael McKinnie (for lending me his expertise on theatre and urban planning), and especially Skip Shand, to whom my debts, personal and professional, are legion. I am, of course, also deeply indebted to my always supportive (and patient) editor at Cambridge, Victoria Cooper, and to the astonishing (and also patient) Tracy Davis, general editor of the series in which this book appears.

My most important debts are to Christine Bold, for her scholarly intelligence, keen insight, personal support, and sense of perspective, and to her and Lewis Bold Wark, to whom I dedicate this book with love and gratitude for being there.

Parts of this book have appeared elsewhere in earlier forms, and are adapted and/or recontextualized here with permission from *Canadian Theatre Review* (parts of Chapters Two and Seven), *Essays in Theatre/Études théâtrales* (Chapter Five), *Shakespeare Quarterly* (Chapter Three), *Gestos* (Chapter Seven), and *The Performance Text*, edited by Domenico Peitropaolo (Chapter Four). The research on which the book is based was undertaken with, and would not have been possible without, the support of a grant from the Social Sciences and Humanities Research Council of Canada (SSHRC).

Introduction

In April 1998, London's Almeida Theatre Company staged
a production of Eugene O'Neill's classic American play, *The
Iceman Cometh*, using a primarily English cast, but featuring
the Hollywood actor Kevin Spacey – star of *LA Confidential,
The Usual Suspects, American Beauty, KPax, The Shipping News*
and other films – in the lead role. The Almeida is a small company, far from any theatre district, with a distinctive reputation
for innovative, respectful, and high quality productions of scripts
from the international repertoire, a company that attracts star
actors working at equity scale for the opportunity to engage in
intelligent work on major scripts. After a successful run at the
Almeida's Islington location, the production transferred, first to
the venerable Old Vic, the cradle of England's National Theatre,
and then to Broadway, where with minor casting changes in response to actor's equity regulations it opened in April 1999 for a
limited run at the Brooks Atkinson Theatre in the heart of New
York's theatre district.

In London, and particularly at the Old Vic, the production gar-
nered rave reviews. Critics invoking European modernist playwrights such as Ibsen, Strindberg, and Beckett were moved by the
play's unrelenting focus on "O'Neill's fundamental argument:
that humankind cannot bear very much reality."[1] "Can we
tolerate truth?" asked Benedict Nightingale. "No. Evasion is our
lot."[2] Kevin Spacey, as Theodore Hickman ("Hickey"), came
in for particularly high praise in London, though one wonders
whether it was for his fine acting, as such, or for his being so convincingly American. As Peter Charles wrote in *Plays and Players*
of the Almeida première, with a telling slippage from "accent"
to "performance," "my only reservation [about the production]
is that the accents of some artists lacked the genuine flavour but

this was more than compensated for by Kevin Spacey's wonderful performance."[3] In any case, Spacey "pretty much cleaned the award racks in England" for his performance, winning, among others, the prestigious Olivier Award.[4]

The Almeida production was also warmly welcomed in New York, where, however, it was reviewed less as a play about avoiding the truth than one about the classic American theme of personal freedom. "O'Neill exalts Hickey's attempt at freedom," wrote J. Cooper Robb, "and uses his search to identify the enemies of liberty."[5] Spacey's performance on Broadway, although it was nominated for a Tony Award, failed to win one; and although Spacey was widely praised, his performance also came in for significant criticism for the first time, most notably by Michael Feingold in *The Village Voice*, who devoted a lengthy paragraph to its shortcomings in depth and complexity.[6]

Why should the receptions of this production be so different, when it remained essentially unchanged in conception, direction, design, and central casting? What accounts for such significantly different understandings of the same play's meaning in the same theatrical interpretation and staging? There are, clearly, many things, both cultural and theatrical, that shape what audiences see on stage and how they understand them, and these things are what this book is about.

Among the many factors that may have shaped critics' and audiences' reading of the Almeida production of *The Iceman Cometh* at the Almeida, the Old Vic, and on Broadway is the cultural politics of location. As an American movie star in an American classic staged in England, Kevin Spacey was in possession of a particular kind of "authenticity," and a particular kind of cultural cachet that made his performance available for a level of praise that was less readily granted in America itself, where, on the other hand (as Spacey himself noted), British actors have been given Tony awards, if for different reasons, "for a long time."[7] Similarly, the somewhat jaded context of European modernism may, in London, have created a range of expectations about a mid-century international realist classic that enabled virtually existentialist readings of O'Neill's play. In New York such readings were less than congenial. There, as an *American* classic, the play was more likely to be read as exploring "classic American" themes.

This book attempts to develop a mode of performance analysis
that takes into account the immediate conditions, both cultural
and theatrical, in and through which theatrical performances are
produced, on the one hand, and received, on the other. It understands *meaning* to be produced in the theatre as a negotiation at
the intersection of three shifting and mutually constitutive poles:

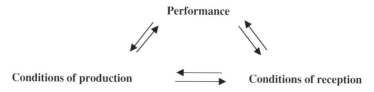

Performance

Conditions of production   **Conditions of reception**

Each corner of the triangle consists of complex and coded
systems – of production, theatrical communication, and reception, all working in concert or in tension with one another to
produce whatever meanings the performance has for particular
audiences. One corner, "performance," refers to the raw theatrical event shared by practitioners and audiences, what is traditionally thought of as the performance "itself." The other two
corners refer to the "material conditions" that shape both what
appears on stage and how it is read, or understood – what has
traditionally been understood to be the "context" within which
the performance happens. This book attempts to flesh out this
triangle and come to an understanding of precisely what constitutes each of these corners, and how they work together in
the contemporary English-language theatre to shape the social
and cultural impact of theatrical productions, that is, to produce
meaning. The book's title, *Reading the Material Theatre*, establishes a tension between its insistence on the materiality (as opposed to textuality) of theatre, and the act of reading, which is
usually understood to constitute what is read *as* text (and is often associated with the interpretation of published play scripts). It
signals at once the non-textual, physical materiality, the ephemer-
ality of the raw theatrical event, and the necessary instability of
the relationships among each of the corners of my triangle. Raw
event – the performance – and the material conditions that produce it and shape its reception can only endure and become
available for analysis once they are together translated into the
realms of discourse and understanding, where they come into

being for critics and audiences alike as "performance texts," and where ultimately their meaning is produced.

The book is divided into two parts. The first attempts to develop and apply a theoretical approach that I am calling "materialist semiotics," one that takes into account the roles of all aspects of theatrical production and reception in the production of meaning in contemporary English-language theatre. Its first chapter sets out to theorize an approach that brings together cultural materialist critique, theories of the semiotics of drama and theatre, and approaches to reception that have been developed in theatre and cultural studies scholarship. Among the principles that emerge from such an approach are the dicta that theory and practice are mutually constitutive, that attention must be paid in writing about theatre (as about all cultural production) to the precise politics of location, and that such writing, too, like theatrical practice itself, is never unlocated, but is always a function of the cultural positioning of the writer.

The second chapter develops and exemplifies the approach schematized in the first through its application to the specific aspects of theatrical production and reception that constitute the corners of the diagram above, while providing specific examples of their operation and ideological coding as produced and read in particular cultural and theatrical locations. The book's method, then, is developed in these chapters in large part through its application in specific circumstances of production and reception, and the book structure that I am sketching here will therefore be more fully articulated as its rationale and theoretical grounding evolve.

While for the sake of clarity Part One deliberately isolates the component elements of both the approach itself (cultural materialism, semiotics, and reception theory) and the production and reception of theatre (training and tradition, working conditions, space, place, and public discourses), it does so with the understanding that these elements do not – cannot – function in isolation from one another. On the contrary, it is the ways in which, and the degrees to which they are in mutually constitutive consort or tension that make both theatrical practice and its analysis so productively complex. For this reason, while the applications and examples provided in Part One are used in isolation to illustrate specific items under discussion, Part Two attempts in several chapters to bring these factors to bear in more fleshed-out ways upon specific productions as case studies. It aims to practice, develop, and test the method that has been articulated in Chapters One and Two with a degree of contextualized thickness across a variety of different cultural contexts and distinct systems of production and reception. These chapters include analyses of the production and signifying systems of a large repertory company in Canada – Ontario's Stratford Festival – and a small not-for-profit company, also Canadian, dedicated to the staging of new work, Toronto's Tarragon Theatre. Also included are New York's Wooster Group, an avant-garde creation company that works out of Manhattan and mounts international tours of techno-postmodern revisionings of American classic dramas, and the English Shakespeare Company, a socialist troupe dedicated to classical theatre and provincial touring that performed in differently coded theatrical spaces in the late 1980s and early 1990s, and entered into negotiations with unlikely partners in the United Kingdom, Canada, and the United States. The final case study is of the global marketplace of international festivals, their fringes, and the companies – including one small southern Irish troupe, Corcadorca – represented at them.

Part 1

Theory and practice

1   Theory: towards a materialist semiotics

A wide range of material factors frame, contain, and contribute to the ways in which audiences understand theatrical productions. This book will outline a practical approach to the analysis of contemporary English-language theatrical productions, one that attempts to take into account what Marvin Carlson calls "the entire theatre experience."[1] The objective is to develop, articulate, and apply to contemporary theatrical practices and productions in the English-speaking world a "materialist semiotics" which combines a cultural materialist approach as it has developed in Britain with theatre semiotics as it has evolved in Europe and North America. The goal is to articulate and apply a method for achieving a more precise and more fully contextualized and politicized understanding of how meaning is produced in the theatre.

Traditional ways of analyzing drama and theatre have tended to focus on what happens on stage or in the script, assuming that theatrical scripts and productions "have" universal meaning that is available for interpretation by audiences anywhere. They treat theatrical performances as the autonomous works of individual creators, products of the determinable intentions of playwrights, directors, and other theatre artists, in which specific meanings are contained and communicated with greater or lesser clarity across the footlights to anyone, anywhere, who cares to receive them. This is the principle on which international tours, co-productions, and festivals function. Most of this work operates on the assumption that artistic inspiration transcends what are considered to be the accidentals of historical and cultural context, that it speaks across various kinds of difference to our common humanity. In doing so, however, such work tends in the interests of what is understood to be universal truth to police the norms and commonsense understandings of dominant cultures, and to efface significant cultural and material differences based on such things as national, political, cultural, and geographical location, together with class, race, ethnicity, gender, and sexuality.

I am interested here, however, in developing modes of analysis that consider performance texts to be the products of a more complex mode of production that is rooted, as is all cultural production, in specific and determinate social and cultural contexts. I would like to consider theatrical performances as cultural productions which serve specific cultural and theatrical communities at particular historical moments as sites for the negotiation, transmission, and transformation of cultural values, the products of their own place and time that are nevertheless productive of social and historical reification or change. I want, that is, to look at the ways in which versions of society, history, nationality, ethnicity, class, race, gender, sexuality, ability, or other social identities can be both instantiated and contested, to different degrees, in a given performance text. And I want to look at the degrees to which the transgressive or transformative potential of a particular script or production functions on a continuum from radical intervention and social transformation to radical containment (that is, the control of transgressive elements in society in the interests of the reproduction of the dominant order). Which end of this continuum each production tends towards will depend, in part, on the material conditions, both theatrical and cultural, within and through which it is produced and received, conditions which function as its political unconscious, speaking through the performance text whatever its manifest content or intent.

My focus, then, is on the ways in which the cultural and ideological work done by a particular production may be seen to have been mediated by the cultural and, particularly, theatrical conditions through which it has been produced by theatre workers, and through which its meaning is produced (as opposed to being merely received, or interpreted) by theatre audiences. Included in this project are considerations of such things as, on the one hand, the conditions of theatrical production, which include the training, traditions, and practices of directing, acting, design, and technical theatre, as well as such working conditions as the institutional and professional structures of theatrical organization and funding, the structures of stage architecture, rehearsal and backstage space, and venue, and the histories, mandates, and programming of producing theatres. They also include conditions of reception such as the spatial geographies of theatrical location, neighborhood, auditorium, and audience amenities, and the public discourses of the producing theatres, including publicity materials, programs and posters, previews, reviews, and the discourses of celebrity. Each of these conditions, to varying degrees in each instance, can involve its own internal contradictions, reinforcing or undermining particular significances or systems of signification; together they relate to one another in varying degrees of congruence or conflict, and these contradictions and conflicts can provide the opportunity for a range of contestatory or resistant readings. And, of course, all of these conditions function within larger social, cultural, and historical contexts, as meaning is shaped directly, performance by performance, by the local, regional, national and global events of the moment.

1. Materialism and semiotics

In trying to develop a mode of performance analysis for contemporary theatre in English, a materialist semiotics that accommodates different social, cultural, and theatrical modes of both producing and receiving theatrical productions, I am attempting to bring two established theoretical approaches productively to bear on one another. On the one hand, the reading practices loosely gathered together under the name "cultural materialism"[2] provide a model for locating cultural production – including the production of theatre – within its historical, cultural, and material contexts, and for the politically engaged analysis of *how meaning is produced* within what Antonio Gramsci, who might be considered the patron saint of cultural materialism, called "the theatre industry" as early as 1917.[3] Cultural materialists, however, have only rarely focused since Gramsci on the specific practices and conditions of production in the contemporary theatre, and, as Keirnan Ryan points out, they have rarely managed to model practices of "really close reading" of particular theatrical productions in particular places.[4] Theatre semiotics, on the other hand, which emerged in Prague in the 1930s and re-emerged in Europe in the 1960s, 70s, and 80s as an attempt to systematize the reading of theatrical codes, has largely fallen into disfavour, primarily because of its increasingly scientific and taxonomic focus on the interaction of different signifying *systems* in the theatre:[5] in its increasing concern with the systematic identification of intersecting signifying *categories*, it, too, failed to provide a practical model for the close reading of specific and culturally located performances. Taken together, however, informed by work done in cultural studies and theatre studies on the reception of media and theatrical productions,[6] and applied to specific productions thickly described – that is, described in rich and fully contextualized detail, taking their larger function within their own cultures into account[7] – the two approaches can inform a materialist semiotics that can illuminate the cultural work done by particular productions. Through a combination of theoretical rigour and located reading, they can provide a model for site-specific performance analysis that takes into account the specifics and politics of location.

2.   Cultural materialism

The principles of the type of analysis that has become known as "cultural materialism" are succinctly outlined by Jonathan Dollimore and Alan Sinfield in their brief general editors' foreword to the 1980s series "Cultural Politics," published by Manchester University Press, and the articulation of the broad project remains, in spite of subsequent developments and refinements, fundamentally valuable and intact.[8] Defining "cultural" in the analytical, anthropological sense as "the whole system of significations by which a society or a section of it understands itself and its relations with the world," and "materialism," in opposition to "idealism," as an insistence "that culture does not (cannot) transcend the material forces and relations of production," Dollimore and Sinfield outline an approach that "sees texts [including, here, performances] as inseparable from the conditions of their production and reception in history; as involved, necessarily, in the making of cultural meanings which are always, finally, political meanings" (ix). "Cultural materialism does not pretend," they insist, "to political neutrality":

[It] does not . . . attempt to mystify its perspective as the natural or obvious interpretation of an allegedly given textual fact. On the contrary, it registers its commitment to the transformation of a social order that exploits people on the grounds of race, gender, sexuality, and class. (x)

Cultural materialism, then, is explicitly concerned with resisting interpretative discourses of the universal and individual, and in paying rigorous attention rather to the realms of the historical and the social, which are, as Sinfield notes, "where meaning is made by people together in determinate conditions and where it might be contested."[9]

In the introduction to his book-length analysis of the theory and practice of cultural materialism, Scott Wilson follows Dollimore and Sinfield in structuring his argument around "the four elements that, in uneasy alliance and fluctuating variation, make up the main strands of cultural materialist practice: *historical context, theoretical method, political commitment,* and *textual analysis,*"[10] and it is these "elements" that provide the frame for my own approach. "Historical context," Dollimore and Sinfield explain, "undermines the transcendent significance traditionally accorded to the literary text and allows us to recover its histories" (vii). But while cultural materialists have tended to focus on the historical contexts for the study of cultural productions of the past, most notably the early modern period and the late nineteenth century, my own focus here is on historicizing the here and now, and on resisting historical teleologies, myths of progress that see the present as the natural state of things, the logical culmination of historical evolutionary development. To historicize the present does involve undermining claims for transcendent significance, but it also involves resisting any naturalized understanding of the writing of history as the construction (and completion) of the justificatory autobiographical narratives of nation and community, masked as the objective or transparent recording of historical fact.

Part of this historical project involves the development of a *theoretical method,* or critical and methodological self-consciousness, in which the critic is her- or himself explicitly located and implicated in history. The critic, that is, consciously brings something – an approach, a politics, a purposefulness, or a way of thinking other than supposed objectivity and neutrality – to the object of analysis. And cultural productions therefore exist and perform their work in a shifting and unstable relationship to the critic, whose position, like that of the work itself, is shaped by social, historical, and cultural determinants. "Theoretical method detaches the text from immanent criticism which seeks only to reproduce it in its own terms," Dollimore and Sinfield argue (vii), and it simultaneously constructs a critical (as well as social and historical) framework from which to engage the text or performance. The critic, therefore, must necessarily locate him- or herself historically, and must acknowledge a lack of critical objectivity, a *political commitment* which, for the cultural materialist, is necessarily a commitment to the transformation of the social order. Convinced that cultural productions, both theatrical and theoretical (or critical), "have a material function within contemporary power structures" and "behave in a direct and meaningful way within contemporary social and political formations," as John Brannigan says, cultural materialists work to expose "cracks and contradictions in the system to allow for some oppositional intervention."[11]

The final element in Dollimore and Sinfield's formulation, "textual analysis," which they say "locates the critique of traditional approaches where it cannot be ignored" (vii), is one to which the practice, as opposed to the theory, of cultural materialism has demonstrated a somewhat intermittent commitment, often focusing more on context than text, more on the politics of (selective) representation than on detailed analysis. As Wilson argues, "[s]ince cultural materialism has now little institutional need or desire to court the attention of close readers, the commitment to 'textual analysis' has waned."[12] I am interested in this aspect of the approach here, however, because I am attempting to determine precisely what cultural work specific theatrical productions *do*. I am attempting to develop a method that brings the analysis of the material conditions for the production of meaning to bear on the close reading of specific performances in the contemporary theatre. Such a method understands the entire theatrical experience as a "reading formation," in which "neither text nor context," as Tony Bennett says, "are conceivable as entities separable from one another."[13] In any case, in theatre as "reading formation" the problem of textual analysis is complicated by the nature of the "object of study," which may or may not, strictly understood, *be* "textual," and which functions at the intersection of a wide range of fleeting, unstable, and impermanent visual, aural, and verbal signifying systems. The theatrical "reading formation," then, becomes "text" – or "performance text" – only as it is translated from raw event into discourse by criticism (including the spectators' recollected experience) as the *constructed* object of analysis – what I have therefore chosen in my title to call "reading."

3.   The semiotics of drama and theatre

Which brings me to the subject of theatre semiotics. As Ian Watson has noted, the "concept of performance as text, and its implication that there is an act of reading involved in theatrical production, has its roots in literary semiotics."[14] Semiotics emerged early in the twentieth century from the work of Swiss linguist Ferdinand de Saussure and American philosopher Charles Peirce, whose work concerned itself with developing "a science dedicated to the study of the production of meaning in society" and was "equally concerned with processes of *signification* and with those of *communication*."[15] Saussure's primary contributions were to provide an analysis of the sign itself, the basic unit of communication, as consisting of a material *signifier*, on the one hand (such as the letters or sounds that constitute a written or spoken word), and on the other a *signified*, or mental concept; and to provide an understanding of *sign systems*, such as languages, from which individual *utterances* derive their meaning relationally. Crucially, as Elaine Aston and George Savona indicate, "the two sides of the linguistic sign are arbitrary, which enables language to be a self-regulating, abstract system, capable of transformation. It is through the interplay of similarities and differences between signifiers that meaning is created."[16] Peirce, on the other hand, and crucially in the development of a not narrowly textual theatre semiotics, classified sign-functions in three categories: *iconic* (indicating a sign that is linked to its object through similarity, as in a photograph, or in the use of a chair on the stage to represent a chair in the fictional world); *indexical* (denoting a sign that indicates, or points toward its object as smoke does to fire, or a knock on the door does to the presence of a visitor); and *symbolic* (indicating a sign that is linked to its object through convention alone).[17]

The application of these theories to the theatre as a sign system emerged in the 1930s and 40s through the work of the Prague School, where the principle was established that everything within the theatrical frame is a sign, that within that frame each of these signs acquires significance *as* a sign that it does not have in everyday life, and that together these signs constitute a complex and elusive symbiosis. Roland Barthes later labeled this symbiosis that uniquely constitutes the theatre "a kind of cybernetic machine," "a density of signs" that Watson refers to as "a complex ostension of interrelated visual and aural images."[18] Not surprisingly perhaps, much of the activity of theatre semioticians in the 1960s, 70s, and 80s involved the identification and classification of the various interconnected "languages of the stage," as scholars categorized and classified signs relating to text, *mise en scène*, character, actor, gesture, space, design, structure, context, and intertext, and established the principle of reading performances as *texts* (rather than simply as the more-or-less ephemeral *interpretations* of dramatic texts, or scripts). This work also included, crucially, in the work of Marco de Marinis, the establishing of the difference between the theatrical performance as event and the "performance text." The latter was understood by de Marinis as the activity of the critic, or reader, in (re)constructing the performance, translating it into the frame of another discourse and rendering it legible ("readable") and mobile – allowing it to travel beyond its originary context as a "*theoretical object.*"[19]

Theatre semiotics as it developed in the 1970s and 80s was criticized on the grounds that performance resists reduction to mere textuality.[20] It was argued that the immanence of the theatrical event *as* event, as performance, or as phenomenon, and as received by audiences exceeds the sum of its sign value as text.[21] Theatre semiotics in its 1970s and 80s manifestations was also criticized for its tendency to treat the theatrical event as contained within the discourses of the producers and the architectures of the stage, and for failing to consider three crucial factors: the larger social and theatrical contexts within which performances occur, the semiology of audience response, and the iconic (in Peirce's terms) relationship between theatre and the life (or material world) it represents. It is these last three failures that were addressed by Marvin Carlson in two books, *Places of Performance* (1989) and *Theatre Semiotics* (1990) which, in attempting to shore up the field of theatre semiotics, moved it into productive relationship with other theoretical approaches, most notably phenomenology and cultural materialism. Carlson's work is particularly important to the development of a materialist semiotics insofar as he argued that such things as "[t]he physical appearance of the auditorium, the displays in the lobby, the information in the program, and countless other parts of the event as a whole are also part of its semiotic,"[22] and that these things as well as the events on stage shape audience reception which is nevertheless by no means passive.

4. Theatre audiences, cultural studies, and the production of meaning

Precisely *how* audiences produce meaning in negotiation with the particular, local theatrical event, fully contextualized (what Carlson calls "Local Semiosis and Theatrical Interpretation," in a section of *Theatre Semiotics* usefully called "Audience Improvisation"), has only rarely been analyzed or modeled in any detail, even by Carlson, and this is the role that the case-studies in Part Two of this book are intended to play. Considerable effort has been made in literary studies, however, to theorize reader response, in work that has been usefully analysed, interrogated, adapted, and applied to theatrical performance by Susan Bennett in *Theatre Audiences: A Theory of Production and Reception*. And models of materialist analysis of audience "use" of popular cultural productions emerged from Cultural Studies in the 1970s and 80s in applied studies of audience response undertaken by David Morley, Janice Radway, Ien Ang, and others. The shared assumption underlying all of this work is that cultural productions neither *contain* meaning nor uni-dimensionally shape behavior and belief; rather they *produce* meaning through the discursive work of an interpretative community and through the lived, everyday relationships of people with texts and performances. Crucially for the purpose of bridging the gap between cultural materialism and semiology, these projects pursued the political objective of identifying ways in which, and degrees to which, popular audiences "answered back," activating meaning in their own interests rather than functioning simply as media dupes. Virginia Nightingale's 1996 book, *Studying Audiences*, provides a valuable survey and analysis of this work, and extends its reach in ways that are both fully congruent with Carlson's work and share some of his vocabulary – arguing, for example, that "the audience–text relation operates along a continuum from impersonation to improvisation."[23]

This Cultural Studies work on audience response was theorized by Stuart Hall in two influential 1980 articles, "Encoding/ decoding" and "Cultural Studies: two paradigms." Hall's essays concerned themselves directly with the politics of the sign and the politics of reception, linking semiotics and materialist theory by making connections and observing disjunctions between the ideologically coded material conditions for the *production* of signs and the similarly coded material conditions in and through which those signs are *received*, decoded, interpreted, and used. He outlines a model of production, circulation, use, and reproduction for the analysis of televisual significations in which power relations at the point of production loosely fit, but do not strictly reproduce, those at the point of "consumption," reproducing-with-a-difference societally dominant hierarchies. Crucially for Hall – and this is where his work fits with cultural materialism – that difference necessarily allows some space, however limited and constrained, for use or reading against the grain. Hall's work is useful here for the ways in which, in application to the theatre, it provides a model for bringing together the cultural and specifically theatrical relations of the *production* of signs (what Hall calls "encoding") – which I have identified as training, rehearsal processes, professional and institutional structures, stage and rehearsal hall architecture, and the technologies of theatrical production – with relations of *reception* (what Hall calls "decoding") – within which I have included the discourses of publicity and marketing, the geographical location and physical amenities of the theatre, and the larger and local cultural context (the technologies of reception) – that frame "the entire theatre experience." Indeed, it is possible to extrapolate from Hall's work a model of performance analysis that fleshes out the triangular model with which this book began, and considers a triangular formation in which conditions of production, the performance text itself, and the conditions for its reception, operate mutually constitutive poles:

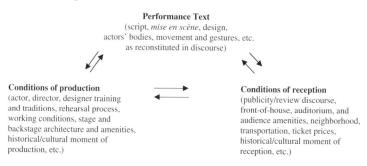

Performance Text
(script, *mise en scène*, design,
actors' bodies, movement and gestures, etc.
as reconstituted in discourse)

Conditions of production
(actor, director, designer training
and traditions, rehearsal process,
working conditions, stage and
backstage architecture and amenities,
historical/cultural moment of
production, etc.)

Conditions of reception
(publicity/review discourse,
front-of-house, auditorium, and
audience amenities, neighborhood,
transportation, ticket prices,
historical/cultural moment of
reception, etc.)

As is clear from this expanded model, each pole of the triangle is constituted by multiple and multiply coded systems of production, systems of communication, and systems of reception, all working in concert or in tension both within their own "corner," and along the axes that hold the poles together and in tension with one another. "Meaning" in a given performance situation – the social and cultural work done by the performance, its performativity, and its force – is the effect of all of these systems and each pole of the interpretive triangle working dynamically and relationally together. The degree to which reception is (pre)determined by culturally dominant contexts and mechanisms of production, and the degree to which resistant meanings are available, depends upon the amount of productive tension and slippage within and among the corners.

Most performance analysis, including theatre semiotics, has concentrated its attention almost exclusively on one corner of this interpretative triangle: the Performance Text. This work considers varying interpretations of different plays, or different theatrical interpretations of a single play, usually understood to be the work of a particular director or company (rather than the production of a particular cultural context or set of theatrical conditions). It most often ignores crucial local specificities of production and reception. But when the Almeida production of *The Iceman Cometh* was read differently by different audiences, fissures appeared, and the divergences in meaning might most obviously be attributed to different conditions and cultures of *reception*. Performance analyses that fail to take these differences into account are in danger of as significant misreading as analyses that fail to take into account conditions of *production*. Reviewers in such respectable journals as *Shakespeare Quarterly*, or *The Shakespeare Bulletin*, for example, routinely compare and evaluate with no awareness of category slippage, stagings of Shakespeare at classical (and classically trained) repertory companies such as the Royal Shakespeare Company with one-off productions by smaller-scale companies with different design and training regimes, such as London's Cheek by Jowl, or by international co-production consortiums such as those coordinated and orchestrated by Robert Lepage's Ex Machina, which has no "home" theatre and mounts productions exclusively for international tours and festivals.

This book, then, is designed to consider conditions of *production*, under the broad categories, first, of training and tradition, and second, of working conditions, within and through which performance texts come into being and make themselves available to be "read"; and conditions of *reception*, spatial and discursive, within and through which audiences perform those readings and negotiate what the works mean *for them*. What follows in Chapter Two attempts to identify and isolate, in the tradition of theatre semiotics, some of the dominant signifying elements in the contemporary English-language theatre, and to analyze them, in the tradition of cultural materialism, as the apparently neutral and value-free but nevertheless deeply coded ideological unconscious of theatrical production. Drawing examples from a range of productions and theatre companies in England, Scotland, Ireland, Canada, and the United States, it attempts to demonstrate some of the ways in which the most common material conditions operating in contemporary English-language theatre tend to function as taken-for-granted delivery systems of the theatre industry. Such systems profess neutrality and aspire to invisibility, but they silently carry considerable ideological weight that can work to reinforce, complicate, or undermine the conscious "thematic" content of the work (and the stated intentions of its creators).

This book relies as heavily as it does on located analysis and case-study work because it is only in its application and in negotiation with specific and located "objects of study" that a materialist semiotics of theatrical production and interpretation can fully or usefully be developed and articulated. Indeed fundamental to the approach is the materialist, cultural studies principle that theory must always be practiced and practice theorized, with theory and its application understood as being mutually constitutive and emerging from particular, local contexts. As a theoretical method, that is, materialist semiotics is differently constituted in and by its different social, cultural, and theatrical applications, even as the method itself differently constitutes in each case the various performance texts that are its objects of study.

The research methodologies that might be expected to accompany such a theoretical approach, however, are more problematic in practice than in principle, particularly when it comes to providing evidence of the ways in which productions have been read, and the specific ways in which the material conditions of production and reception have shaped those readings. This book concerns itself with these questions in four ways. First, it limits the range, not only of productions, but of actual located performances under discussion, almost exclusively to ones that I have seen myself, as a culturally positioned spectator moving from site to site to see and analyze different performances, and investigate them both within their local contexts of production and within various contexts of reception. Secondly, it draws heavily on local reviews of the same productions in different places, contextualizing and locating the reviewers themselves within their cultural and journalistic settings, and considering them neither as consumer reporters nor aesthetic judges, but as providers of evidence of receptions and interpretations – readings – that were enabled by particular local stagings for specific local audiences. Thirdly, the book shifts the focus of its research by taking into account my own, reviewers', and occasionally others' interpretations and responses, *not* as evidence of what audiences-in-general felt and understood – and therefore what the performance "really meant" – but as evidence of meanings and responses that specific performances in particular locations made available. Reviewers' and others' responses, then, serve as evidence of what readings were more or less possible or likely as negotiated meanings for particular audiences, critics, reviewers, and – as a test case across different performances of the various productions under study – myself, as a Canadian academic and theatre director traveling between sites. And finally, as an essential part of the overall project, I consider audiences themselves to be constructed and performed, particularly in terms of class, race, gender, sexuality, ability, and other social positions, by the mutually constitutive technologies of production, performance, and reception that I am studying, rather than, as most social science-based methodologies do, as independent agents operating somehow outside of the loop.

Reading the Material Theatre, then, and the "materialist semiotics" that it articulates and puts into practice, is concerned with the meanings – the social and cultural work – produced and performed by theatrical productions in negotiation with their local audiences in particular cultural and theatrical settings and contexts in the English-speaking theatrical world.[24] Although it employs a theoretical *method*, then, of self-conscious and invested analysis, it does not attempt to create a theoretical template that can be applied to performance analysis in any context; rather it attempts to articulate and demonstrate an open-ended practice in which the theoretical approach, "object of study," and theatrical and cultural contexts are each both malleable and mutually constitutive. What follows in Chapter Two isolates, articulates, and interrogates the most common practices and conditions, primarily theatrical, that obtain in the English-language theatre, and draws examples of the specific ways in which particular practices, traditions, and conditions have shaped meaning in a range of contemporary productions emerging from various national locations. The chapters in Part Two attempt to narrow the focus but deal in more thickly described detail with some of the ways in which theatrical and cultural determinants have worked together (or against one another) in specific instances. I have selected productions from a single decade, recent enough to resonate with the contemporary, but distant enough to allow the cultural contexts for the productions to have registered and to allow sufficient critical distance on my own responses as well as on contemporary reviews and critical accounts. I have quite deliberately chosen to focus on a variety of shows and theatre companies in which contextual circumstances are highlighted in localized readings. This happens either because of unique material conditions of production, such as repertory staging (as at the Stratford

Festival, Ontario), or by the opportunities for controlled comparative analysis of shifting conditions for reception provided by touring, festival performances, co-productions, remounts, or transfers – where the initial conditions for production remain essentially unchanged, but where the shows are read, received, and interpreted in and through different material, cultural, and theatrical contexts.

2 Practice: conditions of production and reception

1. Theatrical training and tradition

Among the material conditions of production that shape meaning in the theatre, training and tradition function as perhaps the determinants least immediately apparent to audiences. They provide a kind of "political unconscious" for productions that is more or less invisible to audiences and taken for granted by theatre workers themselves.[1] The training of directors, actors, designers, organizational and technical personnel in the contemporary English-language theatre, and the traditional practices of the profession passed on through generations of theatre workers, take a variety of forms, but most present themselves as all-purpose preparation for the profession. They claim, that is, to provide practitioners with the full and sufficient range of skills they will need to participate in whatever kind of theatre to which their inclination or opportunity leads them. In so doing, however, such training and such traditional wisdom also most often mask naturalized assumptions about theatrical representation – character, action, focus, and audience perception – that are consequently mystified in productions whose meanings these assumptions help to shape or subvert. This section will examine some of the more prominent training methods (as represented in an informal survey of curricula and texts used in teaching directing, design, technical theatre, and acting in theatre programs in the UK, Ireland, and North America), together with some of the traditional practices learned through apprenticeships and residencies at professional theatres. I will try in this analysis to bring to the surface the ideological underpinnings of theatrical training and traditions in the English-language theatre, and the roles these play as part of the political unconscious that feeds the production of theatrical signs. It is this political unconscious, I suggest, that most often constitutes the cultural work performed by a production, whatever its conscious aesthetic, thematic, or overtly political bent or intent.

i.   Directing

Directors are hired in most English-language theatres, whether commercial or not-for-profit, from among the professional-managerial class, by boards of governors, producers, general managers, and artistic directors, and they do their work within hierarchical structures modeled on the corporate world from positions that might be constructed as "middle management." From this position, directors are understood, at least by their boards and backers, to deliver theatrical productions as "products" for the consumption of audiences who are understood to be the consumers of the theatre industry. These directors are most often trained to function within rehearsal processes as autocrats, creative geniuses whose vision shapes a theatrical production that actors, designers, and technicians – who are constructed in this model as the theatre's working class – are trained to deliver. The standard English-language teaching texts for directing that are most readily available and most widely used are astonishingly prescriptive. They casually employ metaphors of the director as "a good general," a "ship's captain," "missionary," "benevolent dictator," and "guiding genius;"[2] and they invariably describe the "director's job" as beginning by arriving at a single and unifying intellectual or creative "concept" (Morrison, 1; Catron, 8). The director must analyze the script and "find" in it a narrative structure that, as many feminist critics have observed, mimics the male orgasm, one that must include: "inciting incident," "exposition," "foreshadowing," "point of attack," "protagonist's goal," "complication," "climax," and "resolution" (Catron, 39–49). Characters must be analyzed in terms of their goals or "objectives," and must be categorized according to "type": "the protagonist," "the antagonist," "the confidant(e)," "the foil," "the raisonneur," and "the utilitarian character" (Catron, 55, 61–67), all with unitary objectives and linearly reductive forms of psychological consistency. Other aspects of these books are equally prescriptive and equally logocentric, involving such things as the achievement of unity, clarity, and control through the director's "plan of attack" in order to "make the play's intellectual concept clear to the audience" (Catron 8, 9) – though it may in fact be the prescriptions of the method itself rather than the *play*'s intellectual concept that is so clarified.

The directing texts that I am citing, however simplistic they seem, represent what is taught in English-language theatre schools and conservatories, where they are considered to provide "the basics" for directors of any political or aesthetic stripe intending to work in any type of theatre. The result of this training and the directorial practices to which it contributes are visible in many productions in which radical, experimental, or political content, at the conscious thematic level, is undercut or contained by the delivery system itself, which packages *any* content as a product for consumption, and which thereby reinscribes and naturalizes ideologies of consumer society as surely as the packaging and marketing of youth rebellion (punk, rap, and hip-hop come to mind) is contained and neutralized by the contemporary music industry.

There are, however, other approaches to directing, which are usually acknowledged in these same text books through brief chapters about "experimental" methods. Most of these aspire to create a rehearsal process that is open and free of preconceptions, and most of them are celebrated by most scholars and critics. Actor Maurice Good has described Robin Phillips at the first rehearsal for his 1979 production of *King Lear* at the Stratford Festival, Ontario asking members of the assembled company to introduce themselves in turn and say what they thought the play was about. Phillips, speaking last, said, perhaps disingenuously, "my name is Robin Phillips, and I don't know what the play is about,"[3] initiating a rehearsal period that he thereby constructed as democratic exploration (in spite of already having made the major interpretative decision of casting the quixotic Peter Ustinov in the title role). But the prime exemplar of this approach in the English-language theatre is Peter Brook, whose 1970 production of *A Midsummer Night's Dream* and 1968 book, *The Empty Space*, have become landmarks. Thanks to writings by Brook and many of the people who have worked with him his approach is familiar: the rehearsal process is constructed as free exploration of deep, fundamental, primitive, and presumably universal human instincts and impulses that are understood to be transcultural because they are believed to be prior to the shaping (and therefore divisive) influences of language and civilization. Brook's approach is extremely seductive in its mimicry of democratic freedom of choice and its apparent empowerment of actors, who are accustomed to being constructed, in the director-as-dictator approach, as the working class of the theatre understood as industry rather than art form. But, of course, the mere pronouncement of freedom of choice does not level a playing field that is mined with existing power differentials. As is the case with many other freedoms (free trade in its EU and NAFTA forms comes to mind), without engaged analysis and self-reflexivity this approach can serve primarily to mystify inequalities, efface significant cultural differences, and favor the powerful. It becomes clear in reading Brook and viewing many productions by Brook and his followers that what presents itself as free and open exploration in a process designed to liberate actors from their inhibitions often turns out to be the construction of a rehearsal process as "empty space."[4] This "open" process is likely to be silently filled with cultural, historical, and ideological imperatives that "naturally" rush in to fill the vacuum left by the absence of an openly and self-consciously engaged interrogation of the script or performance score. Far from offering unfettered access to universal or transcendent truths, or to a collective, transcultural unconscious, these productions can easily become the unconscious conduits of ideology, and can function, in spite of themselves or the intentions of their directors, as what philosopher and political theorist Herbert Marcuse calls "affirmative culture" – cultural production that silently reaffirms existing power relations in society.[5] Ideology, understood as the taken-for-granteds of a culture, abhors a vacuum, and there is, *pace* Peter Brook, no such thing, in nature or theatrical practice, as a genuinely empty space.

Oppositional directors working within either of these dominant models are confronted with formidable difficulties. On the one hand, they can be discredited by their employment of authoritarian power structures that are willy-nilly inscribed in an industrial model in which they are understood to produce meaning through the theatrical workers under their supervision for audiences constructed as consumers. On the other, their political intentions can themselves be contained or subverted by apparently neutral processes that nevertheless allow the "common sense" of a naturalized dominant ideology to speak through the exploratory process as culturally transcendent truth. Nor are these processes simply functions of director training; they also shape the expectations that actors, designers, technicians and others bring to rehearsals. Any director who fails or refuses to live up to those expectations is likely to be faced with a professionally defensive cast and crew who are concerned to protect their professional reputations in the face of a director who "doesn't understand what actors *do*," or "doesn't understand 'the process'." The company, therefore, in spite of the director's best intentions, retreats into the procedures and practices in which they have been trained, which have worked for them in the past, and which are themselves, of course, as we shall see below, ideologically coded.

This problem is exacerbated by the limitations imposed on a rehearsal process in all but a very few privileged locations in the English-speaking world, designed as a delivery system that is too short to allow for much interrogation, experimentation, or mutual trust when normal procedures are not followed. The process is equally constrained by the exigencies of funding and hiring in a profession without permanent, long-term repertory companies, job security, or any promise of employment that is not dependent, at least in part, upon the cattle market of auditions or the often sycophantic "contacts" and dependencies of what has become a "job market" – with a market-driven need to hire proven "quantities," "properties," "names," or "marquee" attractions.

ii.   *Design and technical theatre*

The limitation that is most immediate and first apparent to a director is the one that dictates, in most of the English-speaking theatre world, a two- to six-week rehearsal period that renders impractical any incorporation of set, costume, lighting, or even sound design into the rehearsal process *as* process, or any attempt to allow the design for a show to evolve alongside its other components. In most theatrical situations directors are forced to arrive at a (single, unitary) "concept" long before they engage in collaborative work with the company, so that they can communicate with their designers, and with their theatres' publicity departments (who need to market the show before it exists), long before they go into rehearsal. Designers are forced, in consultation with the director, to negotiate a design well in advance of rehearsals (or sometimes even casting), and therefore narrowly to circumscribe the options available to actors, who are usually shown a set model, floor plan, and design drawings for costumes – which are often already under construction – on the first day of rehearsals, long before they have begun fully to explore their roles. And most texts used in the teaching of design in the English-speaking theatre reflect, reinforce, and even celebrate this situation. Most begin, for example, with introductory descriptions and illustrations that chart corporatist administrative hierarchies descending from producer or artistic director through playwright and director to production managers, technical directors, and stage managers; on down the chain to "team captains", "foremen," and "heads;"[6] and finally down to cast and crew – a hierarchy that even my own organization of this discussion here mimics and reinscribes. Most of these texts then map the same hierarchies in temporal terms onto rehearsal and production schedules that move from creative and conceptual beginnings involving a *creative* team of producers, directors, and designers, through to drawings and embodiments on the part of theatrical *craftspeople*, before moving on to the final stage and level that is understood as technical application by *workers*. It is these hierarchies and schedules, of course, which are responsible for the familiar "shop-floor" feeling that obtains in many theatres and productions, as creative and onstage personnel position themselves as superior to technicians and crew who in return harbor and voice backstage resentments and disgruntlements.

The most frequently used and reprinted texts on scenography, scene, costume, lighting, and sound design begin with or circulate around material conditions of theatrical production that prevail on Broadway, the West End, and to a lesser extent regional or large, state-funded not-for-profit theatres (such as England's Royal National Theatre and Royal Shakespeare Company or Canada's Stratford Festival) – to the extent that their organizational charts include "Legal Counsel" near the top, and "Company Rep." and "Union Rep." somewhat further down.[7] What is more troublesome is that they tend to naturalize these conditions as simply the taken-for-granted way things are rather than to frame them as culturally determined and determinate, the products of specific historical, political, and economic conditions that function to shape, frame, and contain the designers' work. Also naturalized in these texts – both in introductory sections on the role and principles of design and, more insidiously, in the books' applications and practical instructions on materials, instruments, tools, and technologies – is the role played by design in providing conventional unities and harmonies, supporting linear throughlines, creating spectacle or illusion, and shoring up a model of theatrical performance as the product of an entertainment industry provided for audiences understood to be consumers.

Set design, then, is most often treated as one or more of: the provision of "scenery," most often understood as illusionistic realism, the establishment of setting (place and period), or the provision of decorative background; the construction of appropriate or revealing environments for "characters," naturalistically conceived and identified according to class, taste, and social position; or the provision of atmospheric support or expressionistic reinforcement of what is most often constructed as a logocentric directorial "concept," "central idea," or "theme." Costume-design training is most likely to focus almost exclusively on what Rebecca Cunningham's widely used textbook, *The Magic Garment: Principles of Costume Design* calls its two "Basic functions": first, "Defining character" (including "Setting a character in time and space," "Establishing age," "Establishing the rank or social status," "Establishing personality," and "Reflecting changes"); and second, "Supporting theme, concept, and method" (including "Style," "Color," "Scale," and "Texture").[8] Most of this instruction seems quite unconsciously to accept and reinforce dominant understandings of the role of costumes in the theatre in reinforcing and supporting the "to-be-looked-at-ness" of actors as the object of the voyeuristic gaze of the audience as consumers.[9]

Lighting and Sound Design instruction as reflected in post-secondary curricula and the texts they require share the basic characteristics of scenic and costume-design texts and training (with particular emphasis on atmospherics and, in lighting, focus – colluding with directorial instruction concerning how, through blocking, to manipulate the audience's regard and de-limit their spectatorial choice). These texts and methods tend much more than their more traditional counterparts in set and costume design, however, to focus on industry technology and instrumentalist technique. They devote introductory sections to the organizational placement of lighting and sound designers in the production hierarchy and schedule, nod briefly to the "role" or even "philosophy" of light and sound in the theatre, but turn quickly to such practical topics as how electricity, light, and sound work before proceeding to technical descriptions of equipment, instrumentation, and the procedures of hanging and focusing, plotting, cueing, recording, level setting, and board operation. Many of the published texts in these fields, in fact, are manuals, glossaries, or technical handbooks,[10] and there is a great deal of energy devoted in these texts to the discussion of the peculiar qualities and characteristics of particular brand names of instruments and equipment and the companies that supply them. There are few areas of theatrical training in which one senses so little inclination to question the ideological coding of training that often seems quite comfortable as part of a theatrical industry in co-operation with other industries of its kind.[11]

Actors work, then, not only within the frame of pre-show pub-licity and the audience expectations that it creates long before any rehearsal exploration can take place, but also within concep-tions of their characters that emerge from discussions (to which they have not been privy) between the director and the costume designer, as they work within the confines of a pre-designed floor plan, efficiently taped out in the rehearsal hall by the stage man-ager, which limits them to the space and movement patterns that are thereby made available to them – mapped out long before they begin rehearsals. Finally, late in the process, usually during the last, "tech," week, they most often work within a process in which lighting and sound designers are invited to serve what at that point can only be the instrumentalist or decorative func-tions of illuminating, underscoring, texturing, or decorating a "product" that has been developed largely without their active input – or even knowledge.

However much a director may wish to employ a democratic rehearsal process, then – attempting to allow the full company equal input in the shaping of the show – time, money, training, or experience in "the process" all dictate a model in which a "seminal" idea is floated by a producer and financier, developed by a director as guiding genius and owner, marketed by a publicity department, first implemented by set and costume designers (who have emerged from training and experience that privilege naturalistic, linear, logocentric, and character-based psychological dramas), worked out and applied in rehearsals by actors, decorated and packaged by light and sound designers, built by technicians, and delivered, upon payment, to an audience that is understood, and understands itself to be, consumers. Whatever the nature, content, or conscious theme of the production, *as product*, and as the record of a particular ideologically coded *process*, its central and essentially capitalist message is inscribed, virtually by necessity, within the system itself, and as such it tends to be overwhelmingly culturally affirmative. The possibilities for transgression or subversion linger only in the fissures among the various processes and practices and in the productive tensions that these fissures and fault lines produce.

iii.   Acting

The construction of the performance as either consumer product or empty space is also, and perhaps most thoroughly, inscribed in the training of actors, and considerable attention has been paid to this in recent years as cultural materialists, feminists, and others move "towards a materialist theatrical practice," "performable feminist critiques," or "gestic feminist criticism," to cite a few projects of the 1980s and 90s.[12] The dominant approaches to actor training in English are variations on, conflations of, or mediations between "the American Method" and "the Stanislavski System," and like most theatre training they tend to represent themselves as apolitical, pure, and transcendent technique, adaptable for use in any type of theatre or performance situation. In discussing the Method, or System (words that are invariably capitalized in handbooks), I am using here a representative chapter from Sonia Moore's influential and frequently reprinted handbook, *The Stanislavski System*, rather than Stanislavski's own writings or other more complete or subtle versions of these methods. I do so not because it is the best summary of them, but because it is both widely circulated and representative of how these techniques are most often taught and understood in the English-speaking world, where there is little time at conservatories and schools to take into account the full subtlety and complexity of Stanislavski's own work.

A glance at Moore's chapter "Building a Character," reveals a simplistic, conflated concept of dramatic character and human identity, for example, that is individualist, naturalized, ideologically based, linear, and prescriptive.[13] The following are representative samples of Moore's approach, employing words, metaphors (particularly organic and spiritual), and concepts of character, action, and dramatic structure, which recur throughout the book:

Life will be created on stage if an actor follows the laws of nature. (65)
If an action helps to express the character, it is artistically right; if it does not, it is wrong. (66)
The choice of actions must be guided by the *main idea* of the play and of the role. (66, emphasis in original)
An action on stage, if it has no purpose, merely diverts the audience's attention from the essence of the play. The purpose is what determines the action, and the purpose is to express individual life. (66)
The continuous line of the character's actions, leading to the solution of the super objective, builds *perspective* in a role.[14] (67, emphasis in original)
Work on the role means study of the spiritual content of the play and understanding of the "kernel" from which it came to birth. It is this kernel that determines the essence of the play. (70)
The main idea is the spine and pulse of the play . . . ; the actor must know his [sic] mission in the chain of events of the play . . . Every thought and gesture must be imbued with the light of the main idea of the play. (70–71)
[The actor] must complete the life of his character in his imagination and see a continuous, logical, unbroken chain of events. (71)
A valuable dramatic work is always based on struggles between different persons.[15] (76)
An actor must find the obstacles in the way of his character and try to overcome them. (76)

And finally,

Each character has its own main objective of struggle. (76)

In these examples, "characters" are understood to be "persons" rather than roles or dramatic devices; and following the "laws of nature" is conflated with psychological consistency, narrowly defined, with the pursuit of linear "objectives" through conflict, and with the logocentric pursuit of a single "main idea" as it unfolds in "a continuous, logical, unbroken chain of events." Is it any wonder that a playwright such as John Krizanc complained that his award-winning anti-fascist environmental play *Tamara* was distorted in its Los Angeles and New York productions, and its political implications contained, by "American emotionalism" as inscribed in the work of Method-trained actors who are "so literal [that they] won't tolerate ambiguity"?[16] Is it any wonder that productions featuring actors trained in this approach, directed by directors trained to function as autocrats on the proscenium, "picture-frame" stages of corporately structured theatres, tend so often to function as illustrated lectures, their "messages" serving as the industry's products that audiences can take home with them?

Other modes of actor training exist, of course, and many of these are celebrated by scholars and critics as innovative, liberating, and experimental in much the same way that experimental directors and their empty spaces are celebrated.[17] Indeed, "experimental" directors such as Peter Brook have themselves become directly associated with many of these approaches, most notably those emerging, on the one hand, from the theoretical writings of Antonin Artaud and the physical training methods of Jerzy Grotowski and Eugenio Barba,[18] and, on the other, from vocal techniques developed and circulated widely in Britain and North America through books and workshops by Cicely Berry, Kristen Linklater, Patsy Rodenberg, and their disciples.[19] Most of these methods present themselves as being less prescriptive and logocentric than Moore on Stanislavski, and like the more exploratory directing styles with which they are associated, they make claims to openness and neutrality. These methods attempt in various ways to bypass cerebral, learned actions, reactions, and emotions, in order to "free" the actor's "natural voice" and body, achieving a "neutral" state and providing direct access to purely physical responses to the world, unmuddied by cultural accidentals and therefore closer to a common, primitive, and universal humanity and collective unconscious than are the more prescriptive approaches of the Method. Most of these techniques claim, that is, with intensive discipline to (re)discover a neutral physical state from which to begin, one that is grounded in a human body that is understood to be fundamental, unmarked, a-cultural, and incapable of deception or distortion.

The most actively physical of these methods, in their most fundamental forms as practiced by Grotowski, or by Barba and his Odin Teatret and the theatre anthropology that is associated with it, involve intensive physical training in movement, voice, and skill- or task-based exercises such as stilt-walking, chanting, gymnastics, and other concentrated physical and vocal regimens. These approaches are grounded in attempts to "free" the actor by inducing through concentrated and regimented training a state of intense preparedness, or readiness, through which the body as "instrument" is understood to become immediately responsive, and physically capable of responding, to any stimulus. But, of course, bodies, too, are culturally coded, stamped with learned behaviors, habits, rituals, and cultural practices that are internalized and naturalized,[20] and that tend to surface uninterrogated in rehearsal situations involving apparently "free" improvisation and uninterrogated experiment. "Free" improvisation tends more often towards stereotypically gendered behavior, for example, than does more carefully framed, scripted, or critically self-conscious work, as actors draw automatically upon those impulses and responses to which they have been most deeply socialized. What is "natural," moreover, and appears to be "universal" to an urban, occidental actor, may be quite foreign to a performer formed and socialized, for example, through rural, far-Eastern or Native American cultural, behavioural, theatrical, or performative traditions. The apparently neutral or universal, that is, can quickly reveal itself under scrutiny to be fundamentally ethnocentric.

Dominant theatrical training methods and practices, then, construct the body of the actor ahistorically as a free and empty space – uncircumscribed potential – very much in line with the other empty spaces I have been discussing. But again, like other so-called freedoms, without otherwise directed interrogation and critique this one, too, favors the powerful, and privileges the status quo. Without otherly-directed and conscious shaping, the dominant techniques of contemporary vocal and physical training can simply allow the dominant cultural context, in a sense,

to speak the actor, to "naturally" (or commonsensically) reinforce the ideological unconscious of a dominant culture, thereby
undermining the transgressive potential of any radical or subversive script or creative project.

I have described elsewhere how communist Anglo-Québecois
playwright David Fennario retreated to working with untrained
actors in his working-class community in Montreal after seeing
his plays "improved" within the context of Montreal's "mainstream" Centaur Theatre and the traditional theatrical processes
and wisdoms of director Guy Sprung.[21] It is similarly interesting that the radical director of Toronto's DNA Theatre, Hillar
Liitoja, resists working with professional actors, fearing precisely
the ideological inscriptions of actor training that I have outlined
here. Even within the established dramatic canon, the relatively
short history of successful productions of much-taught and studied socially conscious plays such as those of England's "angry
young men," or of Clifford Odets and the Worker's Theatre in
the United States, or of the late expressionist Eugene O'Neill,
might convincingly be attributed to a failure of training and
rehearsal processes to accommodate styles of playwriting (or
"wrighting") that do not respond to, or are not activated by,
techniques designed to serve a fundamentally naturalist theatre.
This argument is reinforced by the success of New York's Wooster
Group in reviving O'Neill's *The Emperor Jones* and *The Hairy
Ape* in 1993 and 1995, using the "task-based" acting I discuss
below rather than any version of the Method. The English and
Canadian playwright Margaret Hollingsworth hints at this type of
failure to break out of accepted practice in an interview concerning the creation and production at Toronto's Theatre Resource
Centre of her powerful and innovative feminist and anti-fascist
play, *Poppycock*, which was developed through a workshop in
European clowning that, unconventionally, attempted to involve
the working writer in what is normally an actorly process, but
succumbed to the pressures of production:

We got scared and tried to handle the power of what we were seeing
in rehearsal by using more conventional means, which, of course, you
cannot do...We were exploring areas in that rehearsal process that
teetered on the brink of something very new and exciting...But we
simply weren't strong enough to carry through...There were deadlines
to meet and a show to put on.[22]

iv.   Some applications

If it is as difficult as Hollingsworth suggests to break from established practices and procedures at what was one of Toronto's
most flexible and consistently innovative venues and training
centers, the difficulty of mounting and communicating radical
theatre in more established institutions may be considered to
be virtually prohibitive, and it has proven to be so for many
companies. Part of what might be understood as a kind of
schizophrenia in the work of such companies as Glasgow's Tron,
Edinburgh's Traverse, and Toronto's Tarragon Theatres has to
do with a conflict between the fundamentally culturally affirmative training and practices of their directors, designers, actors,
and technical personnel, and their active attempts to tackle socially provocative subject matter in culturally productive ways.
All three theatres are dedicated to the development of national
dramatic repertoires in implicit opposition to the canonical hege-
mony of England and/or the United States, though the explicit
nationalism of each has varied over the years and each now includes productions from the international repertoire. Each theatre also attempts to mount seasons that are socially responsible
and "daring," tackling subject matter that their publicity represents as progressive, provocative, experimental, or controversial.
But because the focus of each is on the development of local
and national *playwrights*, little attention tends to be paid to the
ideological taken-for-granteds of inherited *theatrical processes* (including play-development processes). The result of this is that
provocative subject matter with socially interventionist potential
tends to be both *developed* (through workshop processes that privilege literary value and traditional dramaturgical wisdoms) and
packaged (for delivery through the work of leading actors and directors who will give that work the "best" presentation possible)
in ways that can blunt that provocation and subvert or contain
that potential.

An example is the Tron Theatre co-production with
London's Royal National Theatre, in August through October,
2000, of Scottish playwright Zinnie Harris's potentially scathing
anti-colonial critique, *Further than the Furthest Thing*. The production was mounted at the Traverse Theatre (as part of the
Edinburgh Fringe Festival, where it premiered), at the Tron

itself shortly afterwards, at the Cottlesloe (the National Theatre's third space), and later on an international tour. As written, the script provides the blueprint for an incisive analysis of England's exploitation in 1961, for military and economic purposes, of the apparently "simple" populace, descendants of a shipwreck centuries and generations earlier, of an isolated island modelled closely on the mid-Pacific Tristan de Cunha. In performance, however, this quickly dwindled, partly through the extraordinary and empathetic performance of (Drama Center-trained and National Theatre-experienced) Paolo Dionisotti, to the painful and cathartic tragedy of the psychological adjustment of its characters. The play presented the opportunity for provocative political allegory in Walter Benjamin's sense,[23] resonating actively against the role of Margaret Thatcher's Britain in the Falklands, of Tony Blair's Britain in support of the Gulf War(s), and of the systemic inequities of a neo-colonial culture. Instead, the production played itself out – in the capable hands of a director, Irina Brown (trained in the Stanislavski "System" in Leningrad and with extensive working experience in the traditions of British theatre), a cast and crew trained at such places at London's Guildhall, Drama Center, and RSAMD, and at the venerable Bristol Old Vic, most with work experience at (among other places) the Royal National Theatre, and coached in voice by the National and the Guildhall's Patsy Rodenberg – as conventionally cathartic individual/psychological tragedy of separation and loss.[24] Reviewers praised the production for its "big, majestic structure, and its passionate understanding of what . . . island life, and the loss of it, might mean,"[25] and they (rightly) praised Dionisotti's powerful performance. But they noticed no contemporary relevance or political point.

Some companies do, nevertheless, achieve varying degrees of success in mounting social and cultural critiques by breaking through what might seem from this apparently bleak survey to be the inevitable and perhaps totalizing containments of traditional theatrical training and practices. They do so most often, and most successfully, by being *attentive* to those traditions, by disrupting them, and by probing fissures within and contradictions between them. Two of London's most celebrated companies (Cheek by Jowl and Theatre de Complicite), one explicitly internationalist company located in Quebec City (Ex Machina), and one mainstay of New York's avant-garde scene (The Wooster Group), might serve as test cases in an exploration of the interventionist potential of contemporary theatrical production.

Cheek by Jowl has concentrated for the most part on the classical repertory. The company has achieved much of its very significant popular and critical success, and has directly influenced mainstream stagings of the classics at the Royal Shakespeare Company and Royal National Theatre, largely through the simple expedient of involving, not only both of its co-artistic directors (one a director, Declan Donnelan, and one a designer, Nick Ormrod), but also a lighting designer,[26] *throughout* the conception and rehearsal stages of mounting its productions. Their shows, moreover, involve small, ensemble groups of actors ("we make all our crucial discoveries from watching the actors"[27]), who are deliberately cast as coming from a variety of backgrounds, traditions, and, therefore, epistemologies (ways of knowing). This has led to pared-down productions that are uniquely attentive to the actor as the basic unit of the company's productions: designs are developed in dialogue with, rather than as determining contexts for, the work of the director and actor in rehearsal. And the non-traditional, cross-gendered casting of, for example, a man of colour in the role of Rosalind in the company's famous 1991 all-male production of *As You Like It* (revived in 1994), invites non-traditional readings from audiences thereby rendered attentive to the politics of race and gender construction. This work has resulted in celebratory readings of the company's shows, particularly from an American academy peculiarly attentive in the 1980s and 90s to these politics of gender and racial representation.[28] But the successes of Cheek by Jowl, however important, are nevertheless limited to a considerable extent by the relatively homogeneous and conventional *training* of most of the company, and contained by the thoroughly universalist public *discourses* of the company.

A Cheek by Jowl educational package "meant to be used as a practical document by anyone interested in the performing arts"[29] and made available for purchase during the 1998 run of their production of *Much Ado about Nothing*, includes a familiar – indeed surprisingly old-fashioned – section on "Working with Shakespeare," a brief telling of "The Cheek by Jowl Story" that consists mostly of a list of productions and their related accolades, but includes a statement of "aims" ("to re-examine the great classics of world theatre and to investigate them in a fresh and unsentimental way, eschewing directorial concepts to focus on the actor and the actor's art" [I1]). It also includes a useful section of interviews that constitutes the bulk of the pack: with the director and designer; with music, movement, and lighting personnel; with company, production, and stage management; with costume and wardrobe management; with actors and the casting director; and with marketing, publicity, graphic design, and administrative personnel. Each brief interview addresses questions both of training (or background) and process. Cumulatively they portray a young and exciting company willing to take risks, but one steeped in the uninterrogated discourses of what amounts to conventional theatrical preparation, familiar corporate organization and procedures, and fundamentally essentialist and coercive conceptions of creative freedom and universal "human nature." Declan Donnellan asserts that "[t]here's no such thing as *apolitical* theatre. Those productions of Shakespeare which purport to be apolitical are deeply conservative."[30] Nevertheless, in interviews and in the public discourse of the company, Donnellan and Ormrod, often citing Peter Brook as a major influence,[31] claim to work "without the imposition of a directorial concept," and to concern themselves with "what's [culturally] transcendent in human beings."[32]

As a result, most reviewers outside of the American feminist academy have tended to read Cheek by Jowl productions as refreshingly uncluttered but ultimately familiar reinterpretations and renewals of classic texts rather than as political interventions or disarticulations of those texts and their cultural authority. Even the gendered and racially cross-dressed *As You Like It* and its heroine, Rosalind, tended to be read in Britain in ways that downplayed, neutralized, or contained any potential social disruption it might have performed: "There is no question of forgetting that the actor is a man, but [Adrian] Lester [as Rosalind] makes this less and less important as he lays bare the truth of the role," wrote one representative reviewer, while another found the production to be "a wonderfully warm and surprisingly straight production of the play in which the men playing women are so convincing in the subtleties and nuances of gesture and tone that it comes almost as a shock when the artifice is finally broken." English academics were as likely as journalists to deny the significance of the cross-casting. Jonathan Bate and Russell Jackson argue in *Shakespeare: An Illustrated Stage History*, that "for much of the time [in the Cheek by Jowl production] the actor's gender was forgotten," and Carol Chillington Rutter, in *Enter the Body*, uses the production to shore up an argument that the gender of the male actors who performed women's roles in the Elizabethan theatre was unmarked, no more than "an unremarkable stage convention, no more sensational, anxious, or transgressive when practised by the Lord Chamberlain's men in 1601 than by Cheek by Jowl in 1991."[33] As Lyn Gardner wrote of the company's 1990 production of *Lady Betty*, then, and in spite of procedural space having been opened up for negotiation with the dominant modes of theatrical training and tradition, Cheek by Jowl, at least as read in Britain, most often "relegates politics to a small 'p' in favour of the personal tragedy angle" and other familiar tropes.[34]

Robert Lepage's Ex Machina, a production company specializing in theatre, film, and multimedia whose theatre work has included both revisionings of the classics and large- and small-scale original creations, disrupts traditional practices somewhat more radically, but arguably also succumbs to a degree of containment through subscribing to the dominant discourses of modernist, post-Brook directing, appropriative interculturalism, and late capitalist globalization. Ex Machina is located in a renovated fire hall called La Caserne Dalhousie, with no formal performance space and no local target audience, on the scenic waterfront in lower town, Quebec City, close to Quebec's National Assembly but two hours drive from Montreal, the Province/Nation's theatrical and commercial center. While the space is designed to encourage a focus on creative process over finished product, and to free the company and its artists from the demands of industrial productivity – "a place where people feel they don't have to produce to be productive," as Lepage says[35] – it is also conceived as a kind of multinational, post-industrial production company, where artists from around the world can gather (often electronically, in virtual rather than real space) to create multimedia co-productions funded by multinational consortiums and designed for the international festival and touring marketplace of artistic and diplomatic exchange.

The company's roots, however, are local, and its training and production practices are designed to break from dominant industrial models. While the actual constitution of Ex Machina ebbs and flows, with Lepage and a small core group of collaborators remaining constant, most of the company emerged from a background in improvisation, collaborative work, and *création théâtrale* that breaks with traditional theatrical hierarchies and the rigid demarcation between director, actor, and designer that characterizes the bulk of theatrical training in North America and Europe. Lepage himself, who is also active in the design of his productions and often performs in them, is uncomfortable calling himself an "author" or "director," preferring to use words like "conductor" and to describe his process as one of "translation." He uses the first person plural in describing and attributing responsibility for even his solo shows,[36] and he claims that "the people who are part of our company are not interested in acting that much: they are interested in playing."[37]

Lepage himself and many of his core collaborators were initially trained at the Conservatoire du Québec, which tends to focus heavily on physical and movement work, and they gained much of their creative education and early experience working with Jacques Lessard, Lepage's teacher and collaborator at Quebec City's Théâtre Repère. Indeed, Ex Machina's creation processes emerged from and remains indebted, at a deep structural level if not in the precise details of its application, to the "Repère cycles" developed by Lessard out of his experience in San Francisco with the Anna Halprin Dance Troupe and its applications of architect Lawrence Halprin's RSVP cycles. "Repère," which loosely translates as "starting point," "landmark," or "point of reference," stands for **RE**source, **P**artition, **E**valuation, and **RE**presentation. It denotes a process that begins with concrete *resources*, that is people and things gathered together in place to work on a production; includes *partition*, that is "the exploration and organization of those resources"[38] in improvisations, games, and creative play, followed by a kind of collective scoring of the discoveries made; *evaluation*, the ongoing and increasingly precise delineation of tentative choices and provisional decisions; and *representation*, the public performance that culminates from the process but also serves as the *resource* for its next phase, as the cycle starts again.

This process, particularly its emphasis on collaboration, creative play, and cyclical renewal certainly disrupts the predictability of the industrial model of theatrical production that was the subject of my materialist critique early in this chapter. So, too, does Lepage's tendency deliberately to incorporate into the group collaborators from different cultural backgrounds and/or different performance or artistic traditions that can range, in a production such as *The Seven Streams of the River Ota*, from the sculptural traditions of Japanese theatre through the computerized manipulations of digital video to the musical and performance disciplines of classical European opera. But to describe the Ex Machina process simply as anti-hierarchical, democratic, empowering, or interdiscursively interrogative would be disingenuous. This is so largely because of the near identification of Lepage with the company itself – as director, *auteur*, and guiding genius, with a hand in and ultimate control over all aspects of the productions, including the selection of projects that are often based in his own life: although "he denies himself authority on questions of what art, theatre, and life are," then, as James Bunzli argues, "insofar as Lepage himself and his work are one, he becomes the ultimate authority on what his theatre will be" (98). The role he plays as artist figure at Ex Machina, in fact, is fundamentally continuous with the appropriative traditions of high modernism, in which the artist shapes beautiful and coherent kernels of inscrutable formalist clarity out of fragments drawn from the rag and bone shop of the world – including its "others."[39] And his work, in spite of its presentation-in-progress, is most often remarkable for its discovery or construction of accidental, surprising, and unlikely similarities – parallels and *connections* among and across difference – rather than for any quality of disarticulating disjunctiveness.

Bunzli, in the best article-length study of Lepage's *oeuvre* to date, nevertheless sees "déclage" ("an acknowledgement of gaps, indeterminacies") – operating as the subject of the shows as well as the bases of their narrative and temporal structuration and use of language(s) – as "the main impulse, the principle mode of working, and a major result of his productions" (89). But as Bunzli acknowledges, "[d]éclage does not alienate audiences" (95); rather it involves them in a creative process that is less about "communication" than "communion," and that enjoins them "to experience the shows in an intuitive manner" (97) – as opposed to one that is intellectual, analytical, or interrogative. "There's no moral," Bunzli quotes Lepage as saying to him in an interview. "It's just putting people into a bath of sensations and ideas and emotions. And then they come out of it and do what they want with it" (97). For all their productive processual messiness, then, and their disruption of audiences' consumerist passivity, Ex Machina's productions-in-progress, far from presenting theatrical social *gests* after the politically interrogative fashion of Bertolt Brecht, can tend simply to displace their creative responsibilities for meaning production onto audiences with something resembling the familiar modernist shrug: my name is Robert Lepage, and I don't know what it's about. As Bunzli says, "the importance given the object [as opposed to the idea, or word] – especially in the form of the resource – keeps both the creation and the performance away from debate, logic, and argumentation... The resource and reactions to it are dealt with on an intuitive and emotional level, rather than an intellectual one" (97).

New York's Wooster Group, one of whose productions is the subject of a more detailed case study in Chapter Seven (below), has focused most consistently on radical postmodern deconstructions of classic American plays within what are essentially new creations. Although most members of the company were trained in Actor's Studio naturalism and most work regularly in the commercial world of Hollywood film, under the direction of Elizabeth LeCompte they eschew traditional theatrical practices of character and plot development, concentrate on the precise undertaking and execution of specific performative "tasks" that potentially subvert traditional or capitalist meaning-delivery systems, and have lent themselves to politically radical readings by leading postmodern theatre critics and theorists. The interventionist potential of the Wooster Group rests in part with their independence from the mainstream theatre industry (independence which ironically derives in part from the lucrative Hollywood careers and consequently high public profiles of some of its members), and their ownership of their own fashionably downscale space, The Performing Garage in New York's SoHo, the former home of Richard Schechner's Performance Group. These allow them to break with the pressures of rehearsal scheduling to engage in relatively unfettered "play" as they develop their complex projects over sometimes years of workshops, rehearsals, public presentations, rehearsals, tours, workshops, rehearsals, performances, workshops, rehearsals, remounts, and tours. Even so apparently peripheral a project, at the time, to the Group's central concerns as the radio version of Racine's *Phèdre* that they mounted for the BBC's Radio 3 in the UK in June 2000 warranted an extended rehearsal period: "We were . . . very lucky with this," said Wooster core member Kate Valk, who played Phèdre, "because we have our own permanent rehearsal space in our base in New York, so we could really work at it. We had three months whereas if you were doing this in a Radio 3 studio, we'd have only had three days."[40] In addition to the luxury of virtually unlimited rehearsal time (which also, since the company operates as a collective, circumvents various union restrictions), the company is able, almost uniquely in professional theatre in the English-speaking world, to incorporate more than actors, directors, and dramaturgs in these extended rehearsal processes. "What separates our group from others is that all the technical and design staff are made part of the process from the very beginning, giving everyone a creative role," as performer Roy Faudree says,[41] and this sheer material reality allows the Group to have established the reputation of working "better than any company alive on the complex frontier between live theatre and the dominant screen-and-audio culture of our time" – a frontier that necessarily involves negotiating a kind of interdiscursive tension among the different media involved.[42] But perhaps what most clearly distinguishes the Wooster Group from most companies attempting to push the limits of theatrical representation is their approach to the creation and performance of *roles* rather than dramatic characters. Philip Auslander's 1985 analysis of Willem Dafoe's performance in the Group's *LSD (. . . Just the High Points . . .)* distinguishes between "realistic acting" and "task-based collage," finding both in most Wooster Group shows, but ultimately determining that, "[f]or Dafoe, performance is essentially a task, an activity: the persona he creates is the product of his own relation to the 'paces' he puts himself through."[43] Company members continue to refer to their work as the carrying out of specific tasks, assigned to them by director LeCompte in part for the expressed purpose of avoiding the creation of empathetic, three-dimensional dramatic characters in the naturalistic tradition. Kate Valk, discussing her performance in the Group's production of *House/Lights*, has described the sensory overload provided by reciting lines that are being fed to her live through a headset and imitating choreography on a video monitor in front of her: by enforcing concentration on difficult and immediate physical and mental exercises, the technique almost inevitably distances the performer from any kind of empathetic engagement or identification with the several roles she performs in the show.[44] And this plays itself out for audiences, who "realize," as one reviewer noted of *House/Lights*, "that the entire performance is just one great big distancing device, a highly charged mirror image that confronts and subverts the audience's passivity in witnessing such obvious artifice."[45] Whether the audiences so distanced from Wooster Group performances become engaged in political analysis, or to what degree the shows function as cultural interventions rather than simply aesthetic experiments is an issue to be taken up more fully in a later chapter, but the company itself, like Lepage, is disinclined to assume responsibility for reception. Roy Faudree adopts the familiar (post)modernist line: "How you see the play will depend on you . . . There's no specific way to watch it."[46]

Each of Cheek by Jowl, Ex Machina, and The Wooster Group disrupts conventional and culturally affirmative theatrical practice in its own distinctive way, and each successfully shifts the ground or destablizes the representation to some degree. But effective interventionist theatre perhaps requires both a shift in practice *and* a self-consciously political interrogation of theatrical representation if it wants successfully to resist containment. London's Theatre de Complicite, which specializes in the creation of new and often explicitly political work as well as the explicitly political revisioning of modern classics, might be understood to have challenged the pressures toward containment inscribed in traditional theatrical regimens of training and protocol more successfully than most. The company emerged in 1983 from a broadly international group of practitioners, most of whom had training in mime and movement at L'École Jacques Lecoq in Paris, who wished to work in a manner that was more collaborative and interrogative, and less compulsorily naturalistic, than was readily available in the mainstream English-language theatre. Although the company is located in England, its members, who come from England, Scotland, Wales, Switzerland, Belgium, Spain, Italy, Austria, Canada, Jamaica, Nigeria, and

Vietnam, speak, work, and often perform in several languages, working collaboratively across their cultural and epistemological differences in a creation process that is rooted in the Lecoq belief in the actor, each actor, not simply as interpreter but as creator: "someone who is self-sufficient, who is able to construct the scenario, direct the scenario, and act in the scenario all at the same time."[47]

The training that company members share, although rooted in a concept of neutrality that is easily confused with the state of prepared readiness advocated by Brook and his followers, is nevertheless geared toward the cultivation of a purposefully interrogative attitude among "actors who could collaborate with others and become transformational performers"[48] – an attitude that readily lends itself to political analysis. The neutral mask – the centerpiece of Lecoq training – is, in fact, perhaps best understood as a device that, by insisting upon the exposure of habitual responses and clichés, and at the same time in Sears Eldredge and Hollis Huston's terms, "attacks mumble and scratch naturalism" and the appropriative appetites of empathy:

Peter Frisch has described the kind of actor who says, "Oh, I know that character, that character is just like me," when the truth is that "the character is nothing like they are. They see it though their own neurotic self-image." The neutral mask can lead an actor to reject his habitual identifications in favour of a deeper, simpler understanding of the powers of expression.[49]

Empathy is the fundamental principle of most post-Naturalist acting methods, including most notably Stanislavski's "System" and the American Method. In eschewing the capacity of empathy literally to incorporate the other and thereby efface cultural, political, epistemological, and other difference, the neutral mask reveals its formidable potential as a political tool. It undergirds, to a significant extent, Theatre de Complicite's capacity to "escap[e] both the provincialism of the local and the false promise of 'world culture.'"[50]

Beyond the Lecoq training staple of neutral mask, Lecoq's subsequent introduction of "expressive" mask will have fostered in company members at Complicite the discovery of "attitudes," and exposed "the how and why of people's movement." Together with "[t]he dialectical 'countermask,'" introduced as the third stage in the Lecoq process, which "works against the dominant persona [the actor] has developed, so that the character emerges from contradictions and not from social stereotypes," the expressive mask will have encouraged the cultivation of interrogative, Brechtian social *gests*. Finally, rigorous Lecoq training in clown and *buffon*, introduced towards the end of the Lecoq regimen, will have taught company members the capacity "to forge a link between the ridiculous and the rebel, both battling against social norms."[51]

Like its training methods, Complicite's working processes are both interrogative and collaborative – "endless risk-taking," according to Lyn Gardner[52] – and their shows, like those of Ex Machina (and to a lesser extent the Wooster Group), are understood to be always in progress, never allowed to settle into pure, consumable product. According to Rush Rehm, "the company revitalizes the idea of the ensemble – perhaps the greatest contribution socialism has made to the aesthetics of performance":

The ensemble confronts the world of the play first, before dealing with characters and scenes. Rehearsals involve sharing and developing material used in making the first draft, and group improvisations are an essential component in revising the script. When finally tackling a scene per se, the company takes only short stabs at it, with everyone free to speak any, all, or none of the lines. The script emerges, choices are made. But the aim is neither the traditional "construction" of realistic character nor a postmodern deconstruction of the self. Rather, the goal is to draw the actors – their dialogue and actions – into the world of the story.[53]

Although all of this work, again like the collaborative work of Ex Machina, is subject to the ongoing editorial shaping of its artistic director, in this case Simon McBurney, Complicite is nevertheless very much "[a] company without stars," including the Lepage-style *auteur*.

Complicite shuns the *wunderkind* approach to production, where a play is tackled from the head down or the surface out; where personal preconceptions replace the discoveries that come from a sustained and collective engagement with the material; where visual and aural stimuli substitute for the dramatic event.[54]

Finally, the company's creation and rehearsal processes resist any temptation to subsume differences between company members' social, cultural, and epistemological positioning within the naturalized context of its English location and McBurney's own nationality. Not only do its performers come "from all kinds of disciplines and from different countries," but rehearsals can be held in different languages, in order that "you don't get stuck into a very English way of going about things."[55] And traces of this multilingualism remain to disturb the surfaces of performances themselves. As Benedict Nightingale, among many others, notes, "the performers sometimes express emotion by bursting into their native tongues."[56]

Like those of Cheek By Jowl, Ex Machina, and the Wooster Group, then, Complicite's training and rehearsal/creation processes function to create space for cultural intervention, and work to resist the regulatory containments of the contemporary theatre industry. As Rehm says, "Complicite demonstrates that capitulation to consumerism is no more necessary or desirable than the deracinated model of theatrical 'progress' it represents."[57] Or, in one reviewer's words, "What the company is about is empowerment."[58] Unlike the other companies under consideration, however, Theatre de Complicite has an explicitly political mandate, and this would appear to be crucial. Acknowledging from their Lecoq training "the need to continually listen to the community,"[59] Complicite stresses its relationship to the audience *as* one of complicity: "the word 'complicity' implies a shared understanding," argues McBurney, "not only between the actors onstage but between the actors and the audience." "It pleases me," he says, pointing out the dictionary definition of the term and its implications of shared transgression, "that there should be some sense of illegality associated with what we do," which he considers to be "transformational" – a word frequently used by reviewers to describe the company's border-crossing productions.[60]

Indeed, *The Three Lives of Lucy Cabrol* and *The Street of Crocodiles*, perhaps the company's most characteristic productions – both of which enjoyed long life and extensive international touring (to such places as Buenos Aires, Japan, Australia, Belgrade, and Macedonia as well as destinations in North America and Europe more common for touring British companies) – were at once explicitly political and explicitly concerned with border crossings of various kinds. *The Three Lives of Lucy Cabrol* was adapted by McBurney and his collaborator Mark Wheatley from a short story written by the Marxist art critic and novelist John Berger about a smuggler. *Street of Crocodiles* was adapted, also by McBurney and Wheatley, from the stories of Bruno Schulz, a Galician Jewish writer and art teacher who was shot capriciously by a Nazi officer on a street in Drohobycz in what is now Poland, in 1942.

Street of Crocodiles, originally mounted in London in 1992 at the National Theatre's adaptable Cottlesloe Theatre with remounts and tours extending its life to 1999, sets the childlike imaginative transformations of its central character, Joseph – who is at once an author-surrogate and the central character – against the repressive brutalities of Nazism (see illus. 1). Acted in what reviewers repeatedly refer to as a Babel, or cacophony, of languages that include English, German, Spanish, Yiddish, and others, the production's transformative dramaturgy – "transformation is this

1. A scene from Theatre de Complicite's production, *The Street of Crocodiles*, adapted by Simon McBurney and Mark Wheatley from a short story by Bruno Schulz and originally staged in London at the National Theatre's Cottlesloe space.

company's speciality," remarked Irving Wardle[61] – functioned as a record and continuation of the company's collaborative and interrogative training and practices of creation. As reviewers remarked, the show "encapsulates Theatre de Complicite's method,"[62] in which "character is not the point," and "what happens is less important than what it means."[63] In doing so, the production "shakes the readers free of the blinkers of habitual perception,"[64] evoking in moments from Schulz's stories connections with his life, times, and death to history – as when the sacking of the father's shop vividly recalls Kristallnacht; or when the tyranny of the family's autocratic non-Jewish servant girl, Adela, resonates with the dynamics of fascism; or when Joseph-as-Schulz is finally allegorically killed, fulfilling the ominous threat evoked by the opening scene's jackboots and ringing gunshot and, through musical quotation and resonant stage imagery, also evoking Auschwitz.[65] As Rush Rehm remarks,

by this call to history, Complicite contrasts Schulz's liberating animism, which transforms objects into living beings, with its fascistic opposite, a literal-mindedness that systematically converts humans into inanimate objects, ready for the ash heap.[66]

The company's 1994 show, *The Three Lives of Lucy Cabrol*, which has also had an extended life through remounts and tours, is, like *Street of Crocodiles*, deeply grounded in history, and in the politics of its source story, this time by John Berger, whose early version of Marxism is perhaps too easily encapsulated in the recollection that he (in)famously donated half of his Booker prize money in 1972 to the Black Panthers.[67] Berger has since evolved (by the time of his writing of the tales of Alpine peasant life on one of which *Lucy Cabrol* is based) into what Michael Billington calls "a disappointed Marxist," one whose work is nevertheless rooted in what Berger himself calls "an understanding of and desire of solidarity with the less privileged, which is just as visceral in me and which remains."[68] His focus on peasant experience is based on his belief that "the peasant suspicion of 'progress', as it has finally been imposed by the global history of global capitalism and the power of this history even over those seeking an alternative to it, is not altogether groundless,"[69] and on his suspicion of individualism as it has emerged under market-driven capitalism, where "each person's experience remains an individual problem," and there is no place for collective social engagement. "From this primary suppression of the social function of subjectivity," he argues, in a passage that resonates with post-structuralist and Lecoqian critiques of naturalist understandings of theatrical character, "other suppressions follow":

of meaningful democracy (replaced by opinion polls and market-research techniques), of social conscience (replaced by self-interest), of history (replaced by racist and other myths), of hope – the most subjective and social of all energies (replaced by the sacralisation of Progress as Comfort).[70]

Like Berger, Theatre de Complicite "has always embraced a kind of otherness . . . It is attracted to the marginalized and the dispossessed, and takes them into the centre."[71] "They speak for the urban dumbos, deadbeats and dispossessed in a world where ugliness is endemic and dignity confined to the rich . . . [T]hey animate a theatre of survival, the survival of the poor."[72] McBurney describes Berger's method, moreover, in terms that make transparent its appeal to a company with an affinity to the techniques and politics of Brecht: "The way John perceives the world, you are always allowed to look at it afresh . . . Never in terms of polemic, which can close something down, but in terms of widening it out. He proposes what he sees, and is like somebody waiting for an answer in the way he makes a proposition. What he's left is a space for you to reply.[73]

The Complicite production of *The Three Lives of Lucy Cabrol* was expressly intended "to carry a political charge 'antithetical to the free-market economy at the end of the 20th century,'"[74] conveyed through its transformational creation processes. The story of a peasant woman, Lucy, an eccentric, an outcast, and a survivor (even beyond the grave) who "crosses borders for a living" (quite literally, in her second life as a smuggler), *The Three Lives*, according to Rush Rehm, "captures an essential link between peasant tradition and resistance."[75] It does so by modeling transgression, border crossing, and collective engagement as at once artistic practice and social *gest*. Using actors fluidly as props, barnyard animals, and mountain berries, and insisting upon the disjunctions between actor and role, Complicite in *Lucy Cabrol* creates Brechtian social *gests* that model practices and constitute barriers against consumerist simplicities and samenesses.

The company thereby critiques complicity with dominant ideologies of progress and consumption, and compels audiences
to see freshly – and act differently. Eschewing the production
of empathy with individual character/actors as collusion with
the consumerist individualism and psychologism critiqued by
Berger, the company draws upon its Lecoq training to focus on
the social and historical: "the actors do not play at being peas-
ants," as Rehm argues, "but rather focus on what peasant life
is like: the feel of the wind, the turning of the soil, the cold at
dawn. Earth. Boots. Water. The taste of gnôle. The blood at a
child's birth, and at the slaughter of a pig. Cow's milk. Mother's
milk. Butter . . . [T]he metaphysical dimension . . . grows out of
the necessity for work, the meeting of earth, matter, and human endeavor."[76] In theatrically recreating Berger's story of an
outcast peasant woman's early struggles, transgressive material
successes, and influence even after death, and in doing so by
variously multiplying its focus among the story it has to tell, its
own theatrical processes and practices, and the historical context of both, Theatre de Complicite in *The Three Lives of Lucy
Cabrol* models transgressive transformation as both artistic practice and social critique – or transformative social critique that is
grounded and embedded in productively interrogative theatrical
training and process.

2.   Working conditions

The two topics for discussion which are most prominent backstage, in green-rooms and in theatre bars – money and working
conditions – are as largely absent from the discourses of contemporary theatre criticism as audience amenities and the physical
and discursive spaces in and through which audiences "read"
productions. Yet these fundamental framing circumstances shape
meaning in the theatre to a degree that equals any other, including the largely indeterminable intentions of playwrights, directors, and actors that are the focus of so much journalistic and
academic writing in the field. This section considers, from the
point of view of theatrical production, the ways in which the
structures of theatrical organization and funding shape meaning
in the theatre, and from the points of view of both production and
reception, the impact of the place and space and the histories,

mandates, programming traditions, and micro-cultures associated with particular theatres, on the work produced by those theatres and the ways in which it is received, read, and understood by their audiences.

i.   Funding structures

a. Commercial theatre   Most theatrical organizations in the English-speaking world can be classified as either commercial or not-for-profit. At commercial theatres on Broadway, in Toronto's theatre district, in London's West End, and elsewhere, the theatrical event is explicitly constructed as a product of an entertainment industry. Producers finance productions and/or raise funds from investors in hopes of mounting long-running shows to large audiences paying high prices – "market value" – for entertainment. Shows that don't promise large profits are quickly closed down and written off as losses for tax purposes. In this model, clearly, the theatrical production is understood to be a "property" (hot or not), a commodity whose value is primarily, if not exclusively, economic, and whose participation in dominant models of commercial production is virtually prohibitive of extensive or radical social critique.

A good test case for measuring the potential social and cultural value of this mode of production is perhaps the success of *Rent*, the Tony Award and Pulitzer Prize-winning musical of New York's lower East Side world of "aids, rats and roaches" among the homeless, addicts, bohemians, and wannabe "artistes" that was written by the late Jonathan Larson (book, music, and lyrics) about his own friends and neighborhood. The show was first produced at the New York Theatre Workshop in the East Village early in 1996, was remounted on Broadway at the Nederlander Theatre in April of that year, and has since toured to almost unprecedented international success.[77] Based on *La Bohème*, *Rent* was clearly intended by its creator to be a critique of 1990s American capitalism, and a transgressive celebration of what the show's website calls its "multiracial, multisexual world." Even its co-producer, Jeffrey Seller, saying "[i]f I really wanted to make money I'd go to Wall Street," has indicated that "I came to Broadway because I was excited by the question, 'Can you challenge the mainstream?'"[78] But the show clearly underwent considerable (com)modification early on. Publicity for *Rent* celebrates the democratizing fact that "there are no 'stars' as the show features 21 new, young, talented performers." It also highlights the producers' insistence that the front two rows for each performance be reserved for rush-seat $20.00 sale to those who can't afford the regular $67.50 (in 1996) full price. But the website also narrates a development process in which a more sprawling, perhaps more uncomfortable show was molded by its director, Michael Greif, and dramaturg, Lynn Thomson, to clarify its narrative line, smooth its rough edges, and – employing age-old traditional dramaturgical wisdom – reduce its meaning-as-product to a single, flaccid sentence: "*Rent* is about a community celebrating life, in the face of death and AIDS, at the turn of the century." The completed production ends with a rousing finale with the not unfamiliar, not very transgressive "reprise," in the words of the official website, "of the affirmation that love is all." The show's rave reviews consistently praise its "energy," "enthusiasm," and "exuberance," and describe it as "uplifting" and "cathartic" rather than even remotely socially interventionist. They point to its social effects primarily as the reinvigoration of the moribund Broadway musical, in the way that work from marginalized communities has throughout theatrical history been appropriated in order to bring renewed life to a decadent mainstream without essentially altering it. Serious reviews, even early on, had reservations about "a college-dorm patness to the social politics," as Bernard Dolland wrote in the *New York Times*. "I live around the corner from the real thing," he wrote, "and what I see and hear on the streets has an edge that the earnest practitioners of 'RENT' can't quite summon."[79] In short, *Rent* would seem to have first made it to the stage and to Broadway by undergoing a process of commodification, and the appropriation of the world of its characters as objects of a voyeuristic or consumerist gaze was only solidified by its Broadway and tour packaging, which includes the marketing of souvenir posters, t-shirts, mugs, sound-track CDs, and other paraphernalia that accompany mega-musical success and mark the comfortable assumption of commodity status.

b. Not-for-profit theatre   Not-for-profit theatre in most English-speaking theatrical cultures, although its organizational structures and hierarchies are most often very similar to those of the commercial theatre, relies on public funding, private donations, and box-office receipts to pay its bills. Not-for-profit theatre is neither structured to pay dividends to private investors nor to reward its creators and producers financially with anything other than wages or standard royalties negotiated through agents or professional organizations. In theory at least, this would suggest more flexibility in programming, and the opportunity for more aesthetically or politically alternative productions to contribute more directly or more successfully to the production or negotiation of cultural values than is available in the culturally affirmative world of the commercial theatre. To a certain extent this is true, but public funding is provided for a variety of reasons and functions in a variety of ways, and such funding is not without its own constraints. Theatrical practitioners often feel that their work should receive funding for its own sake and without strings, because of its inherent artistic value or because of the usefulness of the arts as social critique or conscience within civil society. More recently, public funding of the performing arts, in particular, has been defended as good investment, on the grounds of the economic spin-offs it produces, primarily for the tourist industry, at a relatively small cost. Most governments, public foundations, and public-funding agencies, however, either see arts funding as related to other forms of "research and development," in which temporary seed money helps a fledgling industry develop an eventually marketable product, or they espouse a philosophy of public accountability in which the arts are expected to cultivate and represent national values abroad (an ambassadorial role) or community standards at home (an educational role in the production of good citizens).

Occasionally, the principle of public arts funding is thrown into crisis when such funding is withdrawn or threatened. The most visible instance of this in public theatrical space in the United States in recent years is the case of the "NEA Four" – Karen Finley, Tim Miller, John Fleck, and Holly Hughes. In 1990, John Frohnmayer, chairman of the National Endowment for the Arts (NEA), in the face of threats from a far-right federal congress against the NEA itself, overturned grants to the four solo performance artists that had been approved by a peer review panel because of the politicized sexual discourses of the performers, three of whom were gay or lesbian. The intervention provoked outraged responses from the arts community, in part because it was clear that the very principle of "peer review," or "arms-length" public funding – itself perhaps problematic because of the socially reproductive tendencies inscribed in a model in which past success serves as the standard against which new work is judged[80] – appeared to be under attack. But such direct intervention is rare, partly, one suspects, because of the publicity it generates for the performers themselves. In fact this sort of high-profile public intervention, and the controversy it generates, is perhaps most notable as a visible manifestation of a communal crisis of values that can render visible and negotiable the very "community standards" it sets out to uphold.

Far less overt mechanisms of social control function hegemonically within most systems of public funding, which generally provide only a percentage of the revenues required for a given production or season, but which nevertheless generally require that the budgets of their beneficiary theatres be administered through the supervision of volunteer community boards of directors. In many large civic or so-called "regional theatres" in the United States and Canada, or in the "provinces" in the UK, these boards are populated by business and other community leaders (or members of their families whose economic position allows them time for such community service): the same people, that is, who most often constitute corporate and other volunteer boards – including arts and charitable foundations – within the same cities. Apart from times of crisis, when such boards are empowered to fire or to veto the employment of artistic directors or their programs, their primary responsibility, in addition to the routine approval of season plans, budgets, and mandates and the overseeing of the appointment of senior administrative and artistic personnel, is to raise funds, usually from individuals, foundations, or corporations with which they are assumed to be connected. In both capacities, clearly, the (usually unstated) responsibility of such community boards is to ensure adherence to "fiscal responsibility" and "proper community standards" rather than to promote aesthetic or formal risk – not to mention social critique. If they fail in either of these categories, the theatres they oversee are subjected to public and media criticism that reflects badly on the government of the day, and on the very principle of public funding of the arts. In addition to this, of course, the ability of such boards to drum up private – usually corporate – sponsorship relies on a certain conservatism. Corporate sponsors usually consider and budget for their tax-deductible "charitable giving" to the arts as public relations, even advertising, and their corporate logos are prominently featured in the programs and publicity materials of the theatres whose work they support. Not surprisingly, few want their names associated with anything other than secure and uncontroversial "properties": Microsoft does not sponsor lesbian separatism, and Shakespeare is a safer public relations investment than is the unpredictable avant garde.

Smaller theatres, whose work grows from and is targeted at more particularist communities of interest – lesbian, gay, feminist, ethnic, aesthetically experimental, politically alternative, regional, educational, and so on – can occasionally construct boards from among their own communities, though rarely in any theatrical situation can theatre workers constitute a majority of a board, and rarely can such particularist boards guarantee effective fundraising on a significant scale. But even these companies are subject to the unanticipated whims or shifting guidelines of funding bodies. The most egregious case of this in recent years in Britain was the virtually enforced "sabbatical" of London's Cheek by Jowl theatre in 1999 in spite of its being at the height of international acclaim and influence. The company, together with others in its situation such as the formidable Theatre de Complicite, suffered a severe funding cutback because it did not occupy its own permanent performance space – a condition which, as I have argued above, is in part responsible for the fresh and challenging nature of Complicite's best work.

ii.   *Professional regulatory mechanisms and stage management*

Funding, of course, is only one of the external conditions that shape and regulate organizational structures, hierarchies, and practices in professional theatres in the English-speaking world. In addition to the corporate managerial structures discussed above, theatrical organization is framed and driven by a dizzying number of regulations, guidelines, procedures, and working practices. These derive from two sources: police, fire, and municipal policies and by-laws, and agreements negotiated with various professional organizations, associations, and unions. The first regulate the conditions under which certain effects – fire, smoke, gunshots, and so on, not to mention such "community standard" issues as nudity or the representation of alternative sexualities – can be used on stage; and the conditions under which audiences can (or cannot) watch productions – room capacities, washrooms, bar facilities, exit aisles, leg room, and so on. In *Theatre and Everyday Life*, Alan Read examines some of these regimens and regulations, particularly around issues of safety, that have been incorporated into theatrical practice over the centuries and examines some of the ways these have shaped, consciously or unconsciously, what happens in the theatre. In his analysis of the effects of fire regulations, for example, he notes that "hotel fires cut to the quick because of the expectation that a place to sleep is a safe place to sleep."

> But what of theatre? We have come to expect theatre to be a safe place to sleep – but should we? Do we have a right to expect safety where there was once danger? And what price do we pay for that safety – has theatre not disappeared in direct proportion to the restrictions that govern its performance?[81]

What is clear is that, like the discourses of community standards, the *discourses* of safety, and particularly of the regulatory practices of authority – most often issued through non-consultative directives and exercised through unannounced inspections under the threat of shutdown for non-compliance – are those of normative order. They necessarily work against everything from the Dionysian chaos of theatrical ritual to the often anarchic energies of resistant critique. Even "progressivist" models of formal experimentation can be severely inhibited by the unimaginative application of regulations that, designed for the "typical," or average theatrical space and event, can quite unconsciously (and therefore most effectively) police theatrical and social norms.

The second source of regulatory principles and practices that govern the operation of contemporary theatre is the large body of agreements negotiated with various professional organizations, associations, and unions defending the interests of theatre managements, actors, musicians, variety artists, choreographers, fight directors, stage managers, playwrights, directors, designers, technicians, and stage hands – even teamsters, ticket sellers, wardrobe attendants, and press agents. One prominent American handbook for stage managers includes a five-page chart of "independent associations," but notes that it excludes many others – such as "the building trade unions, ASCAP, television unions, the International Ladies Garment Workers, and Sheet Metal Workers," in the interests of economy.[82] Within each of these categories, too, agreements and guidelines exist according to a variety of strictly defined subheadings. Actors Equity in the UK, for example, has different contracts and guidebooks for actors, directors, designers, choreographers, fight directors, and others under each of four categories: West End Theatre, Provincial Touring, Subsidized Repertory Theatre, and Small-Scale Theatre – and similar situations obtain in other countries. Agreements with any one union in any one category can be as long as two hundred pages of small print.

The impact of this situation is most apparent at the contract level, when personnel are first hired (actors' equity handbooks typically include several long paragraphs governing nudity in auditions), but it is most directly felt on the rehearsal room and shop floors, where the person responsible for ensuring that the various regulations and agreements are adhered to is most often the stage manager. The role of stage management, in part, is to assume all regulatory and managerial tasks during the rehearsal and construction periods in order to free directors and designers to be creative and to engage with other creative personnel without conflict. In practice this can involve tactical negotiations and labor relations, and it is too often the case that productive rehearsals are interrupted in mid-flight by the need for a required Equity break, or that theatre workers are strait-jacketed by the requirement that they contribute only according to their own job descriptions. Not only is this contradictory to the supposed freedom of creative inspiration; it is, more seriously, anathema to any social critique of or practical resistance to the disciplinarities, taxonomies, and classificatory systems upon which Euro-American post-industrial epistemologies rest, and which these regulatory structures silently and structurally reinforce.

But stage management in the theatrical hierarchy is also positioned as a non-creative, service function – a craft – gendered female and functioning to enable what is constructed as the much more important, artistic work of directing, typically gendered male. Stage management, then, can work in a number of complex ways to police gendered borders between (female) craft and (male) art on the stage and in contemporary society, while at the same time policing gender roles in the rehearsal hall and throughout the rehearsal process and run of the show.

Stage managers are responsible for a daunting range of (largely service) tasks, such as: scheduling rehearsals, fittings, publicity events, and production meetings; setting up and maintaining rehearsal and performance spaces; establishing and maintaining communications among departments; posting notices; announcing calls; enforcing company rules; maintaining prompt books, props and costumes lists; running technical rehearsals; prompting within rehearsals; recording all cues, and calling them during the run (which of course denies sound and lighting board operators – constructed as technicians – anything but minimal capacity to respond to the day-by-day rhythms of the show); working with house managers; writing show reports; and maintaining discipline and continuity once a show has opened.[83] Stage managers juggle these tasks in large part through the imposition of established and time-proven organizational procedures so conventional that they have themselves hardened into unchallengeable rules. By means of these procedures, many of them borrowed from the management discourses and practices of the business world, the potentially chaotic, Dionysian world of the theatre has become an efficient and productive place to do business. But should it be? And at what cost is this efficiency achieved?

In a rehearsal diary of an extended script-development workshop for Judith Thompson's 1997 play, *Sled*, at Toronto's Tarragon theatre, Scott Duchesne and Jennifer Fletcher note a significant change in direction in the workshop when, after a first week in which the creative team worked together collectively in the rehearsal hall, the stage manager arrived. What had been an exploratory workshop involving a designer, actors, and Duchesne and Fletcher as script assistants, all working with the playwright-as-director in the exploration and evolution of an experimental, expressionist script, growing and spreading throughout an undifferentiated rehearsal space, shifted focus subtly as the stage manager set up shop "with her all-purpose tool box . . . attention to time . . . and . . . air of professionalism":

She set up the room with a long table at one end, behind which she, Judith [Thomson, as director and playwright] and the other actors sat while rehearsals were in progress. This created a proscenium-like performance space with a defined separation between the actors and the audience.[84]

The simple physical act of setting up a worktable shifted what had been evolving as a malleable environment in which actors and others circulated throughout the room, into a divided space between actors and onlookers. The arrival of the stage manager and the efficient practicing of her craft, then, initiated a process in which, as Duchesne and Fletcher describe it, a provocative and unpredictable neo-expressionist script evolved in increasingly naturalistic ways, actors came increasingly to be constructed as the to-be-looked-at objects of a consumerist gaze, and a potentially challenging and interventionist production evolved increasingly as a product for consumption.

In effect, the stage manager is the creation and creature of the theatre as industry, who serves perhaps the least interrogative of theatrical functions. Experimental Canadian writer/performer Daniel MacIvor, whose working practices are collaborative, interdisciplinary, and unpredictable in the extreme, while admiring the industry, tenacity, and geniality of those he has worked with, has nevertheless only half-jokingly described stage managers as "the spawn of the devil."[85] His own company, da da kamera, does not recognize the position.

3.   Space and place

While funding structures, professional regulatory mechanisms, and stage management have their most direct impact on conditions of production, space and place impinge directly on both production and reception. There are few people working in the theatre who have not experienced the shock of moving from the rehearsal hall to the stage only to discover that the production on which they have been working for weeks or months has irrevocably changed. Part of this has to do with a natural progression from what is often an intimate, homey, and safe rehearsal space in which delicate instincts are nurtured in private to a larger, public space, where performances, of necessity, increase in scale, and private explorations insert themselves into the larger public world. But part of it has to do with the ways in which space itself exerts its influence, silently inscribing or disrupting specific (and ideologically coded) ways of working, for practitioners, and of seeing and understanding, for audiences. As Ann Ubersfeld argues, the "theatrical locus" (interpreted broadly as the site at which theatre literally *takes place*), "confronts actors and spectators in a relationship that is closely related to the shape of the hall and the kind of society."[86] The geography of performance is both produced by and produces the cultural landscape and the social organization of the space in which it "takes place," and to shift physical and/or social space is to shift meaning.

Like the more metaphorical bodily, psychic, organizational, discursive, and cultural spaces that have been under discussion so far, the geographical and architectural spaces of theatrical production are never empty. These are spaces full of histories, ghosts, pressures, opportunities, and constraints, of course, but most frequently they are full of ideology – the taken-for-granteds of a culture, that don't need to be remarked upon but which are all the more powerful and pervasive for being invisible. To take the most obvious example, the "picture frame" or proscenium stage (as progenitor of the cinematic and televisual screen) is the closest thing that theatre has to an audience–stage relationship that contemporary English-language theatrical cultures considers to be "normal," and that theatre workers and audiences tend to take for granted. Certainly most theatre practitioners treat it as ideologically neutral, and for most theatregoers the arch, except when explicitly drawn to their attention, disappears from consciousness. Historically, however, the proscenium evolved specifically to inscribe and make manifest a particular monarchical, hierarchical social structure, in which, when it emerged in the seventeenth century, the best seat in the house, the one seat from which the depth perspective was perfect, and the best seat for being seen by the rest of the audience, was that of the king, prince, or duke. The hierarchy of the court was then made manifest in very precise ways by a seating plan organized around relative proximity to the aristocratic presence (which was approximately the same thing as the relative accuracy of perspective on the stage picture).[87] It is not incidental, moreover, that depth perspective in the theatre and the proscenium arch which enabled it emerged at the same historical moment in Europe as the scientific method (with its assumptions of detached objectivity[88]), "Renaissance" imperialism and the colonial project (which positioned the European colonialist as subject and the colonized other as object), humanist individualism, and the beginnings of the (also objectifying) economic system that would develop into industrial capitalism (with its ideological project of objectifying the natural world as "raw material"). Each of these systems, within its own realm, positions the individual (European) human subject as the detached repository of knowledge, value, and (in both senses) "perspective," superior to and separate from the value-free worlds of its objects of observation, consumption, or colonization. Although the historical specificities have shifted and the proscenium no longer functions in precisely the ways that it did when it first emerged in Europe, as Gwen Orel has noted, its capacity to inscribe hierarchies has remained relatively constant: "despite [their] origins in the seventeenth century, the proscenium arch theatres of Broadway and the West End are examples of late nineteenth-century architecture, an architecture heavily gendered and class segregated."[89] Comparable structural, hierarchical, and ideological relationships to those that were visible in shifting ways in the seventeenth through nineteenth centuries are made manifest today in a wide range of old and newly-built proscenium theatres where, now based more directly on economic rather than hereditary stratifications, they are reflected in such things as graduated ticket prices and graduated lists of donor categories in theatre programs, which continue effectively to reflect and reify currently dominant social hierarchies.

But of course depth perspective in the theatre is itself univocal, and inscribes very specific and ideologically coded ways of seeing – ways of seeing that are reinforced by training methods that themselves derive directly from the influence of proscenium stagecraft. Directors, for example, learn to achieve "focus" in ways that are generally considered to be "obviously" good, necessary, and politically neutral, and because proscenium stagecraft is the dominant mode at present, they often employ the same techniques for controlling focus even when working on three-quarter "thrust" or other stage configurations at such spaces as the Olivier stage at London's Royal National Theatre or the famous "Elizabethan-style" stage at the Festival Theatre in Stratford, Ontario.[90] But the achievement of this type of focus is an exercise of power, controlling the audience's gaze and insisting on a unity of vision and perspective that is coercive. It is also a construction of actors' bodies as objects to-be-looked-at, productions as products to-be-consumed, and audiences as passive voyeurs or consumers. Finally, this use of depth perspective conspires with conceptions of psychological depth and characterological unity that are also deeply embedded in most neo-Stanislavskian schools of actor training, with their equally univocal understandings of "through-lines," "objectives," and so on, as we have seen. It is not difficult, then, to see the cultural work performed by proscenium stagecraft and the methods associated with it as, in part at least, the reification of socially dominant, normative values.

This is not to suggest that the proscenium stage is itself the problem, or that other spaces are necessarily "better." All stages and spaces are equally (if differently) charged, and all, including proscenia, can be put to productive use if they are fully understood both physically and ideologically; that is, if they are not taken for granted and considered to be neutral, value free, empty, or natural. I witnessed a graphic, if simple illustration of the way in which even non-theatrical space can shape theatrical creation when I attended a workshop in 1996 by Theatre Labyrinth, an experimental theatre company based in Cleveland, Ohio whose work is rooted in the physical training methods of the late Jerzy Grotowski. The workshop was held in a basement gymnasium in Winnipeg, Manitoba on a cold weekend in early May. It began with physical exercises, moved through individual and group explorations and improvisations based on the bodies, abilities, and imaginations that were in the room, and issued in a very tentative workshop "performance." What fascinated me was the way in which the gymnasium itself, treated as neutral space, and never the object of discussion or focus, nevertheless seemed to shape the result. Movement patterns that emerged during the early stages of the process as the supposedly free explorations of the individual actors' bodies in motion seemed to be generated by the lines and patterns painted on the gym floor, and eventually to be contained by them, as the circles, borders, and boxes of the sports courts seemed to hold the otherwise unconstrained theatrical explorations in check and give them form. Even the narrative that the workshop very tentatively generated seemed to emerge in part from the space itself, as when the circles on the (very cold) floor of the gymnasium's basketball court emerged, late in the workshop and seemingly as the product of no decision by anyone, as igloos.

Theatrical spaces come in many forms. Some theatres have their own purpose-built facilities complete with rehearsal, work-shop, office, and performances spaces, more or less flexible, but at least under their own control. Others own, rent, or find con-verted or multi-use spaces for rehearsals and/or performances, and job out set or costume construction, or even constitute themselves as theatre companies on one-off bases, coming to-gether to do specific projects in found or purpose-built micro-environments (which may or may not otherwise be used for the-atrical performance), and dissolving at their completion. Still others tour exclusively, rehearsing and building their necessar-ily adaptable shows in rental spaces, and performing them in a different venue virtually every night. But whatever the condi-tions, the work performed within them is differently shaped and differently received because of the physical environment it in-habits. In the Western world since ancient Greece, theatre and the cities (most often) in which it happens have tended to be mutually constitutive and have either comprised mutually legit-imating symbolic economies (as is the case with large civic arts centres and opera houses at the heart of large cities) or have in-tersected as oppositional spaces in which civil society might be formed (as is the case with many small converted factories, ware-houses, and retail shops housing "workshop" theatres in "ethnic" or working-class neighbourhoods.) In either case, and however each term may be located on a scale from cultural affirmation to cultural intervention, good theatre makes good citizens, while good theatre and good cities make good civilizations.[91]

i.   Theatre architecture

Whether a performance space belongs to a particular theatre company or not, all performances take place within specific ar-chitectural and geographic frames that serve to shape their mean-ings. As Marvin Carlson has argued, "The way an audience ex-periences and interprets a play [. . .] is by no means governed solely by what happens on the stage," or even by the architec-ture and configuration of the stage proper – proscenium, thrust, apron, or arena. "The entire theatre, its audience arrangements, its other public spaces, its physical appearance, even its location within a city, are all important elements of the process by which an audience makes meaning of its experience."[92] Considerable work has been done on theatre architecture, notably including Iain Mackintosh's book, *Architecture, Actor and Audience*, and Carlson's *Places of Performance*, which has surveyed a wide historical and national range of theatre, situating them within their urban settings and providing semiotic analyses of their interior and exterior designs.[93] But most such studies are, as Gay McAuley argues in her book *Space in Performance*, an exception to the general rule, "concerned with the building as an aesthetic object, rather than with its function in a complex social process,"[94] and there are few scholarly analyses of how space shapes meaning in specific performance situations.

   a. Spaces of production   A considerable percentage of most theatre buildings, and a considerable percentage of the formative time spent in the creation of a theatrical production, involves space that the audience rarely sees, except perhaps in some larger theatres where "backstage tours," employing their own theatricality, guide the public on carefully orchestrated promenades through (usually empty) dressing rooms, workshops, wardrobe rooms, and backstage space, occasionally venturing into sound, lighting, and stage management booths, and perhaps even pointing out lighting grids and equipment, fly galleries, office, and rehearsal spaces. Few audience members or critics, however, sense the ways in which these spaces can shape meaning in the shows that they see, and even among practitioners such considerations rarely rise sufficiently to the level of conscious analysis to significantly structure their working processes.

   The rehearsal hall, where the company works full days for what usually amounts to more than eighty percent of the creative process of mounting a production, is among the most formative of practitioner spaces in shaping meaning in the theatre. It is also the space least frequently under the control of the creative team, or least taken into account *as* creative space in the design of the show. While some few theatres manage to allow significant rehearsal time on the stages where the shows will be performed, most productions are rehearsed elsewhere, moving onto the stage only for a final few days of technical rehearsal, at which point

lights, sound, and costumes are added and actors learn to ad-
just to the size and acoustics of the performance space. Indeed,
most rehearsals for contemporary English-language productions
take place in rented halls and found spaces at some distance from
the theatres that will host them, often in different neighborhoods,
and occasionally even different cities. Many Royal Shakespeare
Company productions, for example, mounted at the concrete
bunker that is the Barbican Theatre, or even at Stratford-
upon-Avon, have been rehearsed at Clapham High Street, across
the Thames and twenty minutes away by Underground from the
Barbican, and a half-day's journey by train from Stratford. The
company's rehearsal halls at Clapham are housed in a renovated
former cinema and car-parts warehouse, the airy capaciousness
of which is at great an atmospheric remove from the windowless gloom of the Barbican as is the near-Brixton South-London
location (together with the sometimes personally dangerous approaches to it) from the idyllic tourist town of Stratford. In either
case, the conditions framing the shows' creation are considerably
different from those that shape its reception. But at least the RSC
has funding not only to rent, but to buy rehearsal space. As Gay
McAuley points out,

young, experimental, and avant-garde troupes can rarely afford the development and rehearsal time they need, and so the law of the market
functions as effectively as state censorship in determining whose voice
may be heard in the theatre. As Lefebvre argues, "space is a means of
control and hence of domination, of power," and one of the major forms
of control is determining who shall have access to what space.[95]

Once they are acquired, and even when they are housed in
the same buildings as the stages on which the shows will be
performed, most rehearsal halls are relatively small rooms with
lower ceilings and only slightly more square footage on the floor –
enough to accommodate the show's floor plan and a row of ta-
bles for the director and stage managers – than the stages upon
which the shows under rehearsal will be performed. This most
often means that productions are rehearsed in more intimate
conditions and circumstances than those in which they are performed, and most working actors are familiar with and conscious
of the ways in which they will need to enlarge their performances
late in the rehearsal process, as well as the inevitable feeling that

something – often a naturalistic conviction and connection nurtured and naturalized by the intimate space – has been lost once the show moves onto the stage, makes the shift from rehearsal props and clothing, and adjusts to the exigencies of light and sound. But few are able to take fully or even consciously into account the ways in which "the rehearsal space," as McAuley says, "never a neutral container... is likely to imprint aspects of its own reality on both the fictional world that is being created and even on the physical reality of the set," particularly the movement of the actors' bodies within it.[96] McAuley gives examples in which such imprinting has taken place in rehearsal, including one in which the unconscious influence of an oppressively enclosed rehearsal space ghosted a floor-bound performance of Genet's *The Maids* when it moved onto an open set with a strong vertical dimension.[97] A production that may have been designed to point heavenward remained stolidly earthbound because of the dictates of a cramped rehearsal space.

The spaces of production, of course, extend beyond the rehearsal hall, and include the size of workshops and loading docks and their physical proximity to the stage; the location of sound, lighting, and stage management booths; the accessibility and disposition of grids, fly galleries, and cycloramas; the number and placement of speakers; the placement, availability, and sophistication of lighting instruments, board, and dimmers; the number and placement of crossovers behind, before, above or beneath the stage; the size, distribution, and deposition of dressing rooms; and the presence, absence, size, or degree of opulence of "green rooms" (actors' lounges) and other company social spaces. Each of these factors participates in specific discourses and brings its own discursive weight to bear on a production, many of them in ways that will become clear in the case studies that constitute Part Two of this book. But to take a single, simple example, it is remarkable to what degree the size, grouping, assignment, and relative opulence of dressing rooms can imprint either a collectivist, ensemble feel to a show in which dressing rooms are communal, or a hierarchical, individualistic, "star-quality" feel to one in which dressing rooms are differentiated. This is particularly true when actors playing minor roles are assigned relatively cramped or squalid communal quarters at some remove from the stage, while leading players are deemed to merit individual dressing rooms close by, with showers, refreshment facilities, and other comforts which allow them to segregate themselves from one another and the rest of the company. Productions of Brecht or other socialist writers at the Olivier stage of National Theatre in London, or the Festival Stage at Stratford, Ontario, never seem to live out or commit to the playwrights' politics in the same ways that they do at the same companies' Cottesloe or Tom Patterson spaces, respectively, where backstage facilities are shared and un-differentiated, or indeed at theatres less symbolically central to their cultures and nations.

   b. Spaces of reception   At the opposite end of the spectrum from rehearsal and backstage "spaces of production," which shape the encoded meanings of what audiences see and hear on stage are those front-of-house spaces reserved for audiences, spaces of reception that to a considerable degree shape the ways in which those meanings are decoded. These spaces include the entrances, foyers, box offices, and lobbies that greet audiences on their arrival, together with the lounges, bars, refreshment stands, snack bars, and even washrooms, where they gather after ad-mission, at intermissions, and occasionally after the show. The degree to which such spaces serve to segregate actors from au-diences, as each group retires to their separate worlds at inter-missions and show's end, and the degree to which they serve as transitional space, a sort of vapour lock between the out-side world and the theatrical event where heterogeneous groups of people become or cease to be audiences during what Baz Kershaw, following Richard Schechner and Victor Turner, calls the "gathering" and "dispersal" phases of performance, has been frequently discussed.[98] But the degree to which such spaces shape meaning by directing audiences' horizons of expectation or containing their post-production response is largely overlooked in theatre criticism.
   Yet the theatrical event begins long before the house lights dim. In his years as artistic director at the Stratford Festival, Ontario, Robin Phillips argued that the production began when the spec-tator arrived at the edge of town, and although he achieved only limited success in his efforts to influence town planning and lo-cal businesses, his years at Stratford were notable for the atten-tion he paid to foyers, lobbies, bars, the disposition of book and

souvenir stands, and front-of-house deportment. But perhaps the most prominent entry point into the theatrical experience, and one to which significant scholarly attention has been given, is the façade or public face of the theatre building itself. These have varied widely over time, as Marvin Carlson has demonstrated in *Places of Performance*, from the enclosed, private theatres of the Renaissance princes through the monumental nineteenth-century palaces of high culture to the street "façade theatres" of Broadway and the West End, and finally once again to en-closed spaces, now those of contemporary real estate develop-ments such as the Lincoln Square Development in New York, "incorporating" Lincoln Center, London's South Bank com-plex, incorporating the National Theatre, and the vast Barbican (re)development, which "contains" the Barbican theatre, in ev-ery sense of the word.[99] All of these designs and spatial relation-ships, of course, are ideologically coded in ways that range from enforcing class differences and interests through "the tyranny of archectonic grandeur"[100] and the segregation of entrances (with nondescript balcony entrances from the side of the building), to cementing the partnership of high culture and commercial real estate. Most of these designs and their attendant ideological codings – or variations upon them – are still operative as "pa-trons" enter theatrical spaces today. Susan Bennett has argued that there is an alternative history of non-institutional venues "where architecture may not play such an important role."[101] I would suggest, however, that the architectural features of the community centers, union halls, and alternative spaces to which she points – like those of the converted factories, store fronts, and warehouses that house so significant a percentage of con-temporary not-for-profit theatrical production – figure equally significantly in the ideological coding of productions held within them, though in these cases such coding is more likely to be community-oriented, populist, or even overtly resistant to dom-inant ideologies.

Front-of-house, foyer, lobby, and lounge areas are today per-haps even more significant than entranceways in terms of their impact on the theatrical experience and the spectatorial produc-tion of meaning, particularly in their framing and preparing au-dience horizons of expectations. McAuley points to the signif-icant and shifting role, in this regard, of the box office, often the first space encountered by the spectator. She notes that "the location of the box office gives some indication of the predominant relationship between spectator and theatre or event (paying customer, member of a club, worshiper at a shrine, etc.)."[102] Here the differences are legion among the clear gatekeeping role of the box office in the liminal, mini-foyers between the street and Broadway auditoria (where box-office personnel figure semiotically as bank clerks), the production-line feel of the row of cashiers in the atrium, far from the performance spaces at Edinburgh's new Traverse Theatre complex, and the friendly atmosphere deliberately inculcated around the box office at Peter Cheeseman's Victoria Theatre at Stoke-on-Trent in the 1980s[103] – echoed since at small theatres everywhere. Increasingly, particularly at large national theatres, multi-venue arts complexes, and international theatre festivals, box offices exist not only in the realm, noted by McAuley, of telephone bookings and credit cards,[104] but also in the virtual spaces of transnational capital and the worldwide web.

Similar differentiations can be made among the artfully arranged brass, glass, and "class" lobbies of upscale civic North American theatres, the shabby-genteel public areas of the West End, and the makeshift spaces of varying degrees of comfort at smaller experimental or alternative venues throughout the English-speaking world. The former, often doubling as galleries or decorated to resemble the foyers of corporate office buildings, featuring flavored coffees, malt whiskies, or micro-brew beers at sleek, efficient bars, can position audiences as patrons or consumers, preparing them to sit back and enjoy the show much as they relax and enjoy the refreshments. The mahogany and faded plush of many older West End venues, sporting plaques to former glories and famous patrons, tend to bear the weight of history and tradition, selling coffee, gin, and white wine at their dress-circle bars, and ice cream from the ushers at the intervals. Experimental venues, on the other hand, can in their various ways position audiences as among the *cognoscenti*, the artistic élite, or the adventurous. And of course even there, as in the lush, department-store lobbies of recent Disney and other theatres purpose-built for international mega-musicals, as McAuley notes, "the commercial activity around the theatre," ranging from restaurants and bookstores to souvenir stands, "underscores the commercial basis for the theatre itself and is to an extent in conflict with the idea of theatre as art,"[105] much less as social commentary. In any case all such amenities carry with them ideological coding that can reinforce, modify, or undercut artistic intent.

A perhaps extreme example of how this can work is the production of *Measure for Measure* directed by the radical British director Michael Bogdanov at Canada's Stratford Festival in 1985. Bogdanov is probably the best-known self-described socialist director of Shakespeare, whose work with the English Shakespeare Company is discussed in Part Two, below. His productions are replete with signs, songs, interpolated prologues, eclectic costuming, and other alienation devices, and they take political stances that attempt to expose the plays' authority figures as capitalist goons. In his *Measure for Measure*, the Duke and his deputy, Angelo, were dressed in tailored business suits, and it was part of Bogdanov's project to make members of Stratford's often similarly dressed, predominantly white, upper-middle-class audience feel complicity in the depravity of their onstage counterparts. Before the production opened, an extended prologue introduced the audience to a Viennese underworld of pimps and prostitutes, who circulated in the lobby handing out business cards and roamed the house inviting spectators to the onstage "club" to dance with exotic figures of uncertain gender. The club, of course, was the script's underworld, and this opening attempt to implicate the audience in its dubious pleasures was revived immediately before the interval, when a highly erotic strip – reviewer Ray Conlogue described it as "a stripper unzipping herself while crooning fellatiously [sic] into a bullwhip microphone"[106] – was interrupted just before its climax by the sirens and flashing lights (throughout the auditorium) of a supposed police raid.

The problems here are clear. Far from feeling implicated as voyeurs or, in the pre-stage show, participants, most audience members, who after all had come to see "Shakespeare at Stratford" with all its high-cultural associations, reacted with either detached amusement – "isn't it clever" – or embarrassment. The police raid was greeted with relief – nobody wanted the stripper to go any further (not at the Stratford Shakespearean Festival), and of course the audience was hustled off, not to prison, but to the comforts of the lavish Festival theatre lobby, its upscale bars, its ice cream, and its gallery of past Festival triumphs.

The precise impact of audience space on spectatorial meaning-making after the show, in the "dispersal phase" of the performance, is difficult to discern, since audiences rarely linger and mingle in these spaces at the end of a production as they do before the show and at the intervals. This may account for the significant role that the extended and choreographed cathartic curtain calls of opera play in orchestrating response,[107] or for the various "talk-back" and post-production discussion sessions that are staged by many social action theatres – or even by mainstream theatres producing "controversial" shows such as Eve Ensler's *The Vagina Monologues* or David Mamet's *Oleanna*. But even without such enhancements the closing of the curtain (or more often the dimming of the stage lighting) and the restoration of the house lights reintroduces the interior architecture and what Carlson calls "the social semiotics"[108] of the auditorium to consciousness, and the time taken by audiences to regroup and assemble themselves in an orderly fashion as they move through rows of seats, up aisles, and back through lobby and coat-check areas to the streets can itself constitute a kind of containment, a restoration of order, or a cathartic return to "normal" life.

c. The auditorium and the stage   Actors and audiences meet at the intersection of the auditorium and the stage, the curtain, the "fourth wall," or the invisible, ineffable barrier between performer and spectator in more interactive modes of theatre. Each space – auditorium and stage – has its own semiotic significance and ideological import. Before the lights dim and the show starts, the auditorium, with its decorations and distractions and the relative comforts of its seating, functions in much the same fashion as do other public areas, except insofar as it begins to constitute the smaller groups in which audiences arrive at the theatre as a single audience. In fixed seating, graduated pricing arrangements, it also encodes and represents larger social or economic stratifications with still more precision, as relative proximity to and visibility of the stage configures social positioning. Once the show starts, however, it is the audience–stage relationship itself that becomes crucial. Each of the five basic configurations of the relative positioning of the audience and the stage tends to encode specific relationships between spectator and performer, depending in part upon the size of the theatre, cast, and audience. The fully-frontal proscenium arrangement, already discussed, with its real or implied arch separating the stage from an audience that faces it, tends to construct the performance as the to-be-looked-at object of spectatorial consumption and to construct the spectator as passive, particularly when the stage, the auditorium, or both are "raked" to slope towards its opposite number. The thrust configuration, in which the audience is arranged around three sides of a platform that extends into its midst, constructs a declamatory space downstage center, acknowledges the audience as populace, and, as in its Greek and Elizabethan variations, lends itself to an understanding of the theatre as a place for listening and a forum for public debate. The arena stage, in which the audience surrounds a central playing area on all sides, lends itself to athleticism, requires fluidity of movement, and can expose the performer in ways that can seem to confer power upon the populace almost as a "mob," while the related traverse stage, which bifurcates the space, placing audience members facing one another across its two sides, can easily encode either dialectics or binary conflict. Finally, environmental theatre, which usually seeks to break down architectural and other barriers between the auditorium and stage, often eschews fixed seating and usually attempts either to capitalize upon an already semiotically charged environment or to create a fully enclosed atmosphere of "total theatre." Depending on how it is used, this can be either the most democratic or most manipulative of staging configurations. In practice, of course, these arrangements blend and blur into one another as proscenia are modified with forestage extensions, thrust stages are stretched to take on some of the qualities of arena staging, traditional theatres are reconstituted as semiotically charged "environments," and so on.

The configuration of the stage, however, is only one element of the audience–stage relationship. Other variables, which include everything from acoustics and sight lines, the degree of continuity or the severity of the break between the materials and design of the stage and those of the audience, the depth of the trough, if any, between the audience and the stage, the height of the stage in relation to the audience and the degree of rake of each, and so on, each of which can determine the degree to which an audience is constructed as a full participant in the making of meaning or is, quite literally, "talked down to." But chief among these factors is sheer size and volume, which includes both audience capacity and such things as the shape and height of the ceiling. Together, these can determine everything from the size and volume of performance required to reach everyone in the house (and therefore the degree of detail and intimacy available) to the degree to which the performance is able to constitute a sense of community within the audience or between the audience and the stage.

A good example of the ways in which audience–stage spatial relationship can shape the meaning and politics of a performance is the case of the Traverse Theatre's production of Scottish playwright Sue Glover's *Bondagers*, a play about the women who were exploited as cheap agricultural labor in the Border regions of Scotland in the late 1800s, and one that was clearly designed by the playwright and the company as resistant feminist history-from-below. The company's study guide for schools – a model of its kind – included material on "Female Troubles," "Sexual Harassment" (including contemporary clips about sexual harassment in the workplace), "A Woman's Lot" (the character of Sara in the play is a single parent), "The Land, the Workers, and Technology" (including a contemporary article entitled "Banks Profit from Job Losses"), the rich worker's dialect employed in the production, and workers' aesthetics, such as music and choreography developed from patterns of work. The play, directed by Ian Brown, opened at the cavernous Tramway Theatre as part of the Glasgow Mayfest on 3 May 1991, was immediately transferred to open 11 May at what was then the tiny Traverse space in the Grassmarket in Edinburgh. It was revived in November of 1993 and again in 1995 at the larger Traverse 1, the main space at the company's new, upscale location behind the Lyceum Theatre and Usher Hall, between Lothian Road and Castle Terrace and directly opposite the newly designated "Festival Square" in front of the Sheraton Hotel. The proximity in time and place of the 1991 performances in Glasgow and Edinburgh provided reviewers the unusual opportunity of commenting on the show in both spaces, and, together with the revivals, provides the materialist critic with the opportunity in retrospect to consider the reviewers' accounts of several incarnations and (dis)placements of the same show.

The Tramway, a former garage for tramcars in an industrial area "across the river" from Glasgow's city-centre shopping area,

is now used as a gallery and a performance space for large-
scale internationally touring productions such as Peter Brook's
Mahabaharata, Robert Lepage's *Tectonic Plates* and *Seven Streams
of the River Ota*, and shows from Moscow's Maly Theatre and
New York's Wooster Group. According to the reviewer of *Bondagers* in *The Scotsman*, the space, "all lofty industrial ceiling, big
floor and rude brick walls, exert[ed] its apt and peculiar magic
once more."[109] There, Glover's play was reviewed as historical
epic theatre and as an all-woman, feminist show about work.
Michael Tumelty, the *Glasgow Herald*'s music critic, focusing on
the music of the language and the rhythms of the play's structure,
described it as operatic,[110] while Joyce McMillan waxed eloquent
in *The Guardian* about this "gorgeous, filmic, lyrical production
in which scenes of dialogue and monologue are swept across the
earthen stage by the spacious rhythms of Pete Livingstone's
music, and by the choric songs and movement of the women
themselves, sowing, reaping, hoeing, shading from work into
dance."[111]

The reviewer for the socialist *Workers Press* described a production that fully lived up to the promise of the company's study
guide, seeing *Bondagers* in its Tramway manifestation as "a play
about women who suffered under a system of agricultural labour
which operated in south-east Scotland and north-east England
in the second half of the 19th century, and continued in some
areas until World War II," and pointing to "the contemporary
resonances of its historical statement."

It challenges the view that history is something to do with "national
heritage," something to accumulate knowledge about rather than to
wrestle with.

It challenges male lip-service to feminist sensibilities . . . It challenges
its audience to grasp the nuances of a complex class structure as it was
seen and experienced by women.[112]

Julie Morrice's review, in *Scotland on Sunday*, also focused on
history "without a glimpse of tartan," and on "the *strength* of
these women,"[113] while Joyce McMillan wondered,

Do men even matter to these women? Yes, but mainly as holders of
economic power or begetters of bairns; the texture of their lives lies in
each other, the shared work, the shared "crack" [talk]. In other words,
once these powerful women break free from their economic bondage to
hinds and husbands, they will be capable of anything.

She also wondered "how Glover's minimal, simple-sounding script will play in the confined spaces of the Traverse."[114]

The answers were not long in coming. When the show opened eight days later at the Traverse's own theatre at 112 West Bow at the east end of Edinburgh's Grassmarket – a tiny, oblong-shaped black hole of a theatre seating about 100, with black, foam-cushioned three-tiered seating modules situated in a down-scale market square – reviews of the production were as different as the spaces themselves. In almost complete contrast to the re-viewers of the Tramway opening just a week earlier, Alasdair Cameron described, in a review in *The Times* entitled "In touch with the local tongues of yore," a show that was "as much a meditation on a now vanished rural life as a piece of narrative." Cameron noticed that "an unexpectedly powerful political di-mension shows the inequities of an uncontrolled tenant-farmer tradition," but mentioned neither feminism nor contemporary political resonance, and in fact focused his review on the aes-thetics of a "ravishingly beautiful" production that he described as "a minimalist Millais painting."[115]

Mark Fisher, in a comparative review published in the Glasgow and Edinburgh *List*, explained the difference in setting between "the sweeping fields of the Tramway and the cramped allotment of the Traverse," finding that "in each space different qualities came to the fore – the patterns of the landscape at the Tramway, the human tragedy at the Traverse."

[I]f at the Traverse the production loses a sense of the epic sweep of the landscape, it also becomes more intimate, the characters growing in individuality, no longer such bleak, exposed figures.

Fisher noted that "the detailed and faithful representation of women's experience is itself a political act," but he also noted that the "more poignant" ending at the Traverse perhaps deflected attention from the social to the aesthetic:

It's too much about collective experience, not individual tragedy, to break your heart, and it's too lyrical to send you out shouting in political anger, but as a piece of sensuous, captivating theatre it's a tremendous achievement.[116]

Revived two years later and then again in 1995 at the Traverse's trendy new, symbolically central quarters which, with its pur-pose-built stone and glass building, complete with upscale

Atrium, restaurants, and bars, took part in the redevelopment of the Lothian Road area for business, the show seemed to have lost most of what was left of its political edge. Richard Loup-Nolan reviewed it in *The Independent* in 1993 as "a subtle and powerful myth about human connectedness; with the earth, with each other and with ourselves," eschewing gender and class analysis for a familiarly depoliticized universalism, while in 1995 Peter Whitebrook considered the play to be "nostalgic" and "sentimental,"

arguably not a drama at all but a poetic illustration of a time, place, and the cyclical historical process, using as a metaphor the agricultural cycle of sowing and reaping, winter and summer.

The remount and the reviewer having removed the play into the safely conservative universalist and asocial realm of the metaphoric, mythopoeic, and seasonal, Whitebrook concluded safely that "while Glover is a writer of great lyrical sensibility, the play is not really about anything."[117]

ii.   Geography and neighborhood

If the shifting meanings of the Traverse production of *Bondagers* had to do in large part with the semiotics of the different theatre spaces in which it was performed, it also had to do, as my comments have suggested, with what Marvin Carlson calls "urban semiotics" – the ways in which the inhabitants of a city intellectually structure their surroundings and hence symbolically position various areas and buildings, including theatres, within the urban landscape.[118]

"*Going to* the theatre" – a phrase that McAuley finds "highly significant" both literally and figuratively for its assertion both that theatre *takes place* and for its assertion that participation in a theatrical event is to take part actively in the realm of the social[119] – is undertaken, if with different associations and resonances, by both practitioners and audiences. The geographical location of the space in the city or elsewhere is therefore significant for the understanding of theatrical production and reception alike. Considerable work has been done by Carlson and others on the symbolic location of civic and other theatres as they have taken their places within or on the outskirts of cities from ancient

Athens to contemporary New York, Toronto, Johannesburg, and New Haven, Connecticut,[120] and in every case, as Susan Bennett has argued, "the milieu which surrounds a theatre is always ideologically coded" and "shapes a spectator's experience."[121] This is true whether the performance takes place in a designated theatre or entertainment district of a major city, near cafés, restaurants, and bars, in proximity to financial, political, or commercial districts, near industrial, residential, ethnic, or working-class neighborhoods, or indeed far away from urban centers in idyllic or commercialized festival towns or isolated pockets of regional culture.

The geographical location of theatres is significant both for the ways in which it is "read" and for the experience of the spectator in getting there. This has to do with factors that include the degree of physical or psychological difficulty involved in traversing familiar or unfamiliar, comfortable or uncomfortable districts, the distance between the theatre and its community (or "target audience"), the proximity and cost of public transportation or parking, and so on. Many large civic theatres located in or near city centers, particularly in North America, serve largely suburban audiences for whom "going to the theatre" means driving significant distances on freeways, dining at downtown restaurants, and paying exorbitant rates for nearby parking. The experience of audiences attending small experimental theatres in New York's East Village, on the other hand, can often feel uncomfortable or threatening, as Bennett points out, and "those who made the journey to Joan Littlewood's Theatre Workshop in the East End of London" often did so as a consciously evaluative, political act of working-class solidarity.[122]

It is worth looking more closely, as an example, at the particularly revealing case of Edinburgh's Traverse Theatre, both in the diachronic context of its own history, and synchronically in relation to a range of other theatre locations in contemporary Edinburgh, to illustrate some of the ways in which the location and disposition of theatres can shape the meaning, not only of the theatre-going experience in general, but of particular productions. Since its founding in 1963 as purportedly "the first 'fringe' theatre in Britain,"[123] the Traverse has inhabited three wildly different spaces in three equally divergent geographical situations in Edinburgh, to the point that it has been, in effect, three very different theatres, its institutional continuities far outweighed by its shifts in geographical location and material circumstance. For its first five years' existence as a theatre club the Traverse – named after an audience–stage relationship in which the performance space bifurcated an audience seated on either side – consisted of a "dirty little rat hole"[124] seating sixty people, located in a seventeenth-century tenement building in James Court, just off the Lawnmarket, on the site of the former house of ill-repute, "Kelly's Paradise." The company's historian, Joyce McMillan, describes the location as "a crumbling former doss-house and brothel barely a stone's throw from the Castle."[125] There the theatre shared its shabbiness with that of experimental theatres everywhere in the 1960s, as its audiences enjoyed the thrill of taking real or apparent social and aesthetic risks while "slumming it" – attending a self-styled experimental theatrical space in a run-down corner of the city center. Sarah Hemming quotes a reviewer of the company's first production of Sartre's *Huis Clos* noting ironically that "[p]olite Edinburgh society watched Sartre's Hell... in Kelly's Paradise, then went upstairs to drink sherry and demolish the cold buffet," and she quotes the theatre's former Artistic Director, Jenny Killick, who points to the censorship powers of the Lord Chamberlain in Britain prior to 1968 in arguing that "the Traverse formed itself into a club so that it could do plays with obscene language or nudity."[126]

"What was it like to go to the Traverse in those early years?" asks Cordelia Oliver in a twenty-five-year retrospective that draws attention to several of the central concerns of this chapter.

Exciting, certainly, for the frisson inseparable from good live theatre was heightened by the contrast between the "shoestring" nature of the surroundings (the place must have been a horrendous fire-risk with all those naked skeins of electric wiring and those positively mediaeval turnpike stairs) with the surprisingly high calibre of so many performance [sic]. Those were the days before the stiffening of fire regulations in public places of entertainment and before the setting, by Equity, of minimum wages for performers. Accomplished, experienced actors would happily come to Edinburgh for "peanuts and hospitality" just to take part in what was, for those days, unusually rewarding material.[127]

To attend a production at the Traverse in its first five years was to attend an "avant-garde" artistic event in the company of those members of the Edinburgh intelligentsia and art crowd associated with the trendy Paperback Bookstore and gallery on Charles Street in a then shabby bohemian location bordering

Edinburgh University, where the theatre was conceived in the minds of its first artistic director, Terry Lane, the first Chair of the Theatre Club, American Jim Haynes, his friend Richard Demarco ("a budding entrepreneur of the visual arts"[128] who displayed there), and other like-minded people. Like the bookstore, the theatre aligned itself with an intellectual elite, an anti-provincialist iconoclasm, and an international avant garde (the theatre hosted performances by the likes of Lindsay Kemp, New York's La Mama under Tom O'Horgan, and The People Show), and its productions signified just such an elitism, iconoclasm, and experimentalism, whatever other meanings each particular show might have evoked.

When the James Court space was declared unsafe in 1969, the Traverse moved quickly into an old stone property built around a courtyard at 112 West Bow, at the east end of the Grassmarket, whence it established itself as the heart of the Edinburgh Fringe Festival throughout the 1970s and 80s. The Grassmarket location at that time, while also downtown and downmarket (and downhill from the Castle, the Royal Mile, and the theatre's former location), had a physical proximity to an open-air street market and to local, working-class pubs and shops that constituted its audience and its neighborhood differently than at the Lawnmarket, but that made the small, still shabby courtyard at the entrance to the theatre a natural location for a kind of unofficial "Fringe central" at festival time, a kind of people's alternative to the perceived stuffiness of the official Edinburgh Festival:

It is free entertainment in the courtyard where many festive things have occurred. Yehudi Menuhin fiddling followed by Lindsay Kemp . . . Jack Shephard declaring Armageddon while the Director of Productions throws water over 300 people . . . John Neville throwing and getting custard pies . . . the Ken Campbell Road Show . . . the emergence of the Low Moan Spectacular . . . Harold Hobson being introduced to the Great Northern Welly Boot Show and on and on.[129]

The increased openness of the location was matched by what McMillan calls the "oddly receptive quality" of the approximately 100-seat performance space itself (there was also a small second space downstairs):

The Traverse in the Grassmarket is a large, oblong garret (with an oddly-shaped foyer and bar on the floor below) about three times the size of

the old Traverse, and capable of seating twice as many people on flexible back seating "modules" – three-tier banks of cushioned seating –
which can be rearranged at will to change the shape of the playing
area. It is more of a relaxed, blank space, much more passive than
the old auditorium; where the James Court theatre was a hot, insis-
tent little pressure-cooker, squeezing intensity out of the most unlikely
situations, the new Traverse is a black hole of a space, requiring to be
filled. (57)[130]

It is perhaps not accidental that the move to this more open location and more accommodating performance space coincided
with a much more pluralist, and much less interrogative sense
of the "mission" of the Traverse under artistic director Michael
Rudman than had prevailed at the Lawnmarket location. Unlike his immediate predecessor at the James Court space, Max
Stafford-Clark, who according to McMillan "had been painstak-
ingly deconstructing and re-constructing the idea of what a 'good
play' and 'good acting' might be in modern terms, and under
what working conditions they were likely to emerge," Rudman
"simply set out, without hesitation, to get hold of the best new
plays around, and to persuade the best available actors to play
in them."[131] Rudman also set the theatre on a renewed organizational and financial footing, and "move[d] the Traverse decid-
edly into the world of 'proper theatre', into the world of proper
wages, proper overtime, conventional administrative structures"
dependence on Arts Council funding, reliance on conventional
routines, payrolls, and so on. But as McMillan argues, this was
not an unmixed blessing:

The Traverse had been created out of an instinctive understanding that
the birth of new kinds of theatre required new structures – a constant rethinking of the physical, social and psychological relationships between
stage and audience, a revolution in the geography and organization of
theatre itself. The early Traverse therefore existed right on the edge of
existing definitions of theatre, on the boundary of theatre and life.[132]

"It's not," McMillan cautions, "that Michael Rudman consciously set the theatre on a more conservative path. Given the
new building, the larger auditorium, the growing establishment
needed to support it and supply it with 'product,' the move towards a more orthodox style of theatre must have seemed entirely
natural and desirable."[133] What is clear is that the move to a new
performance space led to a significant shift in the urban semiotics

of the Traverse, and eventually led in the spring of 1988, under the artistic directorship of Jenny Killick, to the dismantling of the club system. "The club atmosphere is no longer necessary, artistically," argued Sarah Hemming in interviewing Killick at the time, "and, inviting charges of elitism is perhaps even in direct opposition to the complex relationship of fringe theatre to mainstream that is necessary for survival." But as Killick herself said,

I think the really interesting point in the Traverse's history is the time when it accepted public subsidy, accepted the idea of being a member in the Theatre Management Association, accepted that it had to employ Equity members – accepted all this conventional theatre practice and said "We're a grown-up theatre, we want to be part of the mainstream . . . I've inherited this. And sometimes I wonder whether it was a good decision."[134]

Ironically, the same inheritance led to the decision, in the same year, to explore the possibilities of relocating yet again: "we are looking for a bigger building," Killick told Hemming in the same interview, "to make us less dependent on the Arts Council."[135]

It wasn't until 1991, however, that the Traverse moved again, this time to an upscale, purpose-built property in a part of the city altogether different in its urban semiotics from either of its previous locations (see illus. 2). The Traverse is now a theatre complex located beneath a circular glass and concrete atrium housing two performance spaces as well as workshops, box office, and administrative offices, lobby display space, the company's own fashionable theatre restaurant/bar, and two other dining establishments (at least one of which is well beyond the price range of most Fringe audiences). In fact, the two performance spaces are at first blush the least prominent elements of the building, the 216 to 328-seat Traverse 1 located as it is down a flight of stairs from the atrium, its entrance off a corner from the downstairs restaurant/bar, and the Traverse 2, seating 110 and modelled after the Grassmarket space, located deep in the bowels of the building, several windowless flights of stairs below ground level. The new Traverse building is situated in the recently designated "Festival Square" opposite the Sheraton Hotel, and nestled on Cambridge Street between Usher Hall, the city's prime venue for orchestral music, and the venerable Royal Lyceum Theatre, the city's official civic theatre since 1965 and a central venue for

2. The façade of the third Traverse Theatre, Edinburgh.

the Edinburgh Festival's mainstage theatrical productions. It is worlds away from the squalor or anarchy of the theatre's earlier manifestations, so much so that it becomes difficult to see it as in any meaningful way the same theatre as its predecessors. For most of the year, the new Traverse fits naturally in the theatrical landscape of the city as one of its major producing theatres (along with its neighbour, the Royal Lyceum).[136] It is not surprising that the Traverse became in 1999 the first Fringe company to "cross over" to the International Festival, mounting a production of

David Craig's *The Speculator* and Lluïsa Cunillé's *The Meeting* at the Lyceum.

At festival time, in its third location the Traverse serves as one of the hearts of a very different kind of Fringe, one dominated less by the anarchic energies of its early years, and more by the organizing presence of certain key umbrella complexes and organizations. As a festival city, Edinburgh is home to dozens of theatrical and paratheatrical venues, including a range of bars, bistros, galleries, church halls, cafés, courtyards, and comedy clubs throughout the city center. But if the theatre offerings at the International Festival are predominantly housed at the prestigious and historic Royal Lyceum, Edinburgh Festival Theatre, Edinburgh Playhouse, and King's Theatre, the Fringe landscape, as far as theatre is concerned, is dominated by four main venues, each with its own artistic director and staff: the Assembly Rooms (or Scotsman Assembly, to mark its sponsorship by the *Scotsman* newspaper), the Gilded Balloon and Pleasance complexes, and the two Traverse spaces. The Assembly Rooms, Gilded Balloon, and Pleasance jointly publish their own newsprint, tabloid-style Guide to the Fringe, listing only the shows in those three venues, while the Traverse produces its own glossy Festival brochure featuring its own productions. And the locations themselves tell much of the story. The Assembly Rooms consists of half a dozen venues in and around a stately Georgian building located in New Town between Rose and George Streets in a renewed commercial neighbourhood dominated by shops, pubs, and restaurants. It is the home of most of the Fringe's experimental movement and physical theatre, and it tends to draw the bulk of the theatre crowd, those interested in the form itself, and those who tend to follow the arts more generally. The Gilded Balloon consists of five separate venues on and around the Cowgate in the downmarket part of Old Town beneath the Bridges, where its programming is dominated by comedy, stand-up and musical performances, and in-your-face work that does, or promises to, push the boundaries of respectability. The rabbit warren of performance spaces – twelve, at last count, plus a bus – that surround the courtyard, bars, and restaurants of the Pleasance complex and its "annex," Pleasance Over the Road, is situated beneath the geographically dominant "Arthur's Seat" outcropping in a working-class neighborhood in the city center's east end, surrounded by council houses, neighborhood pubs, and social service agencies. Its fringe fare tends towards the working-class populist, the satirical, and the local, and it hosts work by such companies as the socialist 7:84 (Scotland).

The Traverse is at the opposite end of the city center in almost every sense, closer to hotels than housing, and closer now to the city's financial center than to its working classes. Even "Shakespeare's" pub across the road signals the theatre's respectability, its high-cultural associations, and its focus on literary (rather than theatrical or performative) values, as is signalled by the company's selling of published literary scripts at each of its productions.

One of the most powerful and well-received new shows mounted by the Traverse for the Fringe in recent years has been Aileen Ritchie's play, *The Juju Girl*, in 1999, and it is interesting to note the ways in which the geographical site of the theatre within Edinburgh, and its concomitant predominantly white and middle-class audience base shaped the play's production and reception (ironically, given that the urban redevelopment to which the new Traverse building contributed displaced a largely mixed-race, working-class neighborhood). *The Juju Girl* takes on the sensitive issue of Scotland's role as a colonizer in Africa in the nineteenth and early twentieth century in relation to its mythical identity as an oppressed English colony, and in relation to the supposed enfranchisement offered to the so-called "third-world" by today's "liberated" societies. As the show's director John Tiffany said, "In African nations at the present time, and even in Eastern Europe after the Wall came down, we all cheer when capitalism arrives, but never ask ourselves whether this is an appropriate, or even a good thing for the people of those cultures."[137] The powerful play mounted a trenchant critique, but never quite managed sufficiently to ask the question of who Tiffany's "we all" *is*, or to wonder whether the Scottish national identity that it signals might be productively disturbed by the story the play tells, or by a racial mix in present-day Edinburgh that is rarely reflected in present-day Traverse audiences or in the immediate streetscape that the theatre inhabits. Sympathetic reviews of the show, even ones conscious and supportive of its political critique, nevertheless felt comfortable employing a hegemonic (caucasian, western) "we" to characterize "our" sense of

how "we think of ourselves" as "private individuals," with little
sense that the collective may be more splintered, and culturally diverse, than their first-person pronouns suggest.[138] Set in
Zimbabwe/Rhodesia and moving fluidly between the present-day
visit of the white Scottish Kate ("looking for the *real* Africa"[139])
and the missionary sojourn of her grandmother Catherine in
the 1920s, the play confronts such things as the role of Scottish
missionaries in the building of the British Empire, the (racist)
conversion of the "Dark Continent," from "Juju," and the contemporary role of Western liberals in dictating the terms of the
supposed liberation of other cultures – including those of an otherwise homeless woman employed as a maid by one of the play's
contemporary Zimbabwean characters. But, perhaps predictably
given its context and audience, and in spite of a multi-racial cast
and a hauntingly voyeuristic poster image of a Black woman pub-
licizing the show – the woman of color serving as the object of the
gaze but not the central subject of the show – the largely autobiographical play by a white, Scottish writer does not displace in its
writing or staging the white subject from center stage. The dou-
bled role of Kate and Catherine served the Traverse audience
comfortably as the lens through which they might see Africa.
And the show was reviewed almost unanimously as a story of the
self-discovery of Kate and Catherine – Africa used, yet again,
not as intrinsically important, but as a mystical, "othered" location, a site upon which dramas of Western identity-formation are
played out in the ongoing tradition of Conrad. One representative review, noting that the play "upholds [the Traverse] theatre's
reputation," was headlined, "The Juju Girl casts a spell out of
Africa."[140] And reviewer Neil Cooper called it, without irony,
"Possibly the most optimistic play on the Fringe."[141]

iii.   Nomadic and touring theatre

In contrast to the ways in which real estate, its location, and
its maintenance can constrain and frame the cultural work that a
theatre such as the Traverse is able to perform, operation without
a permanent home space by theatre companies such as Cheek
by Jowl, Ex Machina, and Theatre de Complicite can work as
a kind of healthy dislocation to ensure that in at least some of
its senses space cannot be taken for granted, and it virtually

guarantees, on some level at least, *engagement* with space. But there is a downside to this dislocation, too, that might better be called displacement, or perhaps homelessness. As most theatre practitioners have learned, the problem for nomadic theatre companies is the difficulty in finding the rental spaces that they want, and the reality that when such spaces *are* found (or more often some compromise resembling them) they cannot always be controlled, and the company's work gets pulled around by them in unanticipated ways. And, of course, there is little time to find ways of dealing with this problem because the company is often totally exhausted from the constant need to find or create new places to perform.

Part of that exhaustion, for most companies, has to do with the lack of a home, and the constant, healthy, but nevertheless debilitating starting-from-scratch in which even the performance space isn't given or known. But part of the problem also has to do with another kind of nomadism, and another kind of displacement, which is associated with co-productions, with extensive touring, and especially with "the festival circuit," and this has to do with the dangers of losing touch with place. It has to do with actors and audiences losing cultural specificity, and with the generalizing wash that can happen when work is too often or for too long removed from the specificities of its context and begins to develop a fuzzy universalism. Theatre, as the most social and place-specific of the arts, brings with it the need for practitioners to take responsibility for the work they present, and for its material consequences in its actual social and cultural context – the here and now that make theatre and performance different from most other forms of cultural production.

The dangers of displacement and loss of cultural specificity, moreover, apply even to work that is initially both strong and deeply rooted when it is taken out of the cultural context through which it has been produced and has produced its meanings. My thinking about the issues that have eventually shaped themselves into this book began at the DuMaurier World Stage in Toronto in 1996, where I spent much of my time musing about such things as what it means for an artistic director of a festival to select work – constructed by festival brochures in universalist terms as "excellent" – for a festival audience that represents no actual community or society in any recognizable "real world." I wondered about what it means to create theatre for "the festival circuit" rather than for the culture where the company members live and work. One of the things it means, of course, as I will discuss in Chapter Six, is that productions will inevitably tend to be about theatre – about the form itself – and will tend to be admired for virtuosity, innovation, or skill rather than discussed as cultural interventions with particular, grounded meanings for specific audiences.

Two of the plays at the 1996 "World Stage" Festival, Janice Galloway's *The Trick is to Keep Breathing* and Sue Glover's *Bondagers*, discussed above, were from Scotland, from the Tron and Traverse Theatres respectively. Both were very powerful, both emerged from committed feminist perspectives, and both were clearly addressed to the particular concerns of a specific audience. And both were very effective and well received at the World Stage. What interested me, however, was the degree to which the festival context – its placelessness – transformed strong and culturally specific work into mere representation. While reviews of the productions in Britain focused on such things as "social realism" in *The Trick is to Keep Breathing*,[142] for example, Toronto reviewers praised the "fabulously inventive" staging of its director/adaptor, Michael Boyd, and focused on the production's "hugely skilful conjuring of [individual] mental disarray."[143] What's more, both works became "Scottish," and came to *represent* Scotland, in ways that would have been unrecognizable to their home audiences. Where *The Trick is to Keep Breathing* was seen in Britain as part of "a determined effort to de-romanticize Scotland and the Scots by focusing on the ugly realities of cumulative dysfunction,"[144] it was presented in Toronto with an insert advertising Communicado Theatre Company's *Tall Tales from Small People* as "More Great Theatre from Scotland." When *Bondagers* was taken to the Canadian prairie capital, Winnipeg, Manitoba, in 1994, the invitation to opening night included a Tartan ribbon, and reviews – in spite of director Ian Brown asserting publicly that "I don't think the most important thing about Bondagers is that it's Scottish,"[145] – found it "a very Scottish play," and focused on the coincidence of the show's opening on the birthday of the Scottish "Bard," Robert Burns.[146] "As they say in Edinburgh," noted one reviewer – not noticing, of course, that they hadn't – "Bondagers is a bonny play."[147] With the partial exception of the woman reviewer for the agricultural paper, *The Manitoba Co-operator*, who focused on the play's depiction of female agricultural laborers "not unlike . . . the many immigrants who first broke land in Canada,"[148] most critics found the play to be neither feminist nor otherwise political, but simply "life-affirming": "it is really a kind of celebration of life."[149]

I do not, of course, want to say that the work of these and other companies cannot or should not travel or that productive and fruitful meetings across cultures and societies cannot or should not happen. I do want to say, first, that the placelessness of disembodied festivals and touring circuits may not be the appropriate venues for such exchanges, and, more importantly, that nomadic companies and workers in all situations – festivals, touring circuits, and co-productions, in particular – if they wish to engage in active cultural intervention and negotiation beyond the realm of pure aesthetics or formalism, must keep and guard their own sense of place (beyond performing promotionally as cultural diplomats). They must work to function as guerrillas rather than as free-floating signifiers open to appropriation or commodification by contexts and interests over which they have no control. We will return to some of these questions in more detail in Part Two's case study of international festivals.

4.   Public discourses

Among the most powerful influences establishing the horizon of expectations of theatregoers, and therefore shaping their theatrical experience and the meanings they carry away with them from particular shows is what I will call the "public discourse" of the theatre they are attending. This includes, of course, publicity materials relating to a particular show (posters, programs, advertising, pre-show interviews and features, and so on), as it includes reviews and public discussions of the production, all of which can shape response in quite direct and obvious ways. It also, however, includes the cumulative impact of such materials, together with logos, season brochures, fundraising materials, artistic directors' statements, company histories and retrospectives, programming traditions, lobby displays and amenities, even ticket prices and the quality and type of refreshments available as each of these things establishes itself over a season, several seasons, or the life of a company. The cumulative impact of such materials can create discourses of excitement or prestige, exploration or comfort, risk-taking or assured quality. It can associate the theatre in audiences' minds with new work, with outstanding acting or directing, with excellence in design, display, or spectacle, as it can evoke nationalist sentiments, or associations with theatrical classics, lineages evoking real or theatrical royalty, on the one hand, or a history of social disruption or intervention on the other.

It may be illustrative to look briefly at a company's attempt to shift somewhat its programming, its audience base and horizon of expectations, and to do so in part through an attempt to shift its public discourse. When Richard Bradshaw took over as artistic director of the Canadian Opera Company in 1994 he inherited, and initiated an effort to alter, the company's long-standing reputation for producing classical opera in a very traditional manner that focused on vocal delivery rather than innovative theatricality – the operatic staging tradition commonly known as "stand still and sing." In the 1996–97 season, the company took out a series of irreverent, provocative, and text-heavy full-page ads in the Toronto papers for its productions of *Salome*, directed by internationally acclaimed film director Atom Egoyan, *Béatrice and Benedick*, directed by Shakespearean theatre director Robin Phillips, and other productions. The *Salome* ad, featuring a severed head on a serving dish, was entitled "HEY! THIS ISN'T WHAT I ORDERED!" and featured such subtitles as "When Atom Egoyan Yells 'Cut' at the Opera, People Lose Their Heads. But at Least There are no Castrati."[150] The ad was a combination of sensationalism ("opera disturbs, shocks, and excites"), sex appeal ("Table dancing, Circa 30 AD"), star appeal ("Egoyan takes his first Oscar [i.e. Wilde]") and condescension ("Taking in your first opera? Here are some hints"). And the media immediately picked up on the tone of the ads, with Toronto's *The Globe and Mail* offering a preview that featured a photo of Egoyan's own head on a platter and another suggestive photo of a "spa scene" in rehearsal, in an article entitled "Egoyan Serves up Salome."[151] Reviewers also picked up on the marketing, focusing on Egoyan's direction rather than the Strauss score, Richard Bradshaw's conducting, or the performers, and highlighting the filmic dance of the seven veils, which culminated in a brutal, shadowy gang-rape

3. The dance of the seven veils, in the Canadian Opera Company's 1996 production of Richard Strauss' *Salome*, directed by Atom Egoyan and conducted by Richard Bradshaw at Toronto's Hummingbird Centre.

(see illus. 3). The reviews also tended to accept the preview press and marketing suggestions that the opera was "about" such things as voyeurism, sexual abuse, "a dysfunctional family," and "the dark side of the human psyche," set in "a suburban rec-room gone astray."[152] All of this suggests that marketing decisions do quite immediately shape, not only programming, but audience horizons of expectation, the constitution (or at the very least the discursive construction) of the audience, and to at least some extent the ways in which those audiences interpret the productions themselves.

It was clear, in any case, that the company was reaching out for new audiences. First it sought younger audiences (as is apparent from an "18 to 29" discount subscription series that they initiated at the same time, advertised in a brochure featuring an internet-style design and the title, "explore the alternative [:] opera" and the slogan, "Opera for a new age"). But it also wanted to attract theatre audiences (other subscription brochures featured "The Greatest Theatre You'll Ever Hear"), hip audiences from Toronto's trendy Queen Street West rather than the staid and wealthy Rosedale or Forest Hill areas that had been their traditional audience base, and all sorts of others who don't usually go to opera. A postcard distributed in Toronto clubs, for example, in eye-catching pastel blue and yellow with red and white print, reads, in part:

Market Research Finding:
People are more likely to attend the opera as adults if one of their parents took them to performances as children.
Canadian Opera Company conclusion:
So *your* parents didn't take you to the opera? We bet they didn't tell you how terrific SEX is, either.
Never mind what Mom and Dad wanted you to do. There's a lot of uncharted territory out there. Strike out on your own and discover another of life's great experiences.

The marketing decision to target new audiences was clearly allied with artistic decisions around programming and the hiring of outstanding (stage and film) directors who had, in the case of Egoyan, directed sympathetically sexy work such as the film *Exotica* (set in a strip club), that would resonate with their operatic assignments (in this case a production that would include the presumably seductive, but thematically topical "dance of the seven veils"). But the cultural work performed by productions framed in this way was arguably quite complex and conflicted, as was reflected in such conflicting headlines about the same production as "A wickedly marvellous Salome"[153] and "Staged gang-rape makes opera morally and esthetically inert."[154] Part of the complexity is that stage and film directors and their audiences are accustomed to exploring issues of immediate social relevance in their work, while opera traditionally eschews such social reference, and is in any case limited in its interpretative scope by the emotional shaping of the musical score. As reviewer Carole Corbeil asked of the *Salome*, focusing on the emotionally seductive qualities of the Strauss music that accompanied Egoyan's powerful staging of the gang-rape/dance, "is it really possible . . . to plug child sexual abuse into an opera as if it were a theme like any other? What does it do to this opera, and what does it do to the audience?"[155]

The full-page ads disappeared mid-season in 1996–97, as it became apparent that they didn't work for all productions – as the COC's artistic director Richard Bradshaw says, "I don't think

that sick jokes about nuns is necessarily the way you should sell
Dialogue of the Carmelites."[156] In any case, according to the company's marketing director Jeremy Elbourne, the ads seemed to
attract more bemused interest than ticket sales, so the expensive, text-thick ads were discontinued. "The bottom line," says
Elbourne, "was that those ads were noticed by a lot of people
and read by a lot of people and there was really high awareness,
but that didn't translate into ticket sales."[157] But close attention
to the company's marketing of opera in general since then, the
COC itself, and individual productions, proves to be instructive
around issues of how marketing constructs audiences, shapes
meaning, and contributes to the cultural work performed by the
company and its productions.

Clearly one of the difficulties associated with the COC's attempts to reach new audiences has to do with the dangers of
alienating not only sponsors and patrons in an age of cuts to
public funding, but also the traditional opera crowd in Toronto,
identified by Elbourne as being of a median age of 45–55, and
fairly well off. As Elbourne said, in spite of special discount
packages, perks, and special programming, opera, expensive to
produce, is "a high ticket item." (Regular subscriptions to the
1998–99 season ranged from $138 to $660 for the season, with
single tickets from $35 to $130, and the cheaper seats at the
Hummingbird Centre are astonishingly bad, both visually and,
especially, acoustically.) Season promotion, then, moves somewhat schizophrenically among, first, appeals to an audience constructed as already having high cultural sophistication, secondly,
encouragement to young and future audiences to "Get out of
your apartment! Get cultured!", and thirdly, democratic reassur-
ances both that anyone can, with the aid of surtitles "understand
every moment of the action." Opera, the last appeal insists, is
really not as stuffy as some of the company's other ads might
suggest – not to mention the high-art cover designs of show programs and the high-market advertising they frame. The 1998–99
season brochure negotiated this schizophrenia in its note, "What
Should I Wear?" partly by constructing audience dress as part of
the show:

The fact is, when you come to the opera you will see all kinds of fashion
statements being made! Many of our patrons like to dress up and make
a glamorous night of it. But if you decide to dress casually, you won't
be alone!

Single-show, single-ticket promotions tend, on the whole, to be less schizophrenic than do the season marketing or general promotion of opera as a form, and more precisely targeted. Indeed, it is fascinating to observe the company's decisions variously to feature, in its advertising for individual productions, the composer (Beethoven, for *Fidelio*), the director (Egoyan for *Salome*, film director François Girard for *Oedipus Rex*), the designer (book illustrator Maurice Sendak, for *Hansel and Gretel*), the star (Rebecca Caine, for *The Cunning Little Vixen*), the opera itself (*Madama Butterfly*), or even, in the unusual case of the spring 1999 production of *The Golden Ass*, the librettist (the late Robertson Davies, novelist). And these decisions are precisely reflected in the reception and interpretation of the shows, as reviews consistently focused on the music of Beethoven's only opera (the music was powerful, the staging clumsy and uninspired), on the direction of *Salome* and *Oedipus Rex*, (the staging was brilliant, the music not to everyone's traditionalist taste), and on the whimsical Sendak designs of *Hansel and Gretel*.

And the focus is even more precise than that. The marketing campaign for *Hansel and Gretel*, for example, a production designed by a famous illustrator of children's books, devoted much of its energies to a partnership with bookstores and with Maurice Sendak's publisher, including promotions at bookstores throughout Toronto and attractive bookmarks featuring Sendak's drawings. Even the placement of print and radio ads was carefully focused: according to Jeremy Elbourne, the newspaper ad campaign for the "art" production *Oedipus Rex* included placements in the business-oriented *The Globe and Mail* and the alternative weekly, *Now*, and focused on trendy off-Yonge Street rather than conservative suburban postal codes, but didn't bother with what Elbourne regarded as the middle-class mass-market newspaper, *The Toronto Star*, on the one hand, or with the classical radio station, "Classical 96," both of which are marketing staples for the promotion of productions from the canonical repertoire (*Madama Butterfly*, *Tosca*, *La Bohème* and so on).

Occasionally, as with the 1998 production of *The Cunning Little Vixen*, the schizophrenia returns, as ads seemed to micro-target several distinct audiences, with potentially problematic results: some pre-show publicity, notably full-color coverage in *The Toronto Star*, featured the cuddly-cute children in

Sendak-designed animal outfits, other coverage the musical so-phistication of the company's series of Janáček operas, and still others a seductively-posed female star, Rebecca Caine, with the caption "she's a fox!" And reviewers seemed uncertain about what in fact the show was about. William Littler reviewed it as "a unique example of pantheism in music drama,"[158] and fo-cused on its cute caterpillars, grasshoppers and frogs, while Alan Horgan focused on its "sardonic sexual sophistication" and the "animal movements" of Rebecca Caine: "it was difficult to watch anyone else while she was on stage."[159]

At the same time as the COC was reaching out to younger and trendier audiences a new phenomenon emerged, perhaps tangentially related to marketing, but certainly part of making those newer audiences comfortable about opera, and certainly helping to shape audiences' horizons of expectations. A new so-cial awareness manifested itself at the COC that included such things as a seminar with David Henry Hwang and Alexina Louie on cultural appropriation, held in conjunction with the 1998 production of *Madama Butterfly*; stagings of *Salome* and, more surprisingly, *Hansel and Gretel*, that invoke child abuse, and of *Oedipus* that explicitly evokes AIDS; and marketing of *Fidelio* as an opera about political prisoners ("deep in a secret dungeon," the ads read, "lies a political prisoner, half starved but alive"), marketing reinforced by a dedication of the show to Amnesty International. As Elbourne says, "it's just a reflection of how we look at the operas. We're looking at what the dramatic core of the opera is...It's a community thing." Each of these exercises is, of course, welcome, but they all present interpretative problems for a company that hasn't as yet quite solved the tensions among social consciousness, the pragmatics of marketing, and the op-eratic form, in which interpretative innovation can often conflict with the emotional demands of the music, and directorial con-cepts can be readily undermined, whatever the intentions of the creative team. After all, the company may be promoting social justice, but it is still staging shows that are deeply and structurally racist, sexist, or otherwise politically problematic, without man-aging radically to deconstruct their politics.

Thus, in its simplest form, the most interpretatively interest-ing feature of the otherwise charming *Hansel and Gretel* (made charming by the Sendak designs, featured preeminently in the promotions), the suggestions of alcoholism and abuse on the parts of the children's parents, including a number of suggestive associations between their mother and the wicked witch (performed by a man in drag), devolved finally into a demonizing of women in the best misogynist wicked-stepmother tradition. On the other hand, the expectations raised by an expressed awareness of the problems of cultural appropriation in association with shows such as *Madama Butterfly* were disappointed by an unproblematized "yellow-face" production by Brian MacDonald (with many unfortunate resonances with MacDonald's earlier Stratford Festival production of *The Mikado*, also designed by Susan Benson), in which the opera's orientalist and masculinist propensities remained fully intact. What does it mean to market *Salome* as provocative and sexy – including "warnings" about fleeting nudity in the "Dance of the Seven Veils" – and then to stage that dance as a gang-rape and present the show as a serious exploration of child sexual abuse?

Even more problematic, perhaps, was *Fidelio*, dedicated to Amnesty International and advertised – in those ads not dedicated to the music and its suggested analogies with the ode to joy and freedom of Beethoven's Ninth Symphony – as being about "a political prisoner." The artistic decisions in this context were highly problematic. The prisoner was cast in this production as an innocent, middle-aged, white man crushed by a younger Black oppressor-as-villain (the only Black person in the cast, replete with a long leather coat and snappy riding crop), and saved by the combined efforts of a young and long-sufferingly faithful wife and the full deus-ex-machina authority of the (Eastern Orthodox) Church. Are political prisoners best represented or understood in these ways, particularly by a company with an emerging social conscience? Is political oppression to be understood, as here, as the result of personal vendettas against innocent white westerners by evil Black individuals in faraway, exotic places, white westerners who must then be saved by institutional and religious authorities? What does it mean to use marketing and dedications to invoke social concerns or social conscience around a production that makes these choices, and what sorts of cultural work do the productions in fact perform?

Perhaps the most effective of the shows invoking social issues did so most explicitly, and in ways that were most central to the production itself. One of the most successful and rightly celebrated of the COC's productions in recent years, *Oedipus Rex with the Symphony of Psalms* in the fall of 1997 (see cover illustration), brought marketing and artistic interpretation together to reinforce one another directly. The show, produced in a promotional partnership with the AIDS Committee of Toronto (ACT), was very much targeted at a young(ish), hip, downtown audience, advertised in *Now* magazine, and promoted through the use of a fine art photography-style image of a bald and naked male figure curled in the foetal position inside a pristine glass fish tank. The production was designed by the inventive and internationally known Michael Levine, a frequent collaborator with Robert Lepage, directed by François Girard, the director of the art films *The Red Violin* and *Thirty-Two Short Films about Glenn Gould*, and featured as narrator the star of that film, actor Colm Feore. It opened with a powerful choral version of Stravinsky's non-operatic *Symphony of Psalms*, while a huge screen was gradually inscribed with handwritten names of AIDS victims, and shadowy figures with flashlights circulated among the audience wielding books of the dead, eventually surfacing to scribble yet more names on the forestage. When the screen-as-curtain fell – there was no intermission between the *Symphony* and *Oedipus* – chorus members directed powerful floodlights at the audience, and the names of the victims were replaced onstage by the physical remains, piled high in a mountain of decayed, half-naked bodies, of the plague victims in *Oedipus* (see cover illustration). The association between the plague and AIDS is a powerful one, it proved to be extraordinarily moving when physicalized in this way, and it resonated with the stylized passion of Stravinsky's music. And it worked in part, one suspects, because neither the *Symphony* nor *Oedipus* is a traditional opera, the former being a concert piece and the latter more music-theatre than opera, a stripped-down adaptation (by Jean Cocteau) of Sophocles's play, which allowed Girard and Levine to shape their contemporary interpretation more freely, and more theatrically, than is possible in the more traditional operatic repertoire, or even in *Salome*. Even here, however, there were problems. As reviewer Jon Kaplan pointed out:

Oedipus is the cause of the plague in Thebes, but are we to look for a similar single source for the origin and spread of AIDS? That kind of mythology went out a decade or more ago.[160]

More seriously, perhaps, the implied message here may be that the irrational deaths caused by both plagues are inscrutable, without rational, social cause or hope of cure through social intervention. As Kaplan says, then and now, "the citizenry can simply cry out to higher powers for help and relief."

The COC clearly did an outstanding job of reaching out to new audiences in the late 1990s, increasing its subscription base very significantly and introducing into the marketing of their productions as into the productions themselves some social concern and contemporary relevance – and they are to be commended for this. As Richard Bradshaw says, "it's getting away from this wretched elitist tack." But the move is a complex one: the need to keep traditional audiences happy – "I don't want to be irresponsible to a loyal audience that's been here for a long time," says Bradshaw – potentially conflicts with the company's best experimental instincts; an old-fashioned social elitism is potentially replaced by an equally elitist experimental arts crowd; the musical imperatives of traditional opera militate against contemporary class, race, and gender-conscious reinterpretations by directors imported from the worlds of film and theatre; and the exigencies of marketing and fundraising constrain and contain initiatives emerging out of new understandings of the COC's larger community and its new social conscience.

Conclusion to Part One

Part One of this volume has attempted (in the tradition of theatre semiotics) to isolate, identify, and account analytically for the impact of many of the material conditions (in the tradition of cultural materialism) that shape meaning and serve as the political unconscious of contemporary English-language theatre. But, of course, none of the conditions of production and reception that have been outlined here function in the isolation of the analytical laboratory. In fact much of the provocative and productive complexity, not to mention political efficacy, of contemporary theatre operates in the often accidental and unforeseen interstices within and among the different elements that constitute the three corners of the hermeneutic triangle with which this chapter started: Conditions of Production, Performance Text, and Conditions of Reception. Meaning is ultimately produced in the theatre through audiences' lived experience of the entire theatrical event, and the social, cultural, and political impact of the theatrical event lives in the ways in which that experience is knitted into the social fabric of the day.

Part Two of this volume attempts to bring some aspects of the different material conditions of theatrical production and reception out of the artificial isolation of the semiotic laboratory and into productive dialogue with one another as they apply, taken together, in distinctly different local circumstances as discussed in isolation in this chapter. In doing so, it attempts to flesh out a model for the critical analysis of meaning production in the theatre that tries to take a wider range of shaping circumstances into account than is most often done in contemporary criticism.

Part 2

Case studies

3 The Stratford Festival

At the entrance to the Festival Theatre at Ontario's Stratford Festival in the 1993 season, between the ticket-taker and the three central aisles where reviewers are seated, there was a framed excerpt from Eric Bentley's afterword to Stark Young's book, *The Theatre*. The passage was retitled, prominently and in bold-faced type, **"So What Is Required of the Theatre Critic?"** I quote the passage in full as it presented itself to Stratford's audiences and reviewers:

> The perspicacity to read the idea in the performance, and the tact to sense if it is fully expressed and in what details, by what means, by what surprising line readings, by what unpredicted movements. What the critic must not do is accept or reject these movements, these line readings, on their own – as being traditional or the reverse, as being handsome or brilliant or the reverse. He [sic] must see them, feel them, as part of a pattern, the pattern that expresses (if all is well) the pervasive idea.
>
> I am re-stating what I have taken to be the two main principles of Stark Young's theatre criticism. In essence they are traditional, even perennial, nor are they unduly complex. Nonetheless they remain beyond the grasp of most dramatic critics, who seem incapable of the discipline required, the intellectual labour required, and instead blurt out their immediate reactions to the separate parts of the theatre occasion. They register only a brute response to each moment, or perhaps only to certain moments, the moments when they are awake. And since such waking moments follow minutes of somnolence, one senses the lack of connection with what has been going on. Our critics are accustomed to let themselves be as passive as the most helpless, hapless spectator. "Show me!" "Entertain me!" Alas, extreme passivity simply inhibits all real artistic experience.[1] (138)

Setting aside Bentley's notions of unity and intended meaning, his generalizations about sleepy reviewers, and his condescension

105

to audiences – helpless, hapless, and passive as he may think them to be – the fact of the Stratford Festival's reproduction of this passage, recontextualizing it and putting it on display for reviewers and audiences alike – in effect making it part of the public discourse of the theatre – is remarkable.

It is within the context of that discourse rather than "the" perceived "idea of the performance" or the presumed "pattern that expresses ... the pervasive idea" that I want to consider the productions of the 1993 Festival; and this discursive context is too often and too easily ignored in reviews and analyses of productions of Shakespeare at Stratford and elsewhere. I want to ask in this chapter what, and more importantly *how* Shakespeare *means* at the Stratford Festival, and what is produced in producing Shakespeare there. This involves an analysis not simply of the productions "in themselves" (if such a thing were possible), but of the discursive and material contexts from which those productions emerged, not all of them as blatant in their attempts to control and contain audience and critical response as the passage quoted above.

The poster for the 1993 season at the Festival, which also served as the cover for the season brochure and various other publicity materials, consisted of four glowingly golden geometrically-shaped artefacts: a solid, rectangular neoclassical portico; a circular Victorian clock with Roman numbering but without hands; a curvilinear Renaissance-style cupid with a bent, semi-circular bow; and a triangular and apparently *japoniste* fan made from the folded manuscript of a musical score. All of these icons were photographed in soft focus, floating freely against an ethereal background of purples, blues, and pinks that resembled blue backlighting refracted through fine crystal. The poster conjured romantic, nostalgic, and, of course, ahistorical images of a timeless, mythologized, and idealized "past," untouched by historical specificity, and united in a glow of transcendent and golden iridescence. The individual icons were vaguely suggestive of the season's shows: Euripides' *Bacchae*; three plays by Shakespeare; two classic French comedies; *The Importance of Being Earnest*; two musicals, including *The Mikado* (though both *A Midsummer Night's Dream* and *The Imaginary Invalid* were also virtually reconceived as musicals); and a new Canadian history play, Sharon Pollock's *Fair Liberty's Call*. But taken as a whole, and taking into consideration the solid gold Roman-style type

used for the poster, as reminiscent of the letterheads of distinguished boards and corporations as the neoclassical portico was
of the façades of Canada's most august financial institutions,
the poster offered escape to an idealized and comforting tran-
scendence, coupled with a reassuringly corporate sense of security, comfort, and even luxury. This is the visual imagery that
framed the discourse of the Stratford Festival in 1993, and it was
among the most effective in silently shaping the ways in which the
Festival's audiences read and received the season's shows.

This is true partly because many of the shows, notably the
then artistic director designate Richard Monette's *Antony and
Cleopatra* and outgoing artistic director David William's *Bacchae*,
echoed, in their set and costume designs and their publicity
photos, the visual imagery of the poster. As prominent, indeed,
as the poster imagery was a gloriously rich and golden publicity photograph of the appropriately named and exaggeratedly
buxom Goldie Semple, playing Cleopatra, in the encircling embrace of her Antony, the leonine (if prosperously paunchy) Leon
Pownall. This photograph graced the cover of the season's souvenir program and other Festival souvenirs and publications,
and reinforced the poster's rich sense of romantic nostalgia. The
productions themselves resonated within this context as period
and place blended together in a kind of intercultural tourism
for cross-border tourists (34 percent of the Festival's box-office
in the 1993 season was from direct sales to the United States),
which manifested itself most clearly in the "yellowface" Japanese
of *The Mikado*, in the textbook orientalism of *Antony and
Cleopatra*'s erotically exotic Egypt, depicted as an almost archetypal white male fantasy;[2] in the generic and vaguely African prim-
itivism of the masks and straw headdresses of the *Bacchae*; and
even in the appropriated punk and rap of the African-American
street-culture forest of *A Midsummer Night's Dream*, which the
production treated much in the same way as the script treats
India – as exotic fodder for the appropriative voyeurism of a
dominant, tourist audience. But then, as actor Lorne Kennedy
admitted in the promotional "Festival Edition" of the Stratford
Beacon-Herald, commenting on the quintessentially British production of *The Importance of Being Earnest*, artistic director David
William, the play's director, *is* "a living fossil" of that play's
milieu. "He has a direct connection with these people and he's a
cultural imperialist anyway."[3] Many in Canada remember, too,

William's unashamed claim, when he was first appointed to his position, that elitism, in its cultural and intellectual senses, is not a dirty word.

The larger discursive context within which the 1993 season produced its meanings resided in various brochures, press releases, and other written material; in the physical environments of the Festival itself, including audience amenities, gift shops, and ancillary spaces as well as the performance venues; and of course in the season's repertoire and individual productions.

It is immediately apparent that the written discourse of the Festival in 1993 was at once universalist, individualist, essentialist, and literary. It was, as the Festival's literary manager, the late Elliott Hayes, wrote in the season's souvenir program, "all embracing," constructing itself as the encompassing subject, positioned to welcome, comprehend, and contain all aspects of humanity and all human cultures, which are silently constructed as the objects of that consuming subjectivity. What the Stratford Festival "can offer the world," according to Hayes, is "the broad spectrum of dramatic literature and all its various mutations on the theme of what it means to be human." He presented the season's productions variously as "dramatic constructions [that] attempt to elevate the tragic elements of our daily lives to a mythic level," or to "emphasize the universal nature of theatre in a profound and very tangible way," but that can present only the empathetic and usually psychological "struggles" of individual characters, not point toward social solutions, since "art, as religion, can offer no certifiable answers. The artist and the orthodox minister can only offer articles of faith. We accept or reject their offerings according to our own experiences."[4] The universalist/individualist discourse, and its effacement of the historical and social, together with the envisioning of any social change that they might offer, could hardly be more thorough.

Hayes concluded his address with a virtual summary of the neo-Aristotelian, ahistorical, and culturally affirmative qualities of the Festival's discourse. He expressed his hope that,

For some – for many, perhaps – there will be a cathartic moment in the theatre when tears or laughter will bring you to understand that none of us are [sic] truly alone. Euripides – Shakespeare – Molière – Oscar Wilde – are separated by thousands of years, but here at Stratford they are contemporaries.[5]

Clearly, within this context, and congruently with the most conservative theories of the cathartic functioning of great art, few will leave the theatre in a subversive, activist, or even socially conscious frame of mind, whatever they may see on the Festival's stages.

The most widely circulated of the season's contextualizing texts was David William's "Welcome to the 1993 Season," reprinted in slightly varying forms in the season brochure, in all of the season's programs, and in the large and glossy souvenir program, where it is expanded slightly, printed under a photograph of William reclining in casual elegance in a colourful cotton sweater and corduroy slacks, and where it is entitled a "Message from the Artistic Director." In each of its manifestations William's message is clear: we are to see at the 1993 Festival a clearly balanced, binary, and unthreatening exploration of "Order versus the anarchy of Instinct; super-ego and id; sense and sensibility; Apollo against Dionysus," universal and transcendent themes all, and all designed to "appeal, we hope, to all heights of brow" as "a season that will sustain and divert" – and clearly *not* disturb – audiences who are welcomed both as "returning patrons and...new friends."[6] Many of the "returning patrons" (corporate and individual) are listed as donors in the back fourteen pages of the souvenir program under no less than nineteenth categories, ranging from "Major Sponsors" and "President's Club" through "Centre," "Main," and "First Stage;" "Diamond," "Gold," and "Silver Stage;" to "Playwright's Circle," "Supporting" member, and "Supporting Plus;" and finally to various kinds and degrees of benefactors and associates identified by dollar amount, type, and kind of donation.[7] The new "friends," too, were presumably able to afford the Festival's skyrocketing ticket prices, ranging (except for various promotions) from $34.50 to $49.50 (prices have escalated still more dramatically since, to double that amount at the top end) and ranked in equally hierarchical order, with the cheaper seats on the extreme periphery of the theatres, where sightlines and acoustics can be appalling.

These prices are difficult to justify at a publicly subsidized, not-for-profit theatre, particularly when the high-priced sections have tended to expand over the years, pushing the rest further and further to the margins, and when the formerly less expensive seats at the Tom Patterson Theatre (formerly the Third Stage) had moved into line with those at the "main" stages. Canadian government arts-council grants are justified by the theatre, however – in information sheets included in press packages and in the souvenir program – on the grounds of the jobs and tax revenues generated, and on the grounds that those grants amount to only ten percent of the Festival's annual revenue. From a theatregoer's or theatre worker's point of view in Canada, however, when they amounted to by far the largest grants given to any theatre in the country, and when that theatre has staged more American musicals than Canadian plays, the $2,477,000 granted to Stratford in 1993 seemed like subsidizing the rich – and the rich American tourist at that.

How did all of this shape meaning in the Festival's productions of Shakespeare, as "patrons" or potential patrons arrived clutching their $49.50 tickets, each of which prominently displayed the name of that production's corporate sponsor: Dofasco Inc.; Price Waterhouse; the Bank of Montreal; National Trust; Union Gas; Imperial Oil; and so on? How did the productions *mean* for audience members sitting in plush seats that sported brass plaques acknowledging their individual or corporate donors, and reading programs full of upscale and globally "intercultural" (or multinational) advertising for Parisian watches, Jamaican rums, Japanese electronics, Ralph Lauren clothing, and American luxury cars named after Spanish cities? How was meaning shaped by the ad, which appeared in every show's program, inviting the theatre's "patrons" to relocate to Stratford, where "the quality of life is unmatched in North America," particularly for those who may be "travelling by corporate jet" and are desirous of having "'just-in-time' proximity to major Canadian and American markets"? In other words, how did the discourse of the Festival construct its audiences?

Clearly, Stratford in 1993 imagined its "patrons" into being as well-to-do consumers; as having money and leisure to spend on "the finer things of life" reserved for those with privilege and position, including fine cars, fine restaurants, and the fine arts; and as "cultured" people who were constructed in the Festival president's "Salute to Corporate Sponsors," printed in the season's programs, as being capable of recognizing "the enduring role of the arts today," arts which serve "as a testament to the creativity in us all." (Not incidentally, "us all" is represented by the accompanying photographs of the corporate sponsors as exclusively white, male, and middle-aged.) Finally, and above all, Stratford's audiences were constructed as successful people, partners in the success of the theatre itself, which, we were told by Elliott Hayes, "asserts itself as an institution which has been built – and continues to build – on the successive achievements of individual artists." And as we were told in the "Visitor's Guide" to "1993 Festive Stratford" and elsewhere, the Festival "began in a tent in 1953 and is today the largest repertory company in North America, performing on three separate stages and ranked among the great theatres of the English-speaking world." Indeed, according to a brochure called "The Stratford Story," the Festival is more specifically "ranked among the *three* great theatres of the English-speaking world" (my italics), in spite, apparently, of having been "founded in a country where indigenous professional theatre was rare, if not largely unknown," a cultural "vacuum" which without the "vision and perseverance" of a few entrepreneurs (and the help of a few high-profile "consultants" from Britain) might shamefully have remained as "simply another sleepy small town in Ontario."[8]

Clearly, then, Shakespeare at Stratford in 1993 was constructed and read as an intercultural, multinational, and historically transcendent product presented for the pleasure of a privileged and culturally dominant group of consumers for whom "globalization" meant market access, and for whom cultural production was undertaken for the benefit and advantage of those who could afford it.

There was, of course, another set of material conditions through which meaning was produced at Stratford in 1993, conditions that shaped and circumscribed the ways in which directors, designers, actors, and technicians functioned there. Some of these, such as the training and experience of theatre professionals in North America and Britain, are not unique to Stratford, except perhaps in the unusually diverse combination of backgrounds from which the Festival tended to draw. It *is* perhaps worth noting in passing, however, that many of these training methods and processes – such as the Cicely Berry/Kristen Linklater/Patsy Rodenburg schools of voice training, the Alexander technique, and other physical and movement methods, all affirmed by the Festival's corps of eight voice and movement coaches – reinforced the psychophysical and linear conceptions of character, motivation, and action that are already culturally privileged and deeply inscribed in theatrical discourse.[9]

Material conditions specific to the Festival in 1993 included the physical and technical circumstances operating at the three theatres and their auditoria, the functioning of the Festival as a repertory company, and the various traditions, procedures, and processes, organizational and administrative, which had developed at Stratford over its (then) forty years of operation. The company, not unusually in Canada, is organized along hierarchical, corporate principles, with a board of governors dominated by businessmen overseeing the finances and appointing the artistic director and general manager, who report and answer to the board. The various departments for which they are responsible are then run by department heads, managers, and supervisors, in a system that constructs the creative teams in familiar ways as the working class of the theatre, producing and marketing the Festival's shows (and often even themselves, as "stars," "personalities," or "attractions") as products for the consumption of the paying customer. If this seems unsurprising, even normal procedure for a major theatre in the dying days of the twentieth century, that is perhaps a measure of the degree to which consumer capitalism had become the unquestioned and unquestionable "common sense" of the "cultural industries" and the "arts sector," where creative exchange and communication have degenerated with the increasing commodification of culture to the level of commercial exchange. And this structure was and remains deeply embedded in the work that the "employees" of the Festival perform, what is presented on stage, and how audiences understand it.

Stratford was and is not only first and foremost a business; it is important to realize that as the largest theatrical institution in North America it is *big* business. In 1993 the Festival employed 750 people, had a total budget of $24,711,000 (Can.), and had fixed assets with an insured value of $40,381,500. And as in all institutions of its size, there is a certain institutional, structural, and procedural inertia that obtains, and that can defeat even the best-intended creative efforts at change, resistance, or subversion.

The physical plant alone, and the corps of some of the world's best designers, technicians, carpenters, painters, cutters, tailors, decorators, jewellers, milliners, shoemakers, wigmakers, prop-makers, composers, musicians, electricians, and crew, all require employment, even on productions that might be better served by more simple or austere technical support. The sheer quality of the work done by Stratford's staff – and the expectation for excellence-on-parade that this has created over the years – creates a situation in which the "to-be-looked-at-ness" of what is presented can serve, to an unusual and unhealthy degree in an art form that, of course, always relies on the pleasures of looking, to construct the audience as *passive* lookers – voyeurs, consumers, patrons, or investors who must be satisfied that their money has been well spent.[10] If the public discourse of the festival constructed, and continues to construct its audience as white, well-to-do, male, and monolithic, then, the excellence of its physical plant constructs the objects of their gaze as products for perusal and consumption. In 1993 that gaze rested comfortably on a remarkable number of women in lycra body suits – the chorus in the *Bacchae*, for example, and Titania in the *Dream* – together with the scantily-clad strippers of *Gypsy* and the "marquee" breasts of Goldie Semple's Cleopatra, which were made the centre of focus through her costumes to the degree that they became the central theme of the show. Aligned with the interculturally "exotic," which was of, course, gendered female, this objectification of women's bodies was both a contribution to and a product of the Festival's discursive construction of its audience.

If the Stratford Festival functions administratively and ideologically as a corporation, however, it also functions theatrically as a repertory company, in 1993 mounting on its three stages ten full productions, one small-scale trilogy, and several special events. This, too, has many implications for the mounting and meaning of its shows. The repertory system is often celebrated, and justly so, for the ways it can create a healthy company atmosphere, a modicum of job security for theatre workers who are often itinerant and market-dependent, and a creative context in which actors' and others' work on each show imaginatively feeds the other shows on which they work, as various kinds of cross-fertilization feed the creators *and* "consumers" of the shows. To some extent this is true. In 1993, for example, intriguing resonances

were created, for the actor and for audiences, between Colm
Feore's reptilian Oberon in *A Midsummer Night's Dream* and his
fluidly potent (if incongruously masked) Dionysus in *Bacchae*.
For Shakespeare the most interesting and surprising of the resonances created between productions in 1993 had to do with *King
John*, directed at the Tom Patterson Theatre by Robin Phillips,
and Monette's *Antony and Cleopatra*, and many of these resonances were created or enhanced by the fact that the shows shared
many actors. The casting of Goldie Semple as both Constance
and Cleopatra, for example, highlighted the plays' parallel uses
of messenger scenes in which strong women receive the news
of their personal betrayal by powerful men for political reasons.
Similarly, the situation of *King John*'s Blanche, torn apart by her
conflicting loyalties to her husband and family, gained resonance
from the precisely parallel circumstance of *Antony*'s Octavia.
While in the Phillips production Michelle Fisk's Blanche was
quite literally at the centre of an effectively emblematic tug-of-
war involving the full company, however, the same actor's Octavia
was as abandoned by her director as her husband, and left to play
the traditional Stratfordian simpering woman of the tragedies –
weak Shakespearean women that feminist and other analyses in
recent decades have effectively critiqued. Other resonant details
included the intriguingly different portraits of practical men presented by Stephen Ouimette as Philip the Bastard and as Caesar
respectively; the moments in each play in which deserters are
themselves betrayed by their new commanders; and even the
parallel employment of upstage muslin curtains as backdrops,
scrims, and discovery spaces.

Finally, of course, even outside of the single season's repertory,
return visitors to the Festival themselves create resonances by following individual actor's careers, building a memorial repertory
of roles (or even of recycled costumes and furnishings), and taking note of such things as the reappearance in 1993 of Stratford's
previous King John, Edward Atienza, in the role of a peevishly
sleazy Pandulph, or of the evocative echoes in Colm Feore's
Oberon of his earlier roles as Iago, Iachimo, and Richard III.
Such things may be considered to be accidental or irrelevant,
but judging by overheard conversations in lobbies and bars, they
form a considerable part of most audiences' experience of the
plays.

There are constraints to this too, however, some of them more apparent to audiences than others. Casting at Stratford, for example, is a complex procedure, as each director is allowed to hire a minimal number of actors, who then become part of the company's pool, the bulk of which is hired by the artistic director and the "resident director," Robert Beard in 1993. It is from this pool that the majority of roles in each production is cast, after, of course, the labyrinthine complexities of scheduling for shows and rehearsals is taken into account. This can work to actors' and audiences' advantage, as it did when Robin Phillips, in his days as artistic director (1974–80), most often took the career needs of his actors and the experience of his audiences into account in taking personal responsibility for the casting of each season. (But then Phillips tended to himself direct an unprecedented and unsurpassed percentage of each season's shows.) These casting procedures and constraints can also, however, create awkward situations in which directors work with actors they might not otherwise have cast, and actors find themselves stretched in uncomfortable and unhealthy ways, particularly when, as in 1993, the demands of Broadway-style musical theatre and the classical repertory make conflicting claims. The combination of Pompey in *Antony and Cleopatra* with Herbie in *Gypsy* (Peter Donaldson's roles in 1993) can hardly be considered to be healthy cross-fertilization.

There are other, even less apparent rules of repertory as well, rules that are no less constraining. Lighting, for example, is a complex proposition at Stratford, when in 1993 an instrument hang at the Tom Patterson Theatre (the Festival's "third" space) was shared among five shows (including one trilogy) by five different lighting designers, plus a "special-event" "Words and Music Series" of six different evenings. Even at the well-equipped Festival Theatre, where four different designers shared a grid for four very different shows, a certain "house style" almost inevitably obtained, particularly given the significant time constraints on the hands-on use of the busy theatre. At Stratford that style tends to be dictated by the tastes and practices of Michael Whitfield, in 1993 in his twentieth season at Stratford and serving as Resident Lighting Designer. Whitfield's work, for the most part, carries on a tradition of mottled gobos (patterned screens slotted at the front of lighting instruments) and textured atmospherics established by his predecessor, Gil Wechsler, a tradition that tends to create or support a style of heightened theatrical naturalism. The results can be an accommodating softening of a directorial concept, as when in 1993 the potentially subversive and hard-edged pop-rock forest of *A Midsummer Night's Dream* was made more comfortable and more conformative by forest lighting that attempted to reproduce on the facade the polka-dot patterning applied to the stage surface, but through the use of softening, almost dappled gobos ended up consorting better with Mendelssohn than with Motley Crüe, the production's apparently intended inspiration. There is a long-established procedure and technique for lighting at Stratford, and without the informed insistence of a passionately committed director or designer that tradition carries the day almost without question.

Apart from Stratford's repertory system, the theatres themselves and their stages are the most visible and most significant material conditions for the production of meaning at Stratford. In 1993 the Festival operated three theatres. The Avon, seating 1,107 was the company's "second stage." It housed Stratford's only proscenium, was not used for Shakespeare, and can be passed over fairly quickly here. It is worth noting, however, that as the traditional Stratford home not only of Gilbert and Sullivan, but also of financially risky productions of new work or of challenging plays by Ibsen, Chekhov, and Strindberg, it was disappointing in 1993 to see it used exclusively for *The Mikado* and *The Importance of Being Earnest* (the other two theatres were used for four and six productions respectively), both unimaginative if logical choices for this space, and both expected to be money-makers.

Antony and Cleopatra and *A Midsummer Night's Dream*, together with *Gypsy* and *The Imaginary Invalid*, were mounted on the so-called "Elizabethan-style" thrust stage of the Festival theatre, for which Stratford is famous. There is a fiction popular among followers of J. L. Styan and his book, *The Shakespeare Revolution*, together with the publicity offices of Elizabethan-style theatres, that thrust stages, as "empty spaces," are not only "authentic" in some transhistorical sense, but are also genuinely *empty*, neutral, "audience-friendly," and therefore democratic.[11] These spaces, the publicity goes, allow "Shakespeare" to speak directly, as he did to his original audience, to "speak for himself," and be interpreted freely by audiences unburdened by the intrusion of inappropriate scenic decoration. But, as I have argued earlier, ideology abhors a vacuum, and there is no such thing as an empty space. Empty spaces are to the theatre what "common sense" is to critical practice: vacuums to be filled by the unquestioned because naturalized assumptions of ideology.

The Festival stage is a good example. Designed by Tanya Moiseiwitch and built in the 1950s, the stage is very much the product of its time. With its clarity of line and its solidity, its air of dominance, permanence, and authority, the stage is a perfect, internally coherent, and self-contained monument, not to Elizabethan staging, but to post-war modernism (see illus. 4). Whether used as Tyrone Guthrie and Michael Langham have used it, as a series of rostrums for proclamations in turn by highly theatrical characters, or as Robin Phillips has, to draw audiences into identification with naturalistically conceived characters and societies, the stage and the auditorium that surrounds it impose physical conditions that once again construct audiences as the

4. The stage at the Festival Theatre in Stratford, Ontario.

passive consumers of the production as product, and support the replication of capitalist and patriarchal structures.

Power is located stage center at the Festival Theatre – the central pillar of the stage is at the precise geometrical center of the original building, whence it radiates centrifugally throughout the auditorium, nodding intimately towards the top-price seats in orchestra aisle six, but growing increasingly distant towards those seated more cheaply on the peripheries or in the balcony, where sightlines and acoustics are seriously flawed. Whatever the *thematic* content of the productions – which is often a soft-core and self-congratulatory liberalism – any potentially transgressive material that is present is contained and neutralized by a stage and a building that are, to a large extent, themselves the message.

Power was very much in evidence as a central subject of Richard Monette's *Antony and Cleopatra* and Joe Dowling's *A Midsummer Night's Dream* in 1993, both of which concerned themselves more or less directly with power relations and power structures between men and women. In *Antony and Cleopatra* the audience was clearly constructed as male, and their subject position was aligned with that of Antony. The program's plot summary began, quite literally, with "Antony," and the production changed the first line of the script from "this dotage of our general's" to "this dotage of our Antony's," no doubt for clarity. The story was then told in both the summary and the production from the point of view of what Harley Granville Barker, in a passage used for the program note, calls "the once triumphant man of action, [its] hero." As a side-bar to the plot summary, in bold-faced type, the program quotes Antony in act 4, scene 14, "I made these wars for Egypt, and the queen, whose heart I thought I had, for she had mine," constructing Antony and Cleopatra as subject and object respectively, and reinforcing Granville Barker's note that "truly it is [Antony's] passion for Cleopatra that is his ruin."[12] Similarly, the director is quoted in the Festival edition of the local newspaper, the *Beacon Herald* as saying that "the play is about the conflict between duty and desire" (presumably Antony's), and that it "shows the dissolution of Antony's powers to command." In the same article, however, Monette mystifies and naturalizes his reading as neutral and value free by insisting that "I've chosen to balance the play and not interpret the play."[13]

Antony was played by Leon Pownall in a physical form and actorly fashion not easily distinguishable from his earlier performances as Henry VIII at Stratford, or even his incarnation as Long John Silver in 1991. An ageing and overweight sensualist going through a mid-life crisis, Pownall's Antony was dressed by designer Stephanie Howard, "sometimes ... like Lawrence of Arabia and sometimes like the Sheik of Araby," as the *Beacon Herald* puff piece itself put it.[14] In the same newspaper, Pownall claims to see Antony as having "gone native," and he describes "the exquisite romance and lifestyle of the East" in, again, textbook orientalist terms.[15] Clearly this Egypt, represented through the eyes of Antony (and of course Enobarbus), functioned for both the audience and for the characters as a white male fantasyland, where exotic, passionate, and foreign women, some of them Black (though not, illogically, Cleopatra),[16] exist for the sole purpose of transporting "us" beyond the mundane worlds of Caesar, the economy, and affairs of state. Lurching, pompous, and blustery, this Antony was not himself very attractive (I overheard one man ask his companion at intermission what Cleopatra saw in him), but was perhaps an appropriate surrogate for playing out the fantasies of an audience already constructed by the discourses of the Festival as white, male, and middle-aged.

Goldie Semple's Cleopatra was appropriately conceived and costumed to fit the needs of her Antony and her audience. Her outrageously lavish clothes and accessories were for the most part generically exotic rather than specific to any particular place or historical period, appropriating "the other" as represented by rich fabrics and "eastern" fashions in much the same way as the same season's *Bacchae* followed the modernists in appropriating generically "primitive" and "African" masks and materials. According to the *Beacon Herald*, Semple herself saw Cleopatra, not surprisingly, as "passionate," "sensual," and "seductive," "attuned to Eastern intuition as opposed to western logic ... and to a place which is more sensual and imaginative."[17] And if there was more bluster and bust than sex or sap in the relationship between these lovers, at least, in death, "they both transcend," as Semple said, and the fantasy was made both safe and metaphysical. As the audience filed out of the theatre, Antony and Cleopatra could be heard, voice over, replaying their earlier love scenes, presumably rejoined in an eternal gaudy night in Cydnus.

Apart from the Egyptian locations, the production was set by designer Stephanie Howard in a vaguely defined late nineteenth or early twentieth century, with much use of uniforms to differentiate among the armies. Taken as a whole, the costumes suggested an uncomfortable meeting of the Arabian Nights with fascist Italy, which was openly evoked by the uniforms, troop formations, and massive desks (with black telephones) employed for the Roman scenes. This choice, together with the focus on Antony as subject, tended to reduce the talented Stephen Ouimette as Caesar to sneering caricatures of a cartoon dictator. The design had the quality of work by someone who had seen but not understood Robin Phillips' Edwardian settings for Shakespeare, picking up moments but managing them badly, and eschewing both Phillips' historical specificity and the overt and confrontational eclecticism of, say, the Bogdanov/Pennington *Wars of the Roses*, the costumes for which, ironically, were also designed by Stephanie Howard.

Joe Dowling's *A Midsummer Night's Dream* was more thoroughly eclectic than Monette's *Antony*, and more potentially unsettling of audience complacencies. Dowling's Athens combined modern-dress suits for the Duke and his security people with more-or-less Austro-Hungarian uniforms for Demetrius and Lysander that looked to have been pulled from old *Much Ado* stock, adding "roaring twenties" outfits for the mechanicals. His forest, however, was an inflatable rubber and lycra *mélange* of erotic exotica with extensive music and dance deriving primarily from American street culture and the world of rock video.

The stage arrangements and blocking were all dictated by the presence in the forest scenes of a few large, inflatable rubber set pieces, costing $15,000 (Can.) to build, and inspired by the inflatable emergency exit ramps in commercial aircraft. Most observers and reviewers recognized these as male and female genitalia (though at least one academic I spoke with saw them as the ingredients of a ham and Swiss cheese sandwich). In any case, a large, ribbed, and certainly phallic trunk rose from the stage floor to the balcony, connecting a more globular blob on the stage proper to the vaginal folds of another on the balcony level, which was used for entrances and exits. The balcony piece was suggestively effective as Titania's bower, particularly when she led Bottom there in act 3, scene 1, but it was at best confusing elsewhere to see Puck and others crawling through its opening to make entrances and exits. The phallic trunk, on the other hand, was used primarily by Colm Feore's reptilian, bat-like Oberon, who on occasion hung from it by one hand, scuttled up its shaft, or slithered quickly down the shank. Meanwhile, the testicular blob, stage center, served as forest floor, pillow, grassy knoll, and other sylvan sites, but was distractingly prone to causing sleeping lovers' heads to bounce about while Puck and others walked across it.

The set, then, designed by Hayden Griffin, seemed finally to be an example of what happens when a single concept, however provocative and technically innovative, gets out of hand. In spite of an at times jarringly abrupt juxtaposition of styles and periods; in spite of the transgressive sexuality of the forest's eroticism, including transvestite "fairies" as back-up singers for the spotted-snake lullaby to Titania; and in spite of an unusually attractive cross-dressed Thisbe; the design not only caused incidental constraints and distractions in the forest scenes themselves, but it also detracted from the scenes at court. There was the need, at the outset, to disguise the blobs' uninflated presence through the use of an obtrusive red canopy and guy-wires; and at the end to leave one blob onstage at court, illogically, to serve as set piece for the play-within. The design also encouraged a tendency in the acting and conception of the production to let the audience off the hook, partly because of tongue-in-cheek acting in roles such as Bottom (Ted Dykstra), and partly because of the evident lack of logic in *this* Oberon's attempting to help the lovers. There was no felt need to take the whole thing seriously.

There is no question, however, that the forest dominated and dictated the terms for the production, and as a site for potentially creative or even subversive anarchy this could have been productive. The first scene at the court was full of tension between a tyrannical Theseus and "his" Hippolyta, whose long, silent, and upstaging descent from the balcony and cross over the stage to kiss Hermia signalled dissension clearly, even before her peremptory exit on "Come my Hippolyta," which left Theseus publicly embarrassed for "what cheer my love." And the later cutting of "the lunatic, the lover, and the poet" suggests that great constancy was not something for which the production was striving. Although the Duke and his captive Queen seemed to pick up in act 4, scene 1, where they left off earlier, unchanged until Hippolyta forced Theseus to overrule Egeus, making a point, then, of taking his arm on his act 5 reprise of "Come Hippolyta," the resolution did come, seemed to come too easily, and was apparently unrelated, except through plot parallels, to the transformations of the night. Finally, the reasons for Hippolyta's willingness to marry and be reconciled with Theseus, like those for Titania's reconciliation with Oberon, were both unclear and problematic, imposed, disappointingly, by the conventional comic structure, which was treated with Stratford's usual reverence. In any case, the potentially interesting strength of Hippolyta dissolved at the end into the kind of soft-core and token feminism that can generally render liberal feminisms ineffectual.

The forest scenes did not, however, seem to be mediative in conception, though they ultimately served that function almost in spite of themselves. Presided over by a gyrating Puck dressed in a fringed electric blue and yellow body suit with matching yellow face and frizzy blue hair, these forest scenes might best be described as, "The Story of the Night: the Musical." Drawing on commercialized street culture, rock video conventions, and what I think of as "designer punk," Keith Thomas's musical score and John Broome's choreography blended and appropriated the violent social voice of rap and contemporary dance music – the electronic "sampling" of "rock the ground" was a brilliant moment – with the softer, earlier tones of 1950s "do-wap" (dew lap?), together with the occasional foray into, among other things, torch songs, blues, and something sounding suspiciously like Andrew Lloyd Webber. The sound track was for sale in the lobby.

What could have been a frenetic and subversive upheaval at the center of the play – the quarrel between Colm Feore's Oberon and Lucy Peacock's Titania was violent, and their reconciliation violently erotic – was contained somewhat too comfortably by the exploitative commercialization of Black street culture, the colonizing gaze of an audience constructed as consumers, and the lethal embrace of the stage, its institutions, and its traditions. There were elements, such as the ugly intrusiveness of the inflatable forest set-piece into the otherwise elegant court in act 5, in which one could sense the potential of genuinely disturbing subversion of Stratford's high-culture traditions. But, overall, this potential was contained and neutralized by the elegance of the stage's rich natural wood, especially its rich upstage façade (a containment which the designer tried with only partial success to circumvent by applying plastic polka dots to the stage surface and projecting matching polka-dot patterns onto the façade with light); by the poise and grace of actors who had trouble assuming an ugliness they were not trained to; by the mellifluousness of the sound system; and by the sheer quality and conspicuous cost of the set pieces, costumes, and masks.

While actors gushed in interviews about the "pumping eroticism" of the production,[18] suggesting that it would shock, surprise, and even disturb audiences, Dowling drew upon the old chestnut, Jan Kott, to talk about the contemporaneity of the text which would, he assured us, be "spoken as it is."[19] For all of the rhetoric of contemporary relevance, and for all the promised pop-culture irreverence and socially subversive sex, the underlying discursive construction was universalist and conservative, and this conservatism was reinforced by an otherwise incongruous program note from G. K. Chesterton on the structural perfection of the play. The forest, according to Dowling, evokes a Nature that "doesn't change," and a sexual imagination that "we all have."[20] The final blessing, delivered throughout the auditorium by means of a syrupy choral song, with solos by an Oberon who by virtue of his murky make-up and glittery top hat resembled a chimney-sweep refugee from *Mary Poppins*, was a sentimental reversion to a Disneyesque fairyland whose power to disturb had long since been contained.

All this, of course, is familiar and discouraging – what Alan Sinfield has taught us to think of as "Shakespeare-plus-relevance."[21] The eclecticism of the design was ultimately evasive, then, resembling in its ahistoricism as well as its eclecticism the excesses or irresponsibilities of much depoliticized North American postmodernism. The production's ultimate message seemed to be, "see how hip we are? Shakespeare isn't *really* so stuffy: you can feel cultured and hip at the same time!" Puck's epilogue, on the production's lack of offense, was entirely accurate.

Stratford's Third Stage, renamed the Tom Patterson Theatre in 1991 in honour of the Festival's founder and in acknowledgment of its first-stage prices, has traditionally been less likely than the Festival stage to be bound by the dead hand of the past or the constraints of genteel expectation. Housed in a converted barn-like building beside the Stratford lawn-bowling club, and seating a capacity of 500 in 1993 (less than twenty five percent of that of the Festival theatre), the Tom Patterson has little of the air of authority and permanence of Stratford's other stages; in fact, it reverts each winter to its off-season role as a badminton club. The venue has been in use by the Festival for new or experimental works or workshops since 1971, and has through much of its theatrical history been the home of the Young Company, who staged Corneille's *The Illusion* there in 1993. This tradition creates at least an atmosphere of less constraint than obtains at the other stages. It has also created a "third-stage" audience that, in theory at least, is more adventuresome than at the other theatres, more willing to take risks on new work, such as the 1993 premiere production of Sharon Pollock's *Fair Liberty's Call*; on small-scale shows, such as the popular three-play, one-man *Wingfield Trilogy* in 1993; or on "difficult" plays, such as *The Illusion* or *King John*.

In 1993, for *King John* at least, the sense of interpretative freedom was reinforced by the fact that Robin Phillips, the play's director, was artistic director of the Festival from 1974–80, and was in 1987 the original designer of the modular stage since housed at the Tom Patterson, though it was modified and softened somewhat by Debra Hanson, the Festival's Head of Design in 1993. Phillips did his best to restore the extended thrust that he designed in the late 1980s to its original shape and dimensions, and through paint to a colour resembling its original austere bleached pine. As designed, and as used for *King John*, it was a remarkably uncompromising space, which provided audiences with an astonishing range of extreme perspectives on the action, and exposed flaws and hesitations mercilessly. As Phillips uses it, this is among the most challenging stages in the world.

In *King John*, Phillips used it to create, as both set designer and director, and with the help of Ann Curtis's costumes, an internally coherent, historically precise, and theatrically stylized world of the Europe leading up to and engaged in the First World War. If Dowling's *Dream* was failed or half-hearted postmodernism, however, Phillips' *King John* represented the successful, clear, perfectly realized, and ultimately closed *modernist* vision of one of the few Canadian directors with, like most modernists, a recognizable individual aesthetic, one that was precisely served and supported by the austere elegance of the restored third stage. For this production, for better or worse, the material context worked to reinforce the production's aesthetics and politics rather than to subvert them, as in Dowling's *Dream*.

Like many modernist works, Phillips' *King John* was at least in part and at least implicitly about power, form, the power of form, and the forms of power. The period setting, not coincidentally, coincided with the early days of high modernism (and the roots of modern fascism). The production opened with the recruitment-poster image of Kitchener projected upstage, the amplified voices of women singing a First World War recruitment song, and the lurking physical presence of the Pope behind the upstage muslin. The Pope appeared at intervals throughout, always behind the scrim, and always seeming to appear from nowhere to control the action as a personification of hierarchical authority. At the end of the play, the full company assembled (including characters long dead), and as the Bastard spoke his final lines, the audience's eyes were drawn inexorably toward the white rotundity of Rome.

The stage itself was flanked by facing rows of Victorian side chairs, furnished with modern modular pine-and-metal set pieces familiar to Phillips aficionados, and backed upstage by gauze/scrim draping extending from floor to grid. It was, for the most part, brightly lit with clean, white light, and deco-rated sparsely. Blocking was tightly controlled, battle scenes were mimed with expressionist clarity, and visual imagery was consis-tently stunning, underscoring the aestheticism at the roots of modernism.

Phillips and his actors paid the play the compliment of tak-ing it seriously, and avoiding the bluster that often besets what few contemporary productions *King John* receives. The result was a production no less about lies and expediency than is tradi-tional, but one in which the characters convinced themselves, at least, of their sincerity, and one in which the roles of the play's powerful women came to the fore. Janet Wright's Eleanor was very much the power behind the English throne, and contributed to one of the production's most effective moments by ushering young Arthur upstage center, where she stood condor-like, in sil-houette and dressed in black, with her arm enveloping the boy, while downstage, across the full expanse of the thrust, Nicholas Pennell's John insinuated the idea of Arthur's murder into the mind of Hubert, his whispers chillingly amplified throughout the theatre. This was the last scene before the interval, and as the lights faded we saw Eleanor, still in silhouette, facing as through the looking glass the contrasting white and unscripted figure of the Pope behind the gauze.

Goldie Semple's Constance was equally strong, and for once her grief was given its due, in a performance that rendered the men's impatience with her odious rather than sympathetic, as it often is. Her great scene in act 2, scene 3, in particular, was deeply moving, as she managed to hold the stage and our engaged sympathies while concluding the speech collapsed on the floor and partially obscured upstage and off-center. Phillips' and Semple's unconventionally effective control of focus here was brilliantly unsettling, as a scene that is often embarrassing in performance became a centerpiece of the production.

If the strength of the production's women was refreshing (and of course helpful in explaining the collapse of John and of the entire structure of the play world after their deaths), the serious playing of these and other roles also caused some problems for Stephen Ouimette, the actor playing Phillip of Faulconbridge. Usually the touchstone to productions of *King John*, since he can undercut the bluster of the others, the role of the Bastard of Faulconbridge was difficult to place in this production, given the already understated playing of the rest of the cast. I saw the show three times: in preview, half-way through, and late in the run; and what early on was a struggle for Ouimette eventually became one of the show's strengths. Ouimette's Bastard first entered wearing a kilt, the only character in the play to do so, and though he eschewed the Scottish accent that might have been expected to accompany the costume, it was enough to set him apart from both the militant French and the somewhat effete English. (Among the production's brilliant strokes were the English camp's tea-party picnic before Angiers, and the comfit-munching image of Nicholas Pennell's archetypally English King John during Constance's quarrel with Phillip of France in act 3, scene 1.) This Bastard's natural affiliations were with Eleanor and Hubert, and he, more than anyone else, made the audience aware of the cost of politics to those such as Arthur, or, notably here, the soldiers so pointlessly lost in the Lincoln Washes. His ironies in this production were harsher, less amusing than they often are, and the production consequently concerned itself more directly with the social cost of playing politics.

Interestingly, the almost naturalistic focus of the actors on character and motivation, placed in this highly stylized context, resulted somewhat unexpectedly in a withdrawal of sympathies from individual characters. It created for the audience a sense that to focus on the psychological motivations of individuals is to ignore the theatre of politics as a social arena. The action was played out on what was for the most part a brightly lit stage, and the arrangement of the flanking and rarely used rows of chairs seemed parliamentary in its Canadian context, where, as in Britain, the government faces the opposition in a posture of debate across a central stage area (and where in most sittings of parliament the majority of member's places are empty). These chairs were positioned in front of audience members that were themselves brightly lit for much of the production and were lined up like back-benchers – members of parliament without cabinet positions – behind them. The public forum that was the play, then, resonated evocatively during a run that encompassed a leadership convention and election campaign in Canada, in which personality eclipsed the discussion of issues, in spite of the alarming fact that the country's social programs were on the block.

This was not, however, Sinfield's "Shakespeare-plus-relevance," at least not as it is usually understood. The production made no effort to address contemporary issues, or to point up its connections with contemporary Canada. Like most high modernist works, this *King John* was essentially self-referential, existing self-sufficiently in its own and fully realized world, and referring outward only through metaphoric connections made in the minds of audiences. There were no post-structuralist fissures here, none of the *Dream*'s erotic metonymy, and little that could be constructed as subversive, but the production made brilliant and self-conscious use of its own *means* of production, and it exposed and probed within its own form the modes and mechanisms of power. It succeeded on its own terms in a way that no other production did at Stratford in 1993, and it did so by taking fully into account its theatrical context and means of production.

No production of Shakespeare can be assessed outside of the material context within and through which it is produced, any more than can the production of the scripts themselves. At

Stratford, Ontario in 1993, where even more than at most theatres the institutional context tended to function with remarkable directness as an Ideological State Apparatus,[22] funded by government and corporate grants and catering to an audience it constructed as monolithic, the production of Shakespeare is necessarily the reproduction of a complex and shifting but nevertheless conservative, affirmative culture, endorsed by the appropriated, high-cultural image of a universalist "bard of Avon." It is important that directors, designers, actors, and technicians acknowledge and even confront the material conditions within which they work, particularly if they wish to achieve any kind of intervention into the circulation of cultural values – if they wish for their work to be culturally productive rather than simply reproductive. It is equally important for reviewers and critics, in spite of Eric Bentley's manifesto with which I began this chapter and within which Stratford framed its 1993 season, to resist the universalist urge to treat all theatrical production as taking place in a material vacuum, to treat all productions of Shakespeare as somehow comparable theatrical realizations or interpretations of what is "in" the scripts. It is important, then, that reviewers and critics of Shakespearean production, at the Stratford Festival and elsewhere, learn not simply to interpret and analyse production texts *as* texts, but also analytically to read the material theatre itself, and the conditions that shape theatrical production.

4   Tarragon Theatre

Toronto's Tarragon Theatre in the mid 1990s, as represented by its productions of Jason Sherman's new Canadian play, *The Retreat*, in 1996, and of Tennessee Williams's American classic, *The Glass Menagerie* in 1997, represents a relatively straightforward example of the containment of potentially provocative work by unusually homogeneous material conditions.[1] I have chosen this theatre and these productions less for their fascination as interestingly contested sites of the negotiation of cultural values than for their unusual clarity as examples of the operation of containment in action. I am aware of the dangers of inscribing as an analytical model the too simple either/or binary of subversion and containment (with little in between), but the clarity of the Tarragon example, and the degree to which discourses and practices of production and reception can work in relative consort there, make it a useful object of study.

Tarragon Theatre began its life as one of four small theatres in Toronto in the late 1960s and early 70s which set themselves up as nationalist "alternatives" to the then established mainstream Regional Theatre network in Canada, which was considered by many to be inadequately serving the needs of Canadian actors, directors, playwrights, and audiences. The large "Regionals" had been established and federally funded across Canada in the wake of the [Vincent] Massey Commission report of 1952, which had been mandated by the Federal government to report on the state of Canadian culture. These theatres embodied the report's "center-to-periphery" philosophy for cultural dissemination (based on the British model), and functioned for the most part as "branch-plant" operations, taking Art and Culture from the Centre to the supposedly culturally impoverished regions.[2] Tarragon took its place among the small, lower-case regional theatres that emerged in various parts of the country and that usually functioned in a relation of real or rhetorical opposition to the large Regional Theatres. Like other such theatres, Tarragon was considered to be an "alternate" theatre, a term widely used in the 1970s to refer to the theatres involved in what is now most often called "the alternative theatre movement."[3] Most scholars in recent years have become uncomfortable with a mainstream–alternative binary that was strategically useful for certain theatre workers in the 1970s, but that is now considered both to be (re)productive of various kinds of marginalization, and insufficiently nuanced as an analytical category. I am invoking it here, however, as part of a historical discourse that has had, and continues to have, significant material and interpretative consequences.

The mandates and practices of Toronto's so-called "alternates" – which included, in addition to Tarragon, The Factory Theatre Lab, Toronto Free Theatre, and Theatre Passe Muraille – in fact varied considerably, and Tarragon, in particular, has worn the label "alternative" with considerable discomfort. Although Tarragon has always been anxious to position itself "on the cutting edge,"[4] and although its play-development mandate and relatively small budget set it apart from the Regional Theatre network from the beginning, the theatre has produced in its policies, procedures, physical arrangements, public profile, and production history a discourse of stability, balance, comfort, and quality that equally sets it apart from such organizations as Factory Theatre, with its discourse of excitement, adventure, and risk. The Factory has traditionally been understood, in its early years as Factory Theatre Lab ("Lab" was dropped in 1984), to have been in real or imagined conflict with Tarragon, usually over questions of style and subject matter: Tarragon has typically been seen as the home of naturalistic plays on Canadian subjects, with David French seen as its paradigmatic playwright; Factory, meanwhile, has most often been seen as having been a more experimental venue associated with non-realistic plays set in exotic locations, with the early, anti-naturalist work of George F. Walker serving as the preferred example.[5]

Tarragon is located "on the ... edge" of, and literally across the tracks from, Toronto's fashionable "Annex" area (so named because, just northwest of the city center, it was annexed by the rapidly growing city of Toronto in 1887), now an older, residential quarter of the city made up of a mixture of formerly, recently, or soon-to-be renovated homes, largely brick, and peopled for the most part by professionals, artists, and faculty and students of the nearby University of Toronto. This location is, nevertheless, to some degree liminal: the approach to the theatre by public transit involves a potentially uncomfortable walk from Bathurst Street along the poorly lit Bridgman Avenue on the borders of a railway track, and the trains passing by during performances provide regular disturbances to the illusionistic veneer of most performances. The majority of Tarragon's audience, however, arrives at the theatre by car, and makes use of the convenient parking lot on the south side of Bridgman Avenue, and the primary effect of the positioning of the theatre at the edge of the Annex would seem to be its association with that neighborhood's demographic and economic mix, together with its participation in the comforting discourse of "neighborhood" itself. The theatre's audience base is largely derived from the generally "well-off" "professional-managerial class" as defined by Barbara Ehrenreich and John Ehrenreich, with ages ranging from the forties to the sixties, together with an admixture of University students and theatre workers.[6] According to Mallory Gilbert, the theatre's general manager, "a fair number" of Tarragon's audience members are from "the Annex area," and statistics gathered by the theatre in 1995 support her view. Gilbert characterizes the audience as "fairly well-educated . . . very well off," an assessment which my own experience working at and attending the theatre confirms.[7]

The building that houses Tarragon is the site of a former warehouse and casting factory,[8] but its exterior over the years has become comfortably overgrown by trees, bushes, greenery, and a kind of genteel decay. In the same period the interior has evolved through a series of expansions and renovations into a virtual rabbit-warren of offices, workshops, rehearsal halls, and passageways on its second level, with the ground floor devoted primarily to the main, mid-sized performance space, seating just over two hundred,[9] a small, variable-seating "Extra Space," and a (relatively) large lobby with front-of-house facilities and audience amenities that include a refreshment bar serving coffee, juices, bottled water, premium beers, and the theatre's trademark "big cookies." Jennifer Fletcher has characterized the working spaces at Tarragon as democratic in organization and communal in sensibility: "the financial and administrative offices mingle and overlap with the artistic directorship offices," she notes, pointing out that both the late Urjo Kareda, then the theatre's artistic director, and Mallory Gilbert, its general manager throughout the theatre's history to date, always understood the company "as a community or family of workers where a sense of 'collaboration' governs the atmosphere".[10] But the slippage between the discourses of family and those of cooperation, collaboration, and democracy masks the hierarchical structure of the patriarchal family in ways that, applied to the Tarragon (with its artistic director "father figure"[11] and female general manager), are suggestive. Like those of cooperation and collaboration in this context, moreover, the discourses of tolerance and liberal pluralism tend to exist within naturalized hierarchies in which agency is in fact distributed unequally.

The lobby area at the Tarragon in the mid 1990s, congruent with the organizational and written discourses of the theatre, was a relaxed and comfortable living-room area, with well-worn couches, fresh flowers, warm colours, and award plaques and photographs both of previous productions and members of extended "Tarragon family" – including Cleo, the family dog – lining the walls. Both of the theatre's performing spaces created and reinforced a democratic sense of comfortable fairness for both theatre workers and audiences through the use of undifferentiated seating areas, single-price general admission policies,[12] and unpretentious programs with artists' names listed alphabetically (rather than by size of role or reputation), and all workers, except for playwrights – an issue to which we will return – acknowledged equally.

As an organization, Tarragon Theatre has been constructed throughout its history through a discourse of stability and balance that intriguingly blends the fiscal with the philosophical. According to Denis Johnston, Bill Glassco founded the theatre partly in reaction to what he saw as "slapdash production standards" and "offhand squalor" at Factory Theatre Lab, and partly as an attempt to "balance his conservative aesthetic with the experimental quality of the venture."[13] The theatre's early success was interpreted similarly as "a combination of sound management and personal commitment."[14] Indeed, the name Tarragon was itself chosen explicitly "to avoid anything with 'workshop,' 'studio,' or 'lab' in it":[15]

The name "Tarragon" . . . was a reaction against the kind of alternative theatre which promised half-realized artistic experiments. Instead, it offered the imagery of the kitchen: a bright, comfortable work place where carefully chosen ingredients are skilfully combined to bring pleasure to one's guests. It also suggested the well-bred courtesy of the Glasscos' [Bill and his wife Jane's] upbringing, of a style not to be found at Passe Muraille or Factory.[16]

The discourse of the theatre over the years, and indeed the theatre's organizational history since its inception in 1971, has been similarly characterized *by* and *as* a careful *balancing* of ingredients within an atmosphere of well-bred, family-style courtesy. It is a discourse and a history that sort well with a politics of liberal tolerance and fairness adopted and exercised out of a position of social stability and cultural security. Part of this security derives from the social positioning – what Johnston calls the "upper[-]crust" sensibilities[17] – of Jane and Bill Glassco, who founded the theatre, partly "for the fun of it," as "a family operation."[18] But it also derives from the stability and continuity of the operation itself. Uniquely among small Canadian theatres, Tarragon had only two artistic directors over its first quarter-century of history, the second, Urjo Kareda, who remained artistic director until his early death from cancer in 2002, hand-picked in 1982 by the first, Glassco (who remains a board member).[19] When Kareda was selected, moreover, he was on record as a strongly supportive reviewer of Tarragon productions since his praise was registered for the theatre's first show – in his first review as lead theatre critic for *The Toronto Star* – in 1971. Moreover Kareda later wrote of Tarragon and its founding artistic director that

a theatre is a family and Glassco is certainly a father-figure at Bridgman Avenue; the pressures of balancing that with his own private family – his marvellous wife Jane (who also works at the Tarragon) and their three children – must be unimaginable.[20]

Similarly, the theatre's general manager since 1975, Mallory Gilbert, has worked for Tarragon as an administrator since – again in Johnston's characterization – she joined the "founding family" in 1972.[21] Gilbert has also been constructed by the public discourse of the theatre since then as, in Kareda's words, "an extraordinarily family oriented person... But it's a family that's not just her two kids and (ex-husband and friend) John Gilbert, but a very big theatre family within this building [Tarragon Theatre] and across the country."[22] One Toronto theatre critic, profiling Gilbert, discusses her abilities "balancing the books" and working to make Tarragon both "a model of stability on the uncertain landscape of alternative theatre in Toronto," and "the country's most reliable purveyor of new Canadian drama."[23]

It may be thinking too precisely on the publicity, but one might be forgiven for wondering if the cluster of images around family, balance, stability, and sales ("purveyor of new Canadian drama"), works to construct a context within which it is more possible theatrically to ask, or hear, some kinds of questions than others, and in which deconstructions of liberal humanist values and social structures centering on the patriarchal, capitalist economy of the family might be difficult. Indeed, the familial model of heterosexual patriarchy might even be expected to issue less in societal intervention than in an essentially *re*productive economy that has, not surprisingly, been most frequently associated by scholars and critics in recent years with Tarragon's preferred mode, poetic naturalism, of which more below.

There is also an interesting continuity, as I have suggested, between the discourses of comfort, stability, and balance, the theatre's attempts in their productions to present balanced accounts of contemporary issues, and Tarragon's reputation for financial stability and balanced *books* – a reputation that once again sets it apart from organizations such as Factory Theatre, which prides itself on theatrical risk-taking while also always existing precariously at the edge of financial collapse. At a time when Factory had twice in one year seen its loans called in and its doors padlocked, and a time when all arts and social organizations in Ontario suffered from deep federal and provincial cuts, Tarragon, according to its 30 June 1995 financial statement, managed in one fiscal year to increase its revenues and pay $58,640 against its accumulated deficit of $68,613. Again, however, one might be forgiven for wondering if organizational and financial balance frames a theatrical aesthetic and ideological positioning that feature a liberal-centrist political discourse of balance and responsibility, aligning Tarragon more closely with such public institutions as the Canadian Broadcasting Corporation (CBC), which works within a mandated (nationalist) discourse of balance and equal representation, than with any movement in the theatre, the arts, or society that could justifiably be considered to be alternative.

How, then, do all of these geographical, architectural, organizational, and discursive conditions – together, of course, with the training of actors, directors, and designers, the processes of rehearsal and technical production and of new play development – play themselves out in the production of meaning by practitioners and audiences in particular performances? Quite comfortably, in the case of *The Glass Menagerie* in 1997 and Jason Sherman's *The Retreat* in 1996 (at least as it emerged from the rehearsal and development process at the theatre). Indeed, these productions were particularly closely fitted to Tarragon's discourses, working conditions, and methods.

Both productions were framed, of course, by the cumulative discourse and the general physical and geographical context that I have been outlining. Both were also framed directly by Tarragon's traditional interest in poetic naturalism as a style; by the dominant traditions in Canada of actor and director training and rehearsal practices; and by Tarragon's mandated privileging of the playwright and the literary script, together with, in the case of *The Retreat*, its processes of new-play development.

Tarragon from the beginning has been a literary theatre, devoted primarily to the development of the playwright as writer. Both Glassco and Kareda have academic training in dramatic literature, and Glassco's 1971 manifesto, "Why Tarragon?", on the founding of the theatre, articulates a focus on the playwright. As Robert Nunn notes in his entry on the theatre in *The Oxford Companion to Canadian Theatre*,

Tarragon's mandate has always placed the playwright at the centre...There has been virtually no attention to collective creation nor to work in which gesture and image, not language, constitute the commanding centre. A passion for language and a dedication to the playwright define Tarragon's identity and represent its greatest strength.[24]

Within this mandate, Tarragon has always evinced a preference for a style that might best be described as poetic naturalism – a heightened naturalism best suited to explorations of human psychological motivation and interaction in recognizable settings and situations. From the beginning, both Glassco as a director and dramaturge and Kareda as a reviewer and Chekhov scholar showed a deep sympathy for naturalism. In his well-known introduction to David French's first play, *Leaving Home*, produced at Tarragon in 1972, Kareda articulated the "mysterious richness of the naturalistic technique," and the strengths of a style he called "selective naturalism" – naturalism "with the detail carefully gauged and controlled for poetic resonance." "Naturalism," he argued "is an impressionistic method with strict and fascinating formal controls," and he praised Toronto's young playwrights in the 1971–72 season for turning their attention to "old-fashioned, naturalistic drama."[25] It is not surprising, then, that the Canadian playwrights with whom the theatre is most closely associated, from David French in the 1970s to Judith Thompson in the 80s, 90s, and beyond, have tended to work in styles that may stretch the boundaries of naturalism, but rarely break through them. Nor is it surprising that revivals produced at Tarragon have tended to be selected from the naturalistic repertoire – works by Chekhov have dominated, but those of the naturalistic O'Neill, Mamet, and Shepard also show up from time to time.

In 1997 it was the turn of Tennessee Williams, whose early work, *The Glass Menagerie*, felt quite at home within the Tarragon family (see illus. 5). The production was framed in the season brochure in familiar terms that focused on family and on balance, as an "unforgettable tragicomic story of a family – mother, son, daughter – that is both sustained and made vulnerable by its illusions." Williams himself was identified there as "the American theatre's most generous and humane poetic dramatist," but neither there nor in the lengthy program biography was any attention drawn either to the autobiographical character of the play, nor to the scholarly and theatrical revival of interest in Williams as a gay playwright. Finally, the brochure drew attention to the director, Diana Leblanc, who at the time was best known as the director of the critically acclaimed Stratford Festival production of another masterpiece of American naturalism, O'Neill's *Long Day's Journey Into Night*, and to the casting of Martha Henry as Amanda, also closely associated with both

5. Martha Henry and Michael McManus in the 1997 Tarragon Theatre (Toronto) production of Tennessee Williams' *The Glass Menagerie*, directed by Diana Leblanc.

the Stratford Festival through most of its fifty-year history.[26] The choice of Leblanc and Henry is typical of Tarragon practices in hiring and casting from among Canada's leading actors and directors working within the country's dominant tradition.[27] Martha Henry is one of Canada's best and best-known naturalistic actors, trained in the tradition first developed by Stanislavski for productions of Chekhov. She is uniquely suited to and experienced in performing the major roles in classic naturalistic drama (including Chekhov), and (under the direction of Diana Leblanc) she made something of a specialty in the mid-1990s of the female leads in productions of plays by Williams, Miller, and the O'Neill of *Long Day's Journey*, plays closely associated with the American variation on Stanislavski's System known as the American Method – a method that is not incidentally also closely associated with American schools of (normalizing) psychotherapy. In fact, both Leblanc and Henry were trained at Canada's National Theatre School – Henry is famous as its first graduate – where they would have learned, as Denis Salter has argued, an eclectic, depoliticized, culturally unlocated approach to acting rooted in a blend of the Stanislavski System and the American Method, an approach that is deeply ideologically coded and culturally affirmative, and that focuses attention on the realms of the psychological, individual, and "universal" rather than on the social and historical, and therefore the political.

What they won't [have acquired] at the school . . . is systematic training in the kinds of interpretative and stylistic problems which the ideologically-driven theatre of Brecht, Piscator, Meyerhold, and Boal has tried to come to terms with. Nor will they [have received] extensive training in the ritualistically-explorative theatre of Artaud, Grotowski, Schechner, and Brook; nor in the post-modern "pure performance" theatre of Wilson, Foreman, the Wooster Group, and Lepage.[28]

It is interesting that Tarragon's focus on Canada and on what Bill Glassco called "creating a distinctive kind of theatre, one which, hopefully, can make a contribution to this country's culture,"[29] has not led it to explorations of new, specifically Canadian approaches to acting, directing, or design (as did both Theatre Passe Muraille under Paul Thompson and the Theatre Resource Centre under the late Richard Pochinko in Toronto in the 1970s), but has focused exclusively on script development within a received theatrical tradition. It has focused, that is, on the production as *product* rather than on the shaping influences of the processes of production.

Not surprisingly, then, Tarragon's *The Glass Menagerie* was a strong and solid production within a clearly naturalistic tradition. It contained few surprises, and those that it did contain had to do with interpretations of character and unusual delivery of lines. The play rewards this treatment, of course, but one wonders whether another theatre might have taken more care to historicize the show, to pay attention to what Tom calls, in the play's first scene, "the social background of the play": the revolution, followed by the triumph of Franco, in Spain; and "disturbances of labor" and "a dissolving economy" in 1930s America,[30] not to mention Amanda's racism or the social context for, and social cost of, the rugged individualism of the "gentleman caller" (which in the Tarragon production was merely cute). Indeed, one wonders whether the Tarragon's focus on Williams as America's most generous and humane poetic dramatist *precludes*, for example, the interrogation of this autobiographical play as, potentially, a social analysis about two women left literally and figuratively powerless after being abandoned in 1930s industrial St. Louis by the play's three men. When the power literally fails in the middle of the play it is because Tom has spent the money set aside for the electric bill on his membership in the Union of Merchant Seamen, to enable him to escape what the Tarragon production treated as his entrapment at home (77). The power failure might present interpretative choices, the opportunity to highlight Tom's selfishness, perhaps, or perhaps to foreground the family's social and economic positioning within specific historical conditions. In the Tarragon production it was treated – by Amanda and by the production as a whole – primarily as an opportunity for the use of romantic candlelight. What the production focused on was the straightforward presentation of Tennessee/Tom's justificatory autobiography, and the expression of his/their personal psychological angst.

My questions here, I want to emphasise, are not attempts to second-guess production choices or to propose alternative interpretative readings of the script, but to examine what made those choices rather than others possible, probable, obvious, or perhaps even inevitable, to examine some of the often neglected factors that make such choices "natural," or commonsensical, and that frame audiences' production of meaning, whatever production decisions are made. I want to suggest that, for most members of the Tarragon audience, *The Glass Menagerie* did, indeed, function as the self-contained but – in the usual naturalist slippage – also universalist "story of a family...that is both sustained and made vulnerable by its illusions," rather than as a play about the human, material costs of specific historical, social, and political circumstances and decisions in 1930s St. Louis, where it was set, in 1944–45 Chicago and New York, where it was first produced, *or* in 1990s Toronto, where it might have had contemporary political resonances that I suggest were available at Tarragon only through a determinedly resistant reading. It is significant that none of the production's reviewers made any connections with contemporary social issues, or noticed any resonances with contemporary Ontario politics in a period dominated by a particularly oppressive neo-conservative government engaged in its Thatcheresque self-styled "common sense revolution." None noted the fact that the play is about a single mother with a disabled adult daughter who is left at the end to deal with poverty in a time, like that of 1990s Ontario, of high unemployment and economic collapse. Ironically, however, an article by Kate Taylor that appeared in *The Globe and Mail* early in the run of the Tarragon production (and that also featured a National Arts Centre/Royal Alexandra co-production of the play running concurrently in Toronto), was titled "Popular Play Needs *Balancing* Act" (my emphasis), and employed other familiar Tarragon imagery: Taylor unquestioningly accepted the facts (in spite of Tom's statement to the contrary in the prologue) that the characters "should be realistic figures," and that "it is the playwright who, like a good cook, reduces a mess of human muddles to an intensely flavoured tragedy."[31] Taylor's article, working apparently unconsciously within Tarragon discourses of balance and the culinary arts, never questioned the commonsensical presupposition that the play's intended and desirable effect is Aristotelian therapeutic catharsis through identification with "painfully real" tragic situations enacted by sympathetic characters. As theorists from Brecht through Boal to contemporary feminists have argued, however, the cultural work

performed by catharsis is fundamentally normative and affirmative, leaving audiences purged of any potentially disruptive
or socially critical impulses they may have had, while naturalism creates a secure sense of order by delivering its ideology as
normative.

Tarragon's production of *The Glass Menagerie*, then, represented an unusually coherent example of the operation of silent
and relatively seamless ideological containment through material conditions that worked together with one another and with
a relatively self-contained script to keep at bay, if not entirely to
banish, the view from the other side of the tracks.

Tarragon is best known for its production of new work, and it
is perhaps useful to turn to a production of a new Canadian
play written by a Playwright in Residence at the theatre, developed, in part, through the Tarragon "Playwrights Unit," and
therefore shaped at the level of the generation of the script as
well as the mounting of the production and its meanings, by the
discourses and practices of the theatre. One might expect, in
this instance, the relationship between the discursive and other
frameworks and the production of meaning to be clearer, less un-
qualified, less nuanced – and perhaps less open to contestation or
resistance – than in productions of scripts emerging from a different context.

Tarragon's commitment to language and to the playwright as
writer manifests itself in a number of play-development programs
and residencies at the theatre, and although Tarragon claims that
its Playwrights in Residence and members of its Playwrights Unit
have "complete freedom," Scott Duchesne and Jennifer Fletcher
have argued convincingly that most playwrights tend to conform
to the theatre's "house style."[32] Given the material conditions
of trying to make a living as a playwright in Canada, it is not
surprising that writers would see membership in the Tarragon
family as an opportunity to have their work produced there, or
that even within Tarragon's atmosphere of genuine generosity
and tolerance certain pressures would silently come into play.
Indeed, in a forum published in the Canadian theatre magazine,
Theatrum, focusing on Tarragon's Playwrights Unit in 1984–85,
Robin Butt and David Demchuck, members of the Unit, both

commented on such implicit pressures to conform to what Butt calls "a Tarragon esthetic," which Demchuck identifies explicitly as "poetic naturalism." Butt, moreover, notes the political impact of this on the work of the playwrights selected for production at Tarragon: the plays, "usually provocative," he argues, "never quite provoke."[33]

Jason Sherman's *The Retreat* might be considered to be one such play. At the center of the main plot is David, a film producer in Toronto who feels that his company, represented in the play by his hard-nosed partner Jeff, is selling out. David is attracted by both the idealism and the younger female author of a screenplay that has been submitted to him as instructor of a writers' retreat in what is clearly Banff, Alberta (home of one of Canada's leading play-development centers), where the central action of the play takes place. The screenplay, written by Rachel, a teacher in a Hebrew school in Toronto, is based on the story of Sabbatai Zevi, the seventeenth-century Jewish mystic who declared himself the Messiah and then shocked his followers by converting to Islam. *The Retreat* is the story of the affair between Rachel and David at the writers' retreat, the fallout of that affair for David's marriage, family, and business, and its impact on Rachel's understanding of herself, her integrity, and her father Wolf. Rachel's father as a young man had fought for the creation of a Jewish state, but has since become disillusioned with diplomatic compromise and political expediency. At the time of the play's action he is living in an old-age home in Toronto, suffering from a brain tumor, and ranting about the 1993 peace talks between Yassir Arafat and Yitzhak Rabin. Rachel's conversations with her father about Israel, in person and by phone, form a running choric commentary on the rest of the play's action.

The ingredients are available in the script for a serious examination of the intersection of the personal with the political, and specifically with the politics of being Jewish in Canada in the 1990s. As the *Toronto Star* review said, the play "does not shy away from tackling large, important issues, and, on occasion, even risks giving offence."[34] *The Retreat* opens with a monologue by Rachel, who is on the phone defending herself against attacks by members of her school's Parents Committee, who *are*

offended by what she has been saying to the students in her course
on "Israel Today"

Rachel: [W]hat I said was: if these men, these Palestinian men, are
         terrorists, then why don't we call the Jewish settlers on the West
         Bank terrorists too? ... well, I'm sorry the Lifkin boy went home
         in tears ... if I knew he had a brother who lived on the West
         Bank, I ... look, the only way we're gonna have peace is if ... my
         God, I am sick to death of people blindly following this leader
         and that leader and the empty promises of a better life when the
         end result always and forever has been and will be deception,
         betrayal and misery ... and *that* is why it's important for me to,
         yes, challenge these kids to think critically ... (9)

By the end of the play, Rachel is seen retreating, apologizing to
her class, and abandoning her course on Israel today in favour
of a safer one on Jewish mysticism. Sherman, then, here and
elsewhere in the script, evinces an awareness of the potential
for compromise and balance to produce containment, and this
opening monologue establishes the frame for what could be a
provocative, self-reflexive political drama.

The play also evinces considerable and considerably sophisticated Brechtian self-consciousness about the ways in which
dramatic representation, like political representation, and like
religion, can defuse critical analysis and political action – self-
consciousness that may be seen to open a fissure in the production's overall discursive veneer. At one point, for example, Jeff
and Rachel are discussing her screenplay:

Rachel: Okay. A long time ago. The Jews, they get kicked out of Israel.
         They wander. They long to return. They develop the myth of the
         Messiah, a symbol of strength and hope. But that very symbol
         prevents them from acting, from returning to Israel.
Jeff: Like a Frank Capra film.
Rachel: Yes it – what?
Jeff: Frank Capra ... Jimmy Stewart: "Fuck you, Mr. Potter." Okay,
         he didn't say "fuck you," but ... Goes to Washington, whatever.
         Does the big speech to, the oppressor.
Rachel: Uhh ...
Jeff: The hero does the speech, does it up there on the big screen
         and we go, we, in the audience, go, "Hooray. Give it to him."
         Which absolves *us* ...

Rachel: Yes.
Jeff: Of, of...
Rachel: Doing the speech, of...
Jeff: *Acting.*
Rachel: Yes, yes. The Messiah acts on our behalf. It makes us weak because it says: one day *he* will come for you. And when things
get desperate enough, and some guy says" "I am *he*. Follow
me," you don't question it. The followers of Zevi were desperate. And the followers of Zionism were desperate. After the
Holocaust, they were vulnerable to *he* who said, "Let us return to Israel." They didn't question the return. They didn't
question the morality of taking another people's land.

Jeff replies, "I love it. I love that journey you just took me on"
(70–71, emphasis in original).

At Tarragon, nevertheless, the play neither deconstructed its
own politics nor ignored them; rather it put on display at moments such as this the *tools* for a critique of its own representations, and those of theatre in general, but within the Tarragon
context it failed to push the point, or to challenge the audience to
in fact *make* such a critique. And as Jonathan Dollimore argues,

> Nothing can be intrinsically or essentially subversive in the sense that
> prior to the event subversiveness can be more than potential; in other
> words it cannot be guaranteed a priori, independent of articulation,
> context, and reception. Likewise the mere thinking of a radical idea is
> not what makes it subversive: typically it is the context of its articulation:
> to whom, how many and in what circumstances; one might go further
> and suggest that not only does the idea have to be conveyed, it has also
> actually to be used to refuse authority *or* be seen by authority as capable
> and likely of being so used. It is, then, somewhat misleading to speak
> freely and only of "subversive thought"; what we are concerned with
> (once again) is a *social process.*[35] (13)

At Tarragon, in spite of the opportunity the script presented for
social critique, the play's self-reflexivity functioned merely to produce a kind of political catharsis, allowing the audience the pleasure and release of loving the provocative journey the play takes
us on, but, in Robin Butt's terms, never quite provoking us to do
anything about it. Its *verfremdungseffekt* (alienation effect) was,
as in many contemporary theatrical invocations of Brecht, merely
effect.

Finally, the script includes what is a presumably critical representation of the deflection of the political by the personal, and

again a potential space for resistant interpretative strategies. In an earlier conversation, Rachel tells David about the inspiration for her screenplay in the life of her father as an escapee from the Nazis, and as one of Menachim Begin's Betar Boys. David, however – who claims, not to be "a Jew" but to be "Jew . . . ish," and who doesn't "follow Israel" – fails to understand:

David: Don't get me wrong, your father's story is terrific, but what does it have to do with your screenplay?
Rachel: That's what this movie is *about*.
David: Your screenplay.
Rachel: Yes.
David: Is about . . .
Rachel: Israel.
David: I don't see it. I don't get that. Explain that to me.
Rachel: Well . . .
David: I mean, you've written a beautiful screenplay about a *man*, the, the *inner* life, his *struggle*. This stuff about Israel, it's, I mean . . .
Rachel: Are you saying forget about Israel?
David: No, I mean it's up to you. All I'm saying is, don't force it to become *about* something, especially something as ephemeral as, as, a political struggle (44)

In spite of these potentially contestatory traces of self-consciousness, and in spite of the fact that David comes at the end of the play to a desire to research and write about Wolf's life, his motives for doing so, in the Tarragon production, were constructed as being primarily personal, and Rachel's closing question, "do you think this will lead to peace?" arguably had more resonances in reference to the private relationships among Rachel, Wolf, and David than to public policy, social relations, or the Middle-East peace talks. The conviction with which the Method-trained actors portrayed the personal crises of the characters and balanced the presentation, with equal conviction, of their different points of view, also served to resist resolution or the clear political positioning of the script. As the director, Ian Prinsloo said, employing a vocabulary fully congruent both with the major strains of director training in Canada, and with Method-style naturalism,

I focus on the relationships between the characters on stage . . . What is at stake for them personally? They are rich characters. They all have good reasons why they believe what they do. And each of them is right.[36]

These approaches to acting and directing, together with the theatre's framing discourses of family and of genteel and balanced debate, its geographical, architectural, and audience composition, and its "house style," all worked, I suggest, to an extraordinary degree to contain (or themselves constitute a "retreat" from) potential political analysis or provocation within a generalized, polite, and ahistorical liberal pluralism. In fact, I suggest, the entire framing discourse and technology of theatrical practice at Tarragon militate against the production of *The Retreat* itself as being about "anything as ephemeral" – as site-specific and non-universal – as "political struggle." The political commitment of Wolf, Rachel's fight for equal consideration of Palestinian and Israeli settler claims to the West Bank, and even the moral issues surrounding David's betrayal of both his family and of Rachel – issues of *public* morality and responsibility that include gendered and economic power relations and raise such issues as harassment – are all and equally reduced, for their primary interpretative community at Tarragon, to the psychological struggles of sympathetic, naturalistically-realized characters to reconcile – or balance – their Stanislavskian "objectives" with the recognizable "realities" of living in the (implicitly unchanging and unchangeable) world. Change, in this discourse, can only come through individual psychological adjustment to supposed social inevitabilities; political commitment, almost inevitably, is either pathological, misguided or, as in the case of Wolf in the Tarragon production, funny; and tension, produced by dramatic conflict, exists in order to be resolved in formal cadences rather than to move audiences to action, or even to critical thought.

Most members of Tarragon's regular audience, then, will have left the theatre in February–March of 1996 with a healthy and balanced, liberal-minded and tolerant "understanding" that there are two sides to every issue, comfortable in the knowledge that the production had been balanced and fair-minded in its *explorations* of issues which, like the Arab–Israeli conflict, will remain forever unresolved. Above all, they will have left with a sense that they had witnessed "a beautiful [play] about a *man*, the, the *inner* life, his *struggle*." To have done otherwise would have required a significant investment on the part of an audience member intent on reading the play quite consciously from the other side of the tracks, and against the dominant discursive framework of Tarragon Theatre and the material circumstances within which *The Retreat* was produced, and produced its meanings.

5   The Wooster Group

The work of The Wooster Group is known as the ultimate in deconstructive theatre, responsive with a complex postmodern blend of critique and complicity to the mediatization and brutalization of contemporary urban life.[1] This reputation is based on a 1980s staged series of interrogations of classic realist plays, mostly American, that worked to expose those works' compulsory normativity in the construction of American national identity. Through the criticism of David Savran, Philip Auslander, Baz Kershaw, and others, this work has become a key site for debates about the politics of postmodern performance. It seems perverse, then, to read it as pastoral and elegaic, as Elinor Fuchs does in an essay that anticipates the Group's turn to Gertrude Stein in *House/Lights*, first developed in the company's 1996–97 season.[2] But a reading of *House/Lights* in the context of the work and reputation of Stein, of the Group's earlier work, and particularly of the cultural geography of their performance location, positions it not only as pastoral and elegaic, but, in its home location, fundamentally nostalgic. Such a reading highlights a nostalgia that's always been part of the Group's work, and argues that the cultural work it performs is recuperative: as Susan Bennett says, nostalgia is, "in its praxis, conservative (in [both] its political alignment and its motive to keep things . . . unchanged)." This is so, she says, because "the optic of nostalgia insists . . . upon a stable referent" and "works to downplay or . . . disregard divisive positionalities" in promoting "a false and likely dangerous sense of 'we'."[3]

In an unlocated, formalist reading, *House/Lights* does seem continuous with the Group's politically interrogative deconstructions of American classic drama: it brings a 1964 cult lesbian bondage flick, *Olga's House of Shame*, directed by Joseph

Mawra, into productive contact with an American avant-garde classic, Gertrude Stein's *Doctor Faustus Lights the Lights* (see illus. 6). Tossed disruptively into the mix are bodies distorted by prosthetics; voices filtered through sound chambers, supplemented by blips, squawks, and quacks; dancing outsized lightbulbs and a hand-puppet viper-mic; and sound, video, and performance bites ranging from *I Love Lucy, Young Frankenstein,* and Esther Williams, to Yiddish theatre, classical ballet, and Cantonese opera. Most reviewers indeed described the show as deconstructive – some as neo-cubist, some as interrogative, and some as incomprehensible, but most, citing earlier "explosive multimedia deconstructions," as postmodern.[4] But some, noting director Elizabeth LeCompte's ability to "lay bare what was essential and enduring in the original," also saw the show as oddly faithful to Stein, or as a confirmation of the Group's continuity with "the age of Picasso."[5] Far from merely deconstructing its source, *House/Lights* reinforced for many Stein's own deconstructive reading of the Faust legend, her metatheatrical focus on representation, and her understanding of performance as a landscape. Like its source, and for all its frenetic activity, *House/Lights* could work, particularly when performed at the company's home base in New York's SoHo district, as a curiously contemplative exploration of time, art, and nature – the classic concerns of the classical pastoral.

But pastoral landscapes were not new to the Wooster Group in the late 1990s; indeed, most of its work has evoked an idealized past, usually in the form of a "natural" and/or childhood landscape. Even the archetypally deconstructive *LSD (...Just the High Points...)*, Savran notes, "conjures up the dynamics of memory in the tension between the absent 'real thing' and the substitute at hand"[6] in a way that is perhaps definitive of nostalgia. And, significantly, the longing, explicitly in this case, was for a 1960s version of the American avant garde that the belated 1980 founding of the Group almost inevitably positions as a golden age. And in spite of their (anti-) canonical reputation, the Woosters have a more recent history of treating avant-garde (vs. realist) source texts *re-* (rather than de-) constructively. As their SoHo neighbors renovated their classic ironwork lofts, the Woosters in the late 1990s were renovating classics of the

6. The Wooster Group's *House/Lights*, with (l.-r.) Helen Pickett, Kate Valk, Roy Faudree, Tanya Selvaratnam, and Suzzy Roche, directed by Elizabeth LeCompte, first staged at The Performing Garage, New York, in 1996–97.

American avant garde, such as those of the expressionist O'Neill, more honored in the academy than in performance. Does this recuperative tendency at the archetypal American postmodern theatre suggest an amplification of the still unrealized disruptive potential of these texts? Or is it an attempted return to the halcyon days of the American avant garde, when that military metaphor seemed less disjunctive than it does now, and its alignment with national myths of progress – including technological progress – continued to hold sway? The invocation of Stein certainly links the Group with the great American chronotope of Paris in the 20s, and also with key avant-garde moments of earlier productions of *Doctor Faustus Lights the Lights*. After all, the play has become something of a rite of passage for American experimental theatres since it was chosen for the inaugural Living Theatre season in 1951.[7]

In 1990 Richard Kostelanetz called Stein "the greatest experimental writer in American literature, an inventor whose achievements are...scarcely understood, even today, more than four decades after her death."[8] But what does it mean to stage a "classic" of the "avant garde" that, fifty years later, is still ahead of its time? At the very least, to do so drains the term of temporal significance – perhaps especially for the Woosters, who belatedly set up shop in the legendary Performing Garage a decade after the moment Philip Auslander identifies as the onset of postmodernism.[9] Perhaps *House/Lights* marks the Group's nostalgia less as longing for a simpler past than as longing for time itself – for a time when (in several senses) there *was* time. Stein is widely honoured as the "patron saint of the avant garde," in Bonnie Marranca's phrase, "hovering over the artistic landscape, radiating a grandiose personal freedom, delight in invention, and intellectual courage"[10] – all notably mainstream American ideals. As such, Stein evokes nostalgia for a golden age of American avant-garde (as opposed to alternative) art,[11] poised to take its place within, and to renew rather than overthrow, the mainstream. But as Kate Valk, the dramaturg and lead performer for *House/Lights*, asked, "how much have you read of Gertrude Stein?" The work "itself" is largely unread, unseen, and relatively unmarked, positioned to function as both cultural authority and empty landscape. "Its landscape is as abstract as the landscapes we make" says Valk.[12] It is the very abstraction of Stein's landscapes – their lack of social referent – that has made her work recruitable for high-modernist formalism. Thus William Carlos Williams can say "It is simply the skeleton, the 'formal' parts of writing . . . that she has to do with, apart from the 'burden' which they carry."[13] But Stein has more recently been celebrated less for her construction of socially inscrutable modernist artifacts than for her commitment to process, her concentration on the materiality of language, and her role as a proto-feminist. The Wooster Group has similarly conflicted relationships to modernism, politics, and particularly feminism that can seem from outside the country to be characteristically American: LeCompte describes the Group's apparently confrontational politic as unintentional, "an inevitable outcome" – "a *result*, but not the *object*" – of their working process.[14] And yet *House/Lights*, casting women as Faust and Mephisto and staging the objectification of women in *Olga's House of Shame*, is easily read as an interrogation of the construction of gender in America; indeed the show on tour was frequently reviewed this way, though not, significantly, in New York.

One way to approach the apparent tension between the Group's lack of political intent and the frequent reception of their work (particularly outside New York) as politically confrontational is to examine Stein's concept of theatre as landscape,[15] which Fuchs calls "a signature style of contemporary experimental theater" in America, citing "the multifocal scene and the diffused spectatorship it calls for" as "central."[16] But like the American academy's embrace of Bakhtinian dialogism in the 80s, and like its more recent turn to chaos theory for dramaturgical or analytical models (both of which tend to skirt the issue of existing power relationships within apparently empty spaces), the American avant-garde theatre's embrace of theatre-as-landscape can be read as politically naive. Stein's search was for a peculiarly American *balance* within "a given space," balance which she herself called "a definitely American thing." "Nothing really moves in a landscape but things are there," she says, "always in relation."[17] Stein compared herself to Einstein, and it is clear, as Marranca argues, that her technique "has affinities" with post-Newtonian physics "in its development of composition as a field of innumerable centers."[18]

All of this sorts well with the work of the Wooster Group, suggests a parallel between the "chaos" of *House/Lights* and the Steinian theatrical landscape, and serves a familiar American liberal-individualist politic. LeCompte talks of wanting "as many interpretations as possible to coexist in the same time and same space,"[19] (Savran, 53), and Savran argues that the "reagent" in her work is the empowered individual spectator: "the Wooster Group initiates," he says "an Einsteinian project that celebrates the multiplicity of perspectives and only one certainty: that the phenomenon will be different for each member of the audience."[20] Stein herself said that "to me one human being is as important as another human being, and you might say that the landscape has the same values, a blade of grass has the same value as a tree."[21] This fundamentally sentimental politic resonates with the liberal pluralism of the current humanist embrace of chaos theory in such works as William Demastes' *Theatre of Chaos* and Tom Stoppard's appropriately named play *Arcadia*, a post-Newtonian play about a pastoral landscape.[22]

Fuchs also notes Stein's tendency to slip from an understanding of landscape as "spatial and static as opposed to temporal and progressive"[23] to an idealized vision of the "natural." In an analysis that echoes the American avant-garde director Peter Sellars's discovery of "a lyricism and classical repose . . . beneath the busy surface level" of the Wooster Group's work,[24] Fuchs suggests that "landscape to Stein was wholly present to itself, simple and un-anxiety-provoking to the spectator."[25] But in her brief treatment of LeCompte's "edenic dream of returning the earth to the way it 'might have been naturally'," Fuchs also argues that, "for LeCompte, artistic endeavor itself represents (both stands for and depicts) a kind of original sin, a fall from the whole of nature."[26] Contemporary theatre as "art" and technology, I suggest, constructs a contradiction for LeCompte: her own technological urban pastoral and the traditional American dream of progress struggle against an inherited generic vision of technology, and art, as the *death* of the natural – or of the nostalgic belief that the natural has ever existed. In staging a technologically sophisticated performance that "links the [already nostalgic] Faust myth with American history" by linking loss of innocence with technological progress through the invention of electricity, LeCompte stages a tension at the heart of her work. In staging a late play by a modernist artist of the perpetual present that *portrays* an artist's – Faust's – realization "that the perpetual present for which he has bargained has deprived him of hope,"[27] LeCompte evokes postmodern nostalgia for time itself, and for an (American) avant garde as a temporal concept positing a (better) future, as well as an originary past.

Both *Doctor Faustus Lights the Lights* and *House/Lights*, in their "ideal" forms, can be read as contestable terrains, alternately legible as interrogations of the representation of women, as liberatingly open fields, and as sites of nostalgic longing. But performance never exists in ideal forms, and as Kershaw says, location is key to assessing "the political impact of theatre."[28] A located reading of *House/Lights* produces significantly different meanings than does the formalist one I began with. In the literal sense, as far as initial production and reception are concerned, location for the Wooster Group is SoHo ("South of Houston" [St.]), the forty-three-block area of downtown Manhattan founded as an ersatz "neighborhood" between 1968 and 1971, when the art market was thriving, small industry dying, and artists found cheap housing and studio space in vacated industrial lofts.[29] But Sharon Zutkin makes clear in *Loft Living: Culture and Capital in Urban Change* that by 1979, a year before the official founding of the Wooster Group, SoHo was already an urban–pastoral landscape of renovated lofts inhabited by neither industry nor artistry but by what Barbara Ehrenreich and John Ehrenreich call an emerging "professional-managerial class" – children of the 1960s with a (consumer) interest in the arts who returned to the city driving up rent and driving out the previous inhabitants.[30] Zutkin demonstrates that "Far from being...a spontaneous artists' community, SoHo was really a creation of [investment capital]"[31]: developers used "first-wave" artist residents as a "wedge,"[32] effecting changes in zoning bylaws and ousting small industry before they were themselves ousted as "loft-living" became trendy, rents rocketed, and the fleeting, pastoral, SoHo moment was created retrospectively as a product of carefully orchestrated collective memory. Zutkin quotes, and refutes, the manufactured and widely circulated image of "first generation" loft dwellers – "artists and other adventurous souls" – as "urban homesteaders," "lofsteaders,"[33] and "pioneers in the urban wilderness.[34]" It's not without (economic) consequence that Charles R.

Simpson and others construct the district as a pastoral "valley" between the financial high "court" of the southern tip of the island and the skyscrapers of mid-town.[35] And, of course, the renovated living areas of the valley, using "real" materials – brick, iron, and oak (the loft equivalents of natural fabrics) – carve out spacious, open areas that, like all pastoral landscapes, bring art and nature together in contemplative, recreative spaces, retreats from the cramped and hectic life of the city.

This is the SoHo constructed by LeCompte, Spalding Gray, and other members of the Group when discussing the living/ performing space at the Performing Garage out of which all the Wooster Group's work has been created (see illus. 7). Distinguishing themselves from "most people," who are "dislocated," they talk of their space early on as a "clubhouse"[36] out of which, shepherd/artists in an urban-pastoral landscape rich with raw material, "we were just trying to make scenes out of who we were in the room."[37] And this is also the SoHo *re*created for cultural tourists in the 80s, 90s, and beyond, its cast-iron buildings now housing trendy galleries, upscale boutiques, cafés, and still, after all these years, the Performing Garage on Wooster Street, home of the legendary avant-garde Performance Group in its halcyon days, and now the fashionably downscale venue for the movie stars and others that constitute the Wooster Group. Here postmodernism meets late capitalism, as "mainstream" and "avant garde" work less as developmental designations than as marketing labels – Stein's "continuous present" realized as SoHo takes its place with rue de Fleurus and Greenwich Village, not as Bakhtinian chronotopes, but as commodity theme parks: as at Disney, all is now, the avant garde and mainstream coexisting as alternative consumer choices. Thus tourist guides recommend SoHo as a place where "industrious artists mix with industrial workers" and "white-walled, sun-drenched restaurants fill dingy commercial loft buildings."[38] They market the Wooster Group – "a cult among its adherents," "too experimental for mainstream audiences" ("if *Phantom of the Opera* is what you're looking for, don't even *think* of making the pilgrimage to SoHo") – but nevertheless on "the cutting edge of the theatre."[39] "A spirit of adventure is basic equipment for a SoHo theatre outing," one guide warns. "So is an open mind. Bring them and you will be rewarded."[40]

7. The main entrance to The Performing Garage on Wooster
Street in New York's SoHo district.

Another way to approach the politics of location, to revisit my initial reading of *House/Lights*, and to tease out the cultural work it performs *in situ*, is to focus on the way the show has worked for an individual audience member, in this case a Canadian post-colonial subject who grew up in the 1960s, for whom New York is both a mythical theatrical testing ground and a prime tourist destination, and for whom the Performing Garage is legendary: I first saw *House/Lights* in preview at the Performing Garage in the Fall of 1998. I walked south to SoHo from Penn Station on a late October afternoon, making my way down 5th Avenue, through Washington Square and the NYU campus, past the boutiques, cigar shops, cafés and Qigong masseurs of West Broadway, and across Broome, with its trendy store-front galleries, to Wooster St. I stopped at a chic wine bar of brick walls and cast-iron hardware, slipped into a specialty shop for art books and old movies, and took my place in the ticket line – cash only, no plastic – that snaked north from the graffiti-covered shipping-dock door that is the streetfront of the Performing Garage. I stood beneath a plaque about the "SoHo Cast Iron Historical District" and its small-industry past looking across the street at an arched, poster-plastered wall beneath which a homeless man slept on a pile of newspapers. At 7:45 I entered through the narrow south door, squeezed around the corner and found a place among the eighty or so seats at the east end of the tiny "brick-box" space that constitutes the interior of what one reviewer had called "one of the last theatres around doing truly experimental theatre."[41]

Above my head in house center was a phalanx of technicians, equipment, and video monitors. Behind me to my right was the legendary "Liz" LeCompte, and before me a fabulous chaos of ramps, lamps, metal rails, and angled footrests suspended chest-level from the railings; two banks of fluorescent footlights facing forward; video monitors up-left, up-right, and down-center; a lap-top computer mounted onstage down-right on an angled platform; and untold microphones, sliding stools, and see-saw metal platforms. I was enthralled.

First, there were the pleasures of sheer technical brilliance – in the acting, direction, conception, execution, and perhaps most notably the cutting-edge work in live video technology – the pleasures, perhaps, of revisiting the (American) myth of technological progress. Next, there were the pleasures of democratic empowerment in sheer excess of energy and signification: the show meant everything and anything, and the choice, the show seemed to suggest, was up to me. Then there were the self-congratulatory pleasures of recognized revisionism – of seeing new and progressive things done with the Faust story, together with the superior, nostalgic pleasures of viewing from a thirty-five-year distance the chaste leers and gropes that passed for eroticism in *Olga's House of Shame*; the simple pleasures of revisiting clips, sound bites, and reenactments from the pop culture of more innocent times ("I Love Lucy," "Ring of Fire," Esther Williams, and so on); and the surprising pleasures of recognizing the grotesque prosthetic production of "ideal" 50s and early 60s female bodies – all of these allied with the pleasure of Kate Valk's brilliant "Betty-Boop" delivery of Gertrude Stein. Finally, there were the vaguely pleasurable ironies that accompanied all this, ironies that positioned the present as both superior (in knowledge and experience) and debased. But, of course, irony, the signature tone of the Woosters, is a staple of the pastoral, which inevitably contains its temporary sojourn in the simple, natural (but clearly escapist and therefore "artificial") countryside, within a prescribed return, refreshed, to the reified and "naturalized" civilities of court and city life.

I left the show, walking up Wooster St., with "calm of mind, all passion spent" (to invoke Milton's encapsulation of the comforting effects of catharsis), buoyed by the revisionist and renovationist pleasures of the neighborhood, the fable, and its skillful and progressive treatment. As one New York reviewer said "the world that 'House/Lights' portrays may be in atomistic shards, but there's a strangely comforting wholeness in this century-enfolding symmetry."[42] But as I flew out over the industrial wasteland of Newark to return to my work-day world in Southern Ontario, I began to wonder whether my enjoyment of *House/Lights* had primarily to do with nostalgia for an avant-garde theatre in renovated factories that held hope for political change. My sense of repose began to unravel as I sensed in my response a nostalgia – for (political) *progress*, for the 20s, the 60s, the lost days of the avant garde, and the hope it used to bring. I began to share Savran's discomfort with "giddy undecideablity,"[43] as I have long felt impatience with the pleasantly knowing but fundamentally recuperative critique mounted in pastoral dramas from

As You Like It to *Our Town*[44] – landscape plays that "explore the issues" in playful and balanced ways, but leave power *im*balances intact, uninterrogated, and reinvigorated when the pastoral sojourn ends.

Savran's book on the Woosters opens with an epigraph from Nietzsche that articulates, in spite of its origin, a peculiarly American desire for originality *über alles* (including political change), and encapsulates what I fear, in the end, *House/Lights*, in SoHo, in October 1998, for me, was about:

Perhaps . . . we shall still discover the realm of our invention, that realm in which we, too, can still be original.[45]

The reputation and interpretation of the Wooster Group are very different when the company tours, as it frequently does. At a meet-the-artists "rencontre" in Montreal in May, 1999, when *House/Lights* was performed as part of the Theatre Festival of the Americas, I asked Elizabeth LeCompte and Kate Valk what it meant to tour shows that, throughout the company's history, have so often seemed iconically American. They replied that they didn't think of themselves as having a national, or even a New York orientation, but thought of themselves as quite specifically located in Manhattan, and more particularly lower Manhattan, part of a local scene from which their work has emerged and where it has produced its primary meanings.[46] Indeed, in New York, the company is read as off-off-Broadway, a company with a very specific, indeed very narrow interpretative community, not particularly representative of anything beyond themselves. Meanwhile, however, they tend to be read internationally as one of the United States' most important theatres, a leading representative of the American avant garde. Scottish theatre critic Mark Fisher, profiling the company in advance of their performances of *House/Lights* in Glasgow, traveled to New York and was puzzled to find that his New York colleagues, "theatre insiders," were surprised by his plan to take in a Wooster Group performance. What puzzled him "wasn't only that *House/Lights* was easily the most extraordinary thing I saw in a week of theatre-going, it was the idea that the New York theatre establishment hadn't noticed that one of the world's most significant ensembles was on its very doorstep."[47]

Beyond New York, the Wooster Group is invariably described as a New York Company, and is seen as in various ways representative of "what's happening" there. On tour within the US, this can render them the object of critique or resentment rather than praise. In the case of *House/Lights*, for example, early performances of the play in development in Columbus, Ohio, and in Chicago, were greeted with something less than awe. The reviewer for *The Other Paper* in Columbus quoted the company's program notes to the show concerning the juxtaposition of Gertrude Stein with 1960s S&M producing "a shared kitsch-cultural view of female power struggles." The reviewer then commented, "Sounds like the work of a deep mind, doesn't it? Namely, a mind that's spinning its wheels in a meaningless hole of its own making." Describing the erotically charged performance of Kate Valk and the 1960s eroticism of *Olga's House of Shame*, however, and citing a line from the popular American television program, *Cheers* – "this egghead stuff is making me hot!" – the reviewer went on ironically to praise the show's capacity to give Columbus audiences "a rare gift: guilt-free titillation."[48] Even more explicitly, the reviewer for the *Chicago Tribune* felt that "What Chicago gave away is what New York could not – "HOUSE/LIGHTS," the Woosters' new piece, is a marvel of technology, a bravura performance, and pretty much incoherent."[49] The emperor, apparently, had no clothes. Insofar as the show was felt to be "about" anything in its American excursions beyond Manhattan, it was about "destiny, about good and evil, about avoidance of the self, about obsession, about love and dominance and submission," but fundamentally about the equal-opportunity chance "to create your own story."[50] With the exception of dominance and submission, none of these themes was mentioned in reviews of the show in New York or on its international tours.

On tour beyond the US, in fact, the Woosters tend to be read very much and very positively as a trendy, hip, and postmodern New York theatre company, leading exponents (cited almost inevitably in the same breath as the experimental American theatre directors Robert Wilson and Richard Foreman) of what is called the American avant garde. Within the US, LeCompte comments wryly, "avant garde is a European joke. There's nothing avant garde in America. Isn't it a French word?"[51] *In* France, or more specifically at the Festival d'automne in Paris, in performance at the semiotically rich site of Le Théâtre de la Bastille near the site of the former Bastille prison, the storming of which kicked off the French Revolution in July 1789, *House/Lights* seemed at once both very American and very European. Rue de la Roquette, on which the theatre is situated, is a narrow street with a blend of small neighborhood shops and a more recent cluster of galleries, cafés, clubs, and bars that sprang up in the wake of the building of the nearby Opéra de la Bastille in 1989. On the December Saturday evening in 1999 when I saw the show, the short walk from the Bastille metro station took me through a throng of pedestrian traffic. The theatre itself, relatively nondescript, was filled to its capacity of about three hundred, with seats sloping slightly toward the stage. The theatre's small entrance area made available season brochures featuring fine art photography and line drawings, and placing *House/Lights* within the season's context of international contemporary experimental theatre and, especially, dance – *House/Lights* itself being categorized there as both, thereby inviting, as did the rest of the brochure, formalist readings. Reviews of the show (performed in English) placed it most frequently within the contexts of experimental American theatre (particularly the work of Wilson and Foreman), the writing, ideas, and Paris life of Gertrude Stein, and the Woosters' reputation as "le cap de l'avant-garde sophistiquée."[52] For me, the immediate context was the congruent one of having earlier in the day seen a matinée performance of Can Themba's *Le Costume*, directed by the legendary experimental director Peter Brook at his Paris base, the Théâtre Des Bouffes du Nord.

Most Paris reviewers judged *House/Lights* to be "le meilleur spectacle d'avant-garde de ce Festival d'automne,"[53] and Paris audiences, according to a report in *The Guardian* that sorts well with my own experience, "howled with laughter."[54] The show bristled with energy and intelligence in its Paris performances, as if charged by the atmosphere and invigorated by the context. There was little sense of the urban pastoral, or of nostalgia, and no sense of incoherence; rather *House/Lights* seemed to live, as the reviewer for the *Paris Free Voice* observed, in Gertrude Stein's continuous present, and to evoke "Steinian concepts" such as "syncopation and the nature of language being sound and rhythm."[55] For some, the show evoked what seemed to be peculiarly Parisian existentialist concerns about "la réalité de l'être,"[56] while for others it constituted "une magistrale démonstration sur la dualité de nos sens: entre le vrai et le faux, le passé et le présent, l'amour et la haine."[57] For most, however, viewing or reviewing the show in the final weeks of the millennium and at the height of the Y2K scare about global technological failure, it was understood to be a chilling invocation and playing out of Gertrude Stein's own fascination with and fear of technological progress.

House/Lights returned to Europe in June 2000 when it was selected to re-open the cavernous Tramway theatre on Albert Drive in South Glasgow, one of Europe's trendiest venues for the performing and visual arts, after it had been closed for two years to undergo a £3.6 million rehabilitation. The building had been a tramshed in the nineteenth century, stabling many of the three thousand horses used to pull the city's trams until the system was electrified in 1910. It remained the Coplawhill Tram Depot until the coming of trolley cars in 1962, after which it was transformed into a Museum of Transport.[58] The building eventually went to seed, matching the decay of much of the area south of the river in which it was situated. Indeed the environs of the Tramway, which have recently begun to emerge as a mixed and more lively intercultural neighborhood, had became for a time one of Britain's most desperate victims of industrialization and urban blight, the traces of which remain very much in evidence. The building itself, constructed on a large scale to accommodate tramcars and retaining the old steel tracks embedded within its uneven floor, was inaugurated as a theatre space in 1990 to house Peter Brook's epic show *The Mahabharata* in Glasgow when no suitable space could be found for it in London. Almost immediately, as Jackie McGlone wrote in *Scotland on Sunday*, "[t]he once derelict Glasgow Transport Museum became one of the most exciting theatrical spaces in the world...Everyone was making tracks for the Tramway to produce and witness the sort of groundbreaking theatre that used to be shoe-horned into tiny studio spaces the size of a small wardrobe." "There was no question," wrote McGlone, quoting Brook's reference to the space as "an industrial cathedral," "here was a beautiful, rambling space, a space that had its own character, its own nobility, its own background and associations, free from all our old-fashioned notions of theatres with proscenium arches and velvety seats."[59] Over the years the space hosted a checklist of the international avant garde, including Brook, Robert Lepage, Brith Gof, Silviu Puracaret, the Maly Theatre of St. Petersburg, La Fura dels Baus, Wim Vandekyebus, Alain Patel, Michael Clark, Crush, and DV8, not to mention a phalanx of other Scottish companies, or the work in television, video, and the visual arts that has been hosted there. The vast, high-ceilinged brick-built barn has been, indeed, Glasgow's "funkiest contemporary arts venue,"[60] and the renovations seem simply to have made things better, removing obtrusive columns from the Tramway 1 (the main theatre space), evening out the floors, and adding an x-shaped metal staircase leading up to a new bar and restaurant in what had been the old stables, but preserving from the original its industrial scale and unpretentious character – as well as, in spite of the re-roofing, the somewhat forbidding, graffiti-encrusted decay of its exterior.

The programming, too, retained its character, the summer season in which the space reopened featuring, along with the Woosters: *Gravity*, a music and theatre collaboration between a hot young playwright, Zinnie Harris, and composer Marina Adamia; *Desert Rain*, a show that notably featured Nottingham University's "Massive 2" computer among the cast; and *True*, a collaborative international project. In the gallery space of the Tramway 2, running concurrently with *House/Lights*, were three new art exhibitions, one international showcase that included the work of Turner Prize winner Tacita Dean, a group exhibition by five artists from Nantes, France, and one solo exhibition by Sally Osborn, then a recent graduate of the Glasgow School of Art.

All this seemed to sort well with the resonances of the show's Paris performances and its performance venue, though on a physically amplified scale. But to get to *House/Lights* in Glasgow – and few residents of the predominantly South Asian immediate neighborhood frequent the Tramway – it was necessary to drive through labyrinthine and unwelcoming streets, to take a cab or bus, or to board a commuter train from Central Station on Argyle Street at the heart of the city beneath the river to a somewhat forbidding (and largely deserted) outdoor stop at Pollokshields (East). From there, the commuter had to venture up a long flight of deserted stairs and along a street devoid of theatre-district-style restaurants or pubs to the nondescript main doorway of the theatre. This, clearly, was neither SoHo's retro-chic nor the urban bustle of Paris. And again, the show read differently here. The Glasgow audience, according to a review in The *Scotsman*, found itself "caught...somewhere between ex-plosive laugher and sheer slack-jawed amazement."[61] Without the supercharged energy of Paris audiences, those in Glasgow felt more actively focused and intellectually engaged with the production's contemporary resonances than were audiences else-where, as is suggested by the headline of the *Scotsman* review: "Lights, Camera, Interaction: The Wooster Group are in ex-hilarating tune with the times." Reviewers – with one notable and apparently ill-tempered exception that proved the rule[62] – repeated the familiar-in-Europe welcome of the Wooster group as "the cream of New York's theatrical avant garde," celebrated their "achingly hip po-mo credentials," and placed them in the context of, as in Paris, the work of Wilson and Foreman, as well as that of Brook and other Tramway predecessors, including their own earlier work.[63] But they also welcomed the show with some of its most intelligent analysis. This largely working-class city, home of a People's Palace museum celebrating the histories of working people, whose lively arts scene exists primarily to ad-dress a local rather than a tourist audience (as is often the case in Edinburgh), seemed prepared to see the show as a serious politi-cal work engaging with contemporary social issues. The reviewer for the *Sunday Herald* found it to be "an alarmingly sad rendition of modern day alienation and social schizophrenia," in a positive review that nevertheless reflected the *Scotland on Sunday* attack on it as "the art of pessimism."[64] *The Times* (London) astutely reviewed the Glasgow performances in Brechtian terms as "just one great big distancing device, a highly charged mirror image that confronts and subverts the audience's passivity."[65] But per-haps the most acute reviews of the Glasgow performances came from women, who had perhaps had to negotiate the unforgiving neighborhoods of South Glasgow in a different way than had their male colleagues. Only in Montreal, where the show had played at L'Espace Go, the former home of the city's most prominent femi-nist theatre, had *House/Lights'* feminist resonances been so clearly in evidence as at the Tramway, where it was held by Elisabeth Mahoney in the *Guardian*, focusing on the show's disruptively carnivalesque energies and its central female characters, to be in large part "about power and corruption, and more specifically about women and power." Joyce McMillan, in The *Scotsman*, who rightly located Kate Valk's multifaceted performance of Faust, Elaine, and "Margeurite Ida and Helena Annabel" as central, found that the show had to do with "something...about the relationship between scientific curiosity, technological arrogance, and moral decadence," "something about theatre, as a free arena in which actors can finally shape their own relationship with the audience," and "something about women as subjects of their own stories rather than as objects."[66] It is little wonder that Elizabeth LeCompte, complaining that New Yorkers don't really understand the work of the company, has commented that "In Europe it isn't the same. My favourite audiences are the British because they get every nuance."[67] The differences, however, may have less to do with American, European, or British character or intelligence than with the complex geographies of the cities, neighborhoods, and theatrical spaces in which the Wooster Group performs.

6   The English Shakespeare Company

When Jonathan Miller's revival of N. F. Simpson's absurdist comedy *One Way Pendulum* opened at Toronto's Royal Alexandra Theatre in March of 1988, reviewers said "it could have used a better audience." "Canadians," remarked one Canadian reviewer, "do not understand British society."[1] When it transferred to London's Old Vic two months later it was greeted with pleasure and nostalgia by the British press, who reviewed it as the missing link in British comedy between Lewis Carroll and Monty Python.[2]

When Sam Mendes' revival of Jean-Paul Sartre's *Kean* opened at the Old Vic two years later, featuring Derek Jacobi in the title role, reviews focused their attention on English acting from Kean (who had played at the Old Vic "for two weeks in 1831"[3]), through Olivier (whose ghost is said to haunt the theatre, and whose *Othello* most reviewers saw parodied in the last act), to Jacobi himself. Most insisted that, though the play sounded serious, Sartre's philosophical position was less important than the play as a vehicle for a star actor. When it transferred to the Royal Alex, reviewers acknowledged Jacobi as heir to Olivier, but talked mostly about Sartre's adaptation of the 1836 romantic drama by Alexandre Dumas Sr., and found the production strangely unconvincing in ways that were "not entirely the script's fault."[4]

When Richard Olivier's revival of J. B. Priestly's family drama *Time and the Conways* – a play about a late, lamented father – opened at the Old Vic in the fall of 1990, just over a year after the death of the director's father, Laurence Olivier, it featured Lord Olivier's widow, Joan Plowright, and his daughters, Julie-Kate and Tamsin as the play's widow and bereaved daughters. Kenneth Hurren's review in the *Mail on Sunday* opened by noting that "the great Laurence Olivier's finest achievements were at the

Old Vic"; Jane Edwardes, noting the production's "macabre sub-text," opened her review in *Time Out* by commenting that "there are many ways of recovering from bereavement," but that this production was "one of the most peculiar." More than one review opened with the phrase, "this is the one with the Oliviers."[5] The reviews were mixed. At the Royal Alex the following winter the play's philosophical focus on time was more in evidence (and was linked in the program to the restoration of the Royal Alex Theatre itself), but reviewers found the production "tired," "musty," and "arch." According to Ray Conlogue, in a review irreverently entitled "Time and the Oliviers," the production "reproduced what ought to be revivified."[6]

Finally, when the English Shakespeare Company's avowedly socialist, medieval-to-modern-dress trilogy of Shakespearean history plays *The Henrys* (*1* and *2 Henry IV* and *Henry V*) arrived at the Old Vic in 1987 after its successful provincial tour it was widely celebrated, as it was when it was revived in 1989 as part of the company's epic project, *The Wars of the Roses*, covering the eight plays of Shakespeare's two tetralogies of English history. When *The Henrys* opened at the Royal Alex shortly after the first Old Vic openings, the audience left in droves, and in spite of the fact that the owners of both the Old Vic and the Royal Alex, Ed and David Mirvish, were the tour's major sponsors, the company was not invited back to Toronto as part of the international tour of *The Wars of the Roses*.

Philip C. McGuire, in a review of Barbara Hodgdon's *Shakespeare in Performance* volume on *2 Henry IV* which concludes with a chapter on the English Shakespeare Company (ESC), writes that Hodgdon "brings one face to face with an immensely difficult question:"

To what extent is a production culturally specific with respect not only to its origins but also its reception? To what extent are the cultural meanings and cultural functions of a production – especially one that purports to offer "sociopolitical critique" ([Hodgdon] 123) – conditioned, perhaps even altered, when it is performed for audiences in places as culturally different as Hull and Hong Kong, Toronto and Tokyo, Bath and Berlin, Cardiff and Chicago?[7] (103)

In considering this question, I want to focus in this chapter on the gap between socialist principles and what might be seen as neo-imperialist practices at the ESC in 1986–87 under the Management of director Michael Bogdanov and actor Michael Pennington, in order to highlight the ways in which explicitly thematized political content can be altered when the material conditions through which meaning is produced – including in this case the politics of funding, of location, and of cultural meaning-making at the point of "consumption" – are overlooked.

By their own account, Bogdanov and Pennington founded the English Shakespeare Company out of disaffection in the late 1980s with the Royal Shakespeare Company and National Theatre and disgust at the Thatcher government's slash-and-burn policies towards the arts, the provinces, and the Falkland Islands.[8] They wanted to do something "independent of the two big institutions."[9] It is one of several ironies surrounding their venture that this led them to participate in Thatcherite schemes of privatization and cultural imperialism that bore directly on the ways the sociopolitical critique mounted thematically in their production was reworked by its different audiences.

Among the ironies surrounding the ESC venture are the difficulties Bogdanov and Pennington encountered as management negotiating labor disputes with actor's equity and with the company (to whom, in spite of their own politics, Bogdanov and Pennington insist on referring as "actors" rather than workers), and the unacknowledged gender blindnesses which result in their assembling, astonishingly for a socialist arts organization in the late 1980s, an all-male board of directors. Indeed Bogdanov's critique of the Thatcher government, for which he uses Margaret Thatcher herself as a metonym, is itself disturbingly gendered, in that he consistently refers to Thatcher in such gendered terms as "Bodicea," or as "a stern nanny at the helm."[10] Not the least of the ironies, however, circulate around funding, and the fact that, although the decision to tour Shakespeare to the English provinces – frequently iterated as the company's primary goal[11] – was precipitated by early encouragement from the British Arts Council, the company's most significant funding came from the private sector in Ireland and in the colonies. Neither *The Henrys* nor *The Wars of the Roses* toured in Ireland, and *The Henrys* played at the Royal Alex in Toronto with considerable neo-imperialist condescension. Little attention was paid to the theatrical or cultural space or the constitution of the audience there. The site specificity of the Toronto performances, in fact, was left unconsidered in the planning and rehearsal processes, in spite of the leading role they played in funding the entire venture: Bogdanov and Pennington consistently articulated the tour of the English provinces in British anti-centric terms as "the reason we're in business," and they described the Old Vic performances as the climax of the tour. The Toronto performances, clearly, served as its unfortunate but necessary denouement.[12]

The story of the Allied Irish Bank's involvement with the ESC, its first venture into arts funding, is beyond the scope of this chapter, except insofar as England's historical relationship to Ireland, as to Canada, is one of economic exploitation and cultural imperialism. A brief examination of the Mirvishes' involvement, however, as the Canadian owners at that time of both the Old Vic and the Royal Alex, is instructive. In Pennington's account, Ed Mirvish and his son David were attracted to the project because, as the new owners of the Old Vic "they wanted to respond to the deep feeling among English audiences that the Old Vic should [once again] be a fairly regular home for Shakespeare." "Even though our most promising allies, the Mirvishes, were commercial," Pennington says, "we were firmly resting our case from the outset on the principle of subsidy; a commercial management looking for a return would be most unlikely to consider [a budget of £350,000, at that point] for Shakespearean history."[13]

After outlining the background of Ed Mirvish as the son of Lithuanian Jewish immigrants to Toronto who dragged himself up by his bootstraps to become the millionaire owner of Honest Ed's Discount Department Store, the Royal Alex, and finally the Old Vic, Pennington describes the first meeting with the Mirvishes – "the best kind of family concern" – as a cozy family gathering with Ed, Ann, and their son David, that culminated in a commitment of £125,000 to *The Henrys*, plus guaranteed running costs, "on the not very arduous condition that we play six-week seasons at the Old Vic and the Royal Alex at the end of our UK tour." From this point on, each time the Michaels ran into financial trouble bringing populist Shakespeare to the marginalized English regions, "anatomizing the [English] nation," they turned to Canada and the Mirvishes for advances, subsidizing from the colonies a fundamentally English nationalist venture.

"There was," as they say, "a built in profit in Canada of £40,000" for the ESC, the Royal Alex being both the only Canadian destination on the tour and the only venue budgeted, much less guaranteed, to do more than break even for the company.[14]

It doesn't seem to have occurred to Bogdanov and Pennington that the Mirvishes might have had their own reasons for supporting the ESC. They seem to have perceived no conflict between their socialist goals and their understanding of the Mirvishes' wish to restore Shakespeare to the Old Vic; they seem willfully blind to their participation in Thatcherite privatization; and they seem not to have taken the Royal Alex performances into account at all.

What *were* the Mirvishes' goals? Why would Lithuanian-Canadian business tycoons respond to "the deep feeling among English audiences that the Old Vic should be a...home for Shakespeare?" Why would they want to bring a production by the "English" "Shakespeare" "Company" to the Royal Alex? Why did the owner of Toronto's most garish discount department store buy the Royal Alex and the Old Vic in the first place? Clearly, based on "Honest Ed Mirvish" 's folksy autobiography, *How to Build an Empire on an Orange Crate*, and on the books he had published about the refurbishment of both of the Mirvish theatres, the family was in the business of accumulating cultural as well as financial capital. One of these books is in effect two-books-in-one, published back to back. One cover reads, *Royal Alexandra: The Finest Theatre on the Continent*; the other, *The Old Vic: The Most Famous Theatre in the World*. Included is a photograph of Honest Ed with "Her Royal Highness, Queen Elizabeth, The Queen Mother."[15] Ed Mirvish's account of defusing the hostility that was directed at the purchase of the Old Vic by a Canadian retail merchant called "Honest Ed" is also suggestive: "They're calling me a foreigner," he said, "But I'm really just a lad from the colonies."[16]

Ed Mirvish's version of his family's dealings with the ESC, not surprisingly, differs somewhat from that of Bogdanov and Pennington. The discrepancies may in part have to do with Ed's having delegated the management of both theatres to his son, but his account is nevertheless interesting, partly because he erroneously attributes the artistic success of *The Henrys* and *The Wars* (together with Ed's own winning of the title of Commander

of the British Empire "from the Queen"[17]) to Jonathan Miller –
who didn't in fact take over artistic direction of the Old Vic until
1988. More importantly, in spite of Bogdanov and Pennington's
attribution to the Mirvishes of unbridled altruism on behalf of
English theatregoers, Ed Mirvish ends his acount with money
and a moral: "while [the] productions [of *The Henrys*] were artistically great," Ed says, "commercially they were not."

Neither was a money maker. One of the main reasons was that Jonathan
[sic], preferring skilled yet unknown actors, seldom used stars. And
I'd been in the business long enough to know that, even with mediocre
shows, stars *fill* seats. I was incredibly proud of the prestige those Shakespearean productions brought, but we are also in the business to make
a profit.
    So, while it's great to succeed with something daringly different in the
theatre, I still believe, as I constantly told Jonathan:
    **If you ever have the urge to make money, don't fight it. It's not
all that bad.**[18]

Clearly, as in the productions of *One Way Pendulum*, *Kean*, and
Time and the Conways, the Mirvishes' interest in the "English"
"Shakespeare" "Company" was a blend of colonialist Anglo-
philia and a desire to accumulate real and cultural capital. The
Bogdanov desire to change society is nowhere in evidence.

I was not able to see *The Henrys* on their English provincial tour,
and am not able to speak with authority about the meanings they
produced for their target audiences in the English provinces, beyond noting that the reviewers – many of them from London – by
and large approved, though few noticed any interventionist social
critique. It is perhaps worth noting only that the provinces' role
in producing *The Henrys* was limited to their benefiting from the
center-to-periphery nationalist vision of the British Arts Council
and the determination of Bogdanov and Pennington to "allow"
actors their regional accents. Although Bogdanov includes "the
regional problems, the North–South divide, the continuing problems of Wales, Scotland and Ireland" prominently in his accounts of *The Henrys* resonance with Thatcher's Britain,[19] this
tour did not extend to Wales, Scotland, or Ireland, and there is
no evidence that reviewers or audiences in the regions perceived
any regionalist critique. Nor do reviews mention the Falklands,
Henry IV's advice on busying giddy minds with foreign quarrels

to deflect attention from problems at home – "unemployment, housing, and so on"[20] – or other analogies made frequently by Bodganov.

The Old Vic is a semiotically rich theatre that was built in Lambeth, on the Surreyside south of the Thames in 1818 as The Royal Cobourg. The early associations of the district as somewhat unsavory, together with its physical remove from the city, led early on to its conversion to "The Royal Victoria Coffee and Music Hall," a temperance establishment and lecture house, and the theatre over the years has retained its associations with education. But its most resonant contemporary associations are with the theatre's Shakespearean revivals after it was taken over by Lilian Baylis, in 1912, officially adopting its current name, by which it had been known colloquially for some time. Since then, all of the leading Shakespearean actors of the English theatre have performed there, most consistently and notably Laurence Olivier, with whose name the Old Vic is inevitably linked, and who was instrumental in the theatre's serving from 1963 to 1976 as the temporary home of Britain's National Theatre. The Mirvishes bought the building not long after the National Theatre moved to its new location on the South Bank, and almost immediately undertook extensive renovations, completed in 1983, to restore the theatre to "its former Victorian splendor" (though as Marvin Carlson points out, "splendor" is not a word likely to have been applied to the building by the Victorians, and the restoration in fact evoked a mixture of periods – a Georgianized façade, Victorian chandeliers, and a lobby resembling a contemporary luxury hotel).[21] The new Old Vic, then, attempted "to send a message of modern comfort, even opulence, with indices of nineteenth-century elegance," "signs validating the Vic to contemporary audiences as a legitimate historical and cultural artifact."[22] The upper circle was named for Lilian Baylis and features a bust of Shakespeare, while the right and left stage boxes in the auditorium were named for Laurence Olivier and Shakespearean director Tyrone Guthrie, who both directed at the Old Vic and founded Canada's Stratford Shakespearean Festival.

Reviewers of *The Henrys* at the Old Vic focused on "the stunning renewal of the Old Vic [as] showplace," and on Shakespeare. "Rejoice!" trumpeted the *London Daily News*, "Shakespeare is back at the Old Vic." Michael Coveny, in *The*

Financial Times, said "it was almost like old times at the Old Vic on Saturday."[23] The primary audiences explicitly targeted by Bogdanov – people who "a) have not gone to Shakespeare for a long time and b) may never have gone to the theatre before and couldn't care less whether Shakespeare lived or died"[24] – don't seem to have attended; at least their presence isn't registered in reviews. Ironically, too, given the company's stated intentions, reviewers noted that the ESC was "helped by being able to stage their cycle in a proper theatre like the Old Vic" as opposed to the less suitable spaces it had occupied in the provinces.[25] Pleasure at the Mirvishes' architectural restoration of the Vic, the restoration of its repertoire to Shakespeare, and the urban renewal of its South-Bank neighborhood, all overrode analysis, particularly socially engaged analysis of the production as sociopolitical critique. There is certainly no evidence that such critique was perceived to have extended to the South-Bank renewal that was so unproblematically celebrated by Ed Mirvish in his account of the purchasing of the theatre:

From its early days as an industrial slum when added police patrols were needed to control the rabble, and the Waterloo Bridge Company offered theatre-goers free tolls to entice them across the bridge, the district is now so upscale that Old Vic patrons can soon cross the street to Waterloo Station and ride the celebrated Chunnel to France. Even better for us, hundreds of Parisians can cram into the Chunnel, zip beneath the English Channel, and scoot across the street smack into the Old Vic.[26]

What did surface in the London reviews was acknowledgment of the productions' (and Bogdanov's) interest, explored through eclectic costuming, in social and historical process. As Andrew Rissik noted, representatively, in *Plays and Players*, "we watch the passing of time, the transitional agony by which one kind of government becomes another." "Here, for the first time in my theatregoing experience we chart the changes in the national character."[27] An Anglo-Québecois reviewer of the production at the Old Vic – one who had, however, participated in the rehearsal process – was virtually alone in pointing out and taking seriously resonances with the Brixton riots, the Falklands war, and Thatcher's Britain, and particularly in asking "what...is this mild-mannered Canadian millionaire doing with Marx and

Shakespeare?" And David Mirvish answered: "They're all Marx-ists in British theatre ... I'm sure Michael will deliver a first rate show."[28]

At the Royal Alex, however, where the also-restored turn-of-the-century theatre sits at the heart of Toronto's commercial entertainment district, near the CN Tower, the Skydome (home of the city's professional baseball team), Roy Thomson Hall (home of the Toronto Symphony), and the City's giant Convention Centre, reviews were different. In part because of the opulence of the theatre, the discursive construction of the production in Anglophilic program notes and upscale advertising, and the price of the tickets (which, as reviewer Jon Kaplan noted, rendered the production beyond the means of those "who would most enjoy" – and perhaps differently understand – the shows[29]), the very few who mentioned the shows' sociopolitical agenda did so in interview features with Bogdanov. But no Toronto reviewers read them as explorations of historical process, and most considered the eclectic costuming to function essentially in historically appropriative metaphorical ways, removing the action from the realms of history and the social, where change happens, to that of timeless and universal truth. Thus one saw "a timely reminder of the awesome genius that was Shakespeare"; another considered the costuming to have made period disappear altogether, "to make chronology invisible"; even the reviewer for the alternative weekly, *Now*, wrote that "[w]hat [the costuming] signifies is that the themes of the play are timeless and universal."[30] The disaffection of the show's creators with the RSC and the National were likewise not in evidence, as promotional features marketed their credentials with "Britain's prestigious Royal Shakespeare Company and National Theatre," and featured the patronage of "Sir" John Gielgud and "Dame" Peggy Ashcroft.[31] Did the committed socialists Bogdanov and Pennington have no interest in or control over marketing, ticket prices, or the public discourse of the productions?

The most immediately apparent difference between the reception of *The Henrys* at the Old Vic and Royal Alex rests in a surfacing at the Alex of a pervasive Englishness, servicing the Mirvishes' colonialist Anglophilia and their accumulation of cultural capital, while constructing the ESC team, in spite of their best stated intentions, as cultural imperialists rather than

anti-centrist English folk (or class warriors) on tour in the
provinces. Resolute Englishness, in postcolonial Canada, reinforces rather than contradicts "timeless universality," and not
only did this production market "English stagecraft at its best,"[32]
but it was greeted with considerable colonial cringe. Reviewers
searched for appropriately "English" comparisons, vocabularies,
and discursive frames through which to describe the action. John
Woodvine, only in Canada, was described as a " huge, charming,
George Formby of a Falstaff" in the *Henry IV* plays, and "[an]
Alistair Cook-like chorus in *Henry V*; "Aunchient Pistol" (this
spelling was not used in the program, but was introduced by the
reviewer) wore a "Teddy-boy jacket" – not a style that crossed
the Atlantic; and publicity materials saw "bobbies on bicycles"
where English critics had seen Thatcherite thugs.[33]

This last example points towards one of the problems of cultural translation that were encountered by the production. It is
difficult, in Canada, to take "bobbies" seriously, or to consider
them to fulfill Bogdanov's frequently stated intention in his mod-
ernizations" "to put the viewer at ease by seeing in Shakespeare's
world something with which he or she is at ease in their own," to
make audiences "identify with people."[34] The cumulative effect
of several such slippages, in which significances and resonances
shifted considerably between their encoding and their decoding,
is significant. What did Canadians experiencing their own versions of French–English conflict make of the "Fuck the Frogs"
banner that accompanied the English to France in *Henry V*?
Was it for them, as for Bogdanov, a sign of "th[e] same bigoted
xenophobic patriotism" that is represented by Henry's army as
football hooligans shouting the archetypically English " 'ere we
go, 'ere we go, 'ere we go?" in one of the show's most celebrated
scenes?[35] What was made of the inscription on Pistol's T-shirt,
"Never mind the bollocks, here comes Pistol" – in a country
where "bollocks" signifies "English" more than – well, anything
else – and "English" signifies "Culture?" (The slogan's citation
of the also quintessentially English Sex Pistols' then decade-
old first punk rock album went under the heads of Canadian
reviewers.)

Perhaps the most complex example of signifying slippage circulated around what many – including Bogdanov – considered
to be "something of a symbol for the ESC style"[36] – the spiky,

8. Andrew Jarvis as Gadshill and Colin Farrell as Bardolph in the English Shakespeare Company's 1987 touring production of *Henry IV, Part One* in *The Henrys*, directed by Michael Bogdanov.

punk haircut sported by Gadshill that Bogdanov calls "Mohican" (curiously evoking James Fenimore Cooper), but that most in Canada would call a "Mohawk" (see illus. 8). For me and my friends growing up Catholic in Ontario, these were called "Iroquois cuts," and their first resonance, good settler/invader Catholics that we were, was with what we learned to think of as the savage torture and murder of the "Canadian Martyrs," Fathers Brébeuf and Lalement, near Midland, Ontario in 1649. In England "Mohock" derives from an early appropriation of supposed Indian savagery, and its applications range from the gangs of "rakes" who roamed eighteenth-century London over-turning carriages[37] to the rebellious street punks Bogdanov intended to invoke, together with the subsequent fashion state-ments that re-crossed the Atlantic in the 1980s to infect subur-ban middle-class youth in shopping malls. In Canada, for some, the style and its name have not yet lost their complex and un-comfortably appropriative postcolonialist resonances, as became very clear a few years after *The Henrys* were performed in Toronto when "real" Mohawks took on the Quebec police and Canadian Army in an armed standoff over the building of a golf course on Mohawk land at Oka, near the Quebec-Ontario border.

As a consequence of the production's combination of resolute Englishness, its lack of engagement with the site-specific reso-nances of its metaphorical vocabulary, and resilient readings of it as a source of universal truth, I suggest, the ESC played a cultural role in Canada as Ideological State Apparatus not un-like that of the RSC in England – perhaps even reinforcing, on the level of Repressive State Apparatus, the kind of cultural work performed by the British troops in the Falklands or the Canadian Army at Oka.

At the Royal Alex audiences voted with their feet, and made themselves the object of some scorn by doing so. Pennington explained that Alex subscribers represent "the conservative end of a rather conservative city,"[38] and Bogdanov that

the problem is subscription audiences. Deadly theatre. Ed and David rely on their subscribers to provide 75% of their income. They have thirty-eight thousand subscribers. Their seat prices are, for Toronto, very high. Therefore what young following they have is very small, few being able to afford the cost of a ticket. The average age of our audience [there] must have been closer to sixty than fifty; some had held seats at the theatre (the same seats) for as much as twenty years. They come the first Thursday (or the second Wednesday, or the third...) of every month. It was a ritual performed with Pavlovian precision. People left *The Henrys* both during the performance and at the interval.... Some thought the interval was the end! Frankly, many did not know what they were coming to at all.[39]

Setting aside the shift from class to age, and the avoidance of responsibility for such things as ticket prices and marketing in the making of meaning, Bogdanov and Pennington reveal, for Marxists, an astonishing disregard for the gap between what is thematized in a production and what is located – an astonishing removal from engagement and responsibility that manifests itself as condescension rooted in a failure or refusal to understand their audiences or do their homework: Bogdanov caricatures with ludicrous inaccuracy the supposed English-Canadian cultural exodus from "Montreal, Ottawa [which he mistakenly believes to be in Quebec], Quebec itself" when "a law was passed making French the first language of the province of Quebec," and he misidentifies Toronto's important Theatre Passe Muraille, where the women members of his own company performed a benefit during the run of *The Henrys*, as "a theatre club called the Place Muraille."[40] This sort of clumsiness, carelessness, and cultural caricature resonates rather uncomfortably with Henry V's attitudes to the French (or Margaret Thatcher's to the Falkland Islanders).

Some Toronto reviewers sided with Bogdanov, and distanced themselves from what they characterized as the audiences' lack of sophistication. John Bemrose, reviewing for the national news magazine, *Macleans*, seemed to agree with Bogdanov and Pennington, noting that "the Royal Alex's conservative audience – many of whom are season subscribers – is less enthusiastic [than audiences at the Old Vic had been]. But if *The Henrys* fail to strike a spark in Canada it may also suggest that local audiences are not yet willing to take their Shakespeare fresh, strong – or in massive doses."[41] Interestingly, however, Bob Pennington, writing in the local tabloid, *The Sun* – a paper that represents a working-class audience the ESC might have been expected to reach, but that the city's well-to-do have little to do with – wrote that "the determinedly strong, regional accents . . . could take time for Canadians to attune to[,] while having chanting, soccer-style thugs carry 'F . . . the Frogs' banners as they join Henry V's invasion fleet may also be a little too insular for general appreciation here."[42]

One person's "insular" may be another's cosmopolitan, but it is clear that using colonial resources to fund an English national project and then taking the unmodified product abroad with no engagement with the specificities of local cultural meaning-making can have unfortunate, unforeseen, and culturally imperialistic results. It is clear, too, that theatre criticism and practice, particularly for those who believe, as Bogdanov claims to, that the only reason to do theatre is to initiate social change, must go beyond purely thematic, metaphoric, or historically allegorical considerations of contemporary relevance. At the points of both production and reception, both critics and practitioners need to pay closer attention than did the ESC to the politics of funding, sponsorship, and marketing; to the politics of location; and to the complex localized politics of cultural meaning-making.

7   International festivals

In a consciously provocative opinion piece in the spring 1992 issue of *Theatre Forum*, Ritsaert ten Cate asked in his title, "Festivals: Who Needs 'Em?" In the process of attempting to answer the question ("travel agents, who can offer package deals" is the closest he seems to get, quoting an apparently "deadly serious" American student (87)) ten Cate raises some issues that remain crucial to any discussion of the cultural work performed by international festivals at the turn of the millenium. He focuses his piece on a familiar, mutually reinforcing binary – and I suggest that this binarism is itself part of the problem – one that seems to set artists/producers against the economic and other interests of governments and "the part of society that provides cash backing for a festival (an overlapping, but essentially different part of society from that which makes up our audiences" [87]). It's "'us' against 'them,'" he says (86). But his essay also touches on less familiar, and I think more useful territory, including such things as "the presentation of our registered cultural trademarks" (87) and "a move toward multiculturalism which seems inspired more by pragmatic reasoning, political opportunism, and the availability of funding than ... by any involvement of the heart" (87). Noting ruefully that "we have witnessed just how successfully the arts can be incorporated as a useful aspect of consumer society," he argues, against his own "better" instincts, that festival organizers "must consider what their own *function* is within the larger context of a mélange of art and society and the world, and also how that function might help move us all toward a future – perhaps even a future somewhat better than the present day they observe around them now" (86, emphasis in original). It is this question, together with those of "the presentation of our registered cultural trademarks" and of multi- or interculturalism (and its relationship to multinationalism, or globalization) that I want to take up here, in spite of ten Cate's own manifest opposition to any consideration of the potential "usefulness" of "art" in a festival context. And finally, I want to address the question of how, and in what ways, the recontextualizing involved in remounting productions at international festivals that emerged from particular cultural contexts or were designed for specific local audiences changes the cultural work that they perform and the ways in which they are read.[1]

International Festivals are first and foremost marketplaces. The major festivals such as Edinburgh and Avignon (together with the neo-Elizabethan theatres functioning as festivals in a different sense that sprang up in North America following Tyrone Guthrie's first, in Stratford, Ontario) were founded in the wake of the Second World War. As Dennis Kennedy has argued, they operated as fundamentally modernist institutions and as destinations for cultural tourism.[2] They served to shore up cultural fragments against "our" ruin, functioning as museums, pillaging and exhibiting decontextualized cultural artifacts in much the same way modernist artists themselves pillaged African masks and "oriental" forms of ritual expression. Today Edinburgh, Avignon, and other festivals such as Montreal's Festival du théâtre des Amériques, Toronto's tellingly named DuMaurier World Stage, and the annual migrating (and even more aptly named) European Cultural Capitol festivals, function primarily as manifestations of a theatrical version of late-capitalist globalization, postmodern marketplaces for the exchange, not so much of culture as of cultural *capital*. The audiences for these festivals constitute communities (as opposed to consumer groups) only insofar as they share what can primarily be understood as a formalist interest in theatre itself. And the capitol/capital pun is operative: the festivals increasingly function as National showplaces, in which the "Culture" of nations, often with financial support from national governments and within the context of various organizational and diplomatic interventions from their foreign offices and embassies, is on display for a world and audience that is thereby constructed as an international market for cultural and other "industries." These festivals, that is, display national cultural products in much the same way that other products are displayed and promoted at international trade fairs and through aggressive government/business trade delegations. A representative example is my own country's "Team Canada," led by the Prime Minister, provincial Premiers, and corporate CEOs to specially targeted markets around the world, including, frequently, so-called "Third World" countries whose populations have borne the heaviest brunt of late twentieth-century globalization.

As I indicated in Chapter Two of this book, my first serious thinking about international festivals emerged from the experience of seeing two extraordinarily strong Scottish productions – Tron Theatre's *The Trick is to Keep Breathing*, adapted from Janice Galloway's novel of the same name, and Traverse Theatre's *Bondagers*, written by Sue Glover – at the DuMaurier World Stage in Toronto in 1996. For their home audiences in Glasgow and Edinburgh respectively these had both been powerful, detailed, carefully textured and culturally specific feminist interventions, and they were equally well received at home and at or on the World Stage. What intrigued me, however, was the degree to which the festival context – it's apparent placelessness – transformed strong and culturally specific work into mere representation (in two senses): 1) metaphor, analogy, or "local color," allowing audiences and critics to detach themselves from the specific social issues under active negotiation in the plays and retreat into discussions of theatrical form and technique; and 2) *national* representation, as the work came to represent Scotland in ways that would have been unrecognizable in Glasgow or Edinburgh. The (Canadian) Scottish Studies Foundation turned out to both shows in full force and set up booths in the lobby to celebrate and appropriate work that had little to do with serving the nationalist, culturally affirmative, and fundamentally sentimental role of cultural ambassadorship – to say nothing of the nostalgia of expatriate communities. The shows became "registered cultural trademarks" – if not in the sense that ten Cate intended, perhaps in an even more pernicious one. And similar things happened when, for example, the Little Theatre of Vilnius presented its operatic rendition of the nineteenth-century Russian romantic poet Mikhail Lermontov's *Masquerade* at the DuMaurier World Stage in 1998. The long and slowly paced show had enjoyed extraordinary popularity within its beleaguered home community, and it brought out the supportive Lithuanian community of

Toronto in droves, but a great many others could be seen handing in their simultaneous-translation headphones and heading
for the exits at the first intermission.

The "main-stage" international festivals, moreover, maintain
a strong trace of their origins in post-war modernism, tending as they do to feature the often inscrutable, formalist, high-
modernist work of theatre companies, most of them either
in receipt of significant government subsidy or funded as co-
productions by a number of festivals – or both. These productions appear by invitation only and are often more notable for cultural cachet than popular appeal. Indeed, at Edinburgh in 1999,
the International Festival's theatre offerings were dominated by
exquisitely crafted and self-consciously high-cultural avant-garde
productions from Holland, Germany, and Poland, almost all of
which were subtitled, slowly paced, bleak, brilliantly performed,
and sparsely attended. Anthony Thorncraft unequivocally identified the programming as "elitist."[3] The productions it featured,
like those of Robert Lepage's explicitly "international" company,
Ex Machina, with no performing space in its home location in
Quebec City, and those of Robert Wilson, Peter Sellars, and
others, are, of course, *staged* for the international "community,"
tend to be based on classics or other sources that already have
transcultural authority or resonance, and tend to be similarly
received and celebrated in most festival contexts. Lepage's solo
show, *Elsinore*, for example, based on *Hamlet*, which was performed in both English and French as it toured the Festival circuit, functioned in 1996 at both the Festival de Otoño in Madrid
and at the DuMaurier World Stage in Toronto, as elsewhere,
as a kind of meta-critical commentary on the play and on theatre itself. It deliberately heightened the play's cultural iconicity
by foregrounding and combining such familiar emblems as the
"to be or not to be" speech and the address to Yorrick's skull;
it used the familiar but old-fashioned Victor Hugo translation
when it was performed in French (rather than using or com-
missioning a new Québécois translation); when performed in
English, even in Canada, it adopted something jarringly like a
"standard English" accent (Lepage, when he first performed the
show, was coached by the National Theatre of Great Britain's
Patsy Rodenberg); and it provided a visual context that conjured supposedly transnational Western humanist icons (such

as da Vinci's drawing of the male body inside a circle inside a square, and Eadward Muybridge's serial photographs of a naked man running) rather than local or site-specific references or resonances. For better or worse, and with the connivance of national governments interested in cultural showcases as promotional opportunities, an increasing percentage of theatrical production is taking this form, as the cultural economies of nations become increasingly globalized.

When other kinds of show from "othered" places are performed at these festivals, the results of decontextualizing can be extreme. When Brazil's Grupo Galpao, a socially interventionist street theatre, staged the neo-medieval biblical pageant *Street of Sorrows* in Portuguese at the Premiere Dance Theatre at the DuMaurier World Stage in 1998, the result was disconcerting in the extreme. The first act, a folk nativity play featuring a tiny, bald, and bearded Christ "child" that was designed to be performed in the street – the people's space – was incongruously mounted within a chalk circle inscribed on the traffic loop/loading dock area that adjoins the upscale Queen's Quay shopping mall in which the theatre is housed. Actors and spectators then proceeded up the mall's shiny metal escalator and through the glass and class of the mall into the theatre proper, where the sculptural relief of abandoned crutches, lanterns, and devotional objects that framed the proscenium became uncomfortably folkloric rather than operating as a collective testimonial of faith. What in Brazil had been a healing theatre-of-the-streets, staged for the small and impoverished villages of the Minas Gerais – the company boasts that seventy percent of its audience doesn't go to theatre – became in Toronto intercultural tourism of the most intrusive kind. It was also considered by some I talked to in Toronto to be offensively racist in its depiction of the Biblical Jews. In any case, it was reviewed as "more of an adventure in anthropology than in theatre."[4] But even less stark examples of such decontextualizing abound. The RO Theatre of Rotterdam's adaptation of Maxim Gorky's *The Lower Depths* at Edinburgh in 1999, one of the bleakest productions I have ever attended, saw its stark presentation of the desperate lives and deaths of men and women in a shelter transformed into something resembling voyeuristic display when the harsh environment of the shelter was framed by the relatively lush surroundings – and corresponding

ticket prices – of the recently renovated nineteenth-century Royal
Lyceum Theatre, with its Henry Irving and Ellen Terry rooms,
located at the heart of Festival festivity in Festival Square, next
to "Shakespeare's" pub, and right across from the Sheraton
Edinburgh.

But Edinburgh is not limited to the International Festival, and
not all international festivals are the same, including the ways
in which they negotiate the tension between the local and the
global. Some of the large-scale festivals, such as the DuMaurier
World Stage, simply incorporate work already going on in the
city as part of the festival, bringing new audiences to local theatres while expanding the range of festival offerings at little cost.
The downside to this is that new Canadian work mounted on
low budgets with three-week rehearsal periods as regular parts of
a theatrical season is judged against specially selected highlights
of the international repertoire, often work that has enjoyed long
gestation periods of rehearsal and development and that has been
in repertoire for years. The Festival du théâtre des Amériques,
on the other hand, features a considerable amount of strong local work in the main program – indeed government funding for
the festival is contingent upon its doing so – but it also features a
"Nouvelle scène" series consisting of new and experimental local
work that is often among the most exciting at the festival. But,
of course, like the rest of the program, this work is selected by
the festival's artistic director, who is also responsible for government and corporate fundraising. If the Nouvelle scène work is
often aesthetically experimental or avant garde in nature, then,
it is unlikely to serve any genuinely alternative function, as such
shows as Scottish playwright Joan Ure's feminist plays *Something
in it for Ophelia* and *Something in it for Cordelia* did when they were
deliberately mounted at the Edinburgh Fringe opposite International Festival mainstage productions of *Hamlet* and *King Lear*.

But the Edinburgh festival's negotiation with the local was initiated outside the bounds of the festival proper, has taken on a life
of its own, and has arguably gotten out of hand. The Edinburgh
Fringe, now also an international festival, has long since sur-
passed its parent in numbers of productions, artist/participants,
and audiences, as well as in economic importance to the city,
producing over 1,300 shows by the turn of the millennium,
involving 14,500 performers and attracting an audience in excess

of 800,000 – three times that of the International Festival.[5] And this is the second type of festival, or the second aspect of festivals, that I want to consider, where the market is in "real" rather than, or as well as, symbolic or cultural capital, and the organizing structure is modeled directly on what is called free enterprise. The myth, of course, is that the Fringe is where the truly experimental, anarchic, avant-garde energy of the festivals that inhabit Edinburgh each August lies (there are also film, television, and book festivals), together with its *local* (versus global) or *alternative* import and resonances. But if this was ever the case it isn't any more. In fact, like the Fringe phenomenon that has captured Canada, where a circuit of "fringe" festivals spreads across the country each summer in association with no recognizable mainstage, and where participants are chosen purely by lottery, the "original" Edinburgh Fringe is the archetypal theatrical model of global free trade, where virtually anything goes. Theatre companies from around the world mount productions in literally dozens of venues across the city "on spec," handing out flyers and hustling for audiences and press recognition in hopes of, at a very long shot, breaking even – but more importantly establishing a reputation, becoming known, and making contacts with potential producers or co-producers of their work. Physical theatre rubs shoulders with stand-up comedy and competes for audiences with pop music, musical comedy, "talks and events," and such things – listed as fringe events in its official brochures – as "The Sensory Secrets of Malt Whisk(e)y and Cheese," a "Tutored Whiskey Sampling," or "The MacEwan's 80/ [ale]- Edinburgh Literary Pub Tour." In this context, few theatre companies – pushed, as Ger Fitzgibbon argued as early as 1990, "towards soft content and hard sell"[6] – can afford to produce experimental, avant-garde, or alternative work unless it is also sensational or has sufficiently broad popular appeal to draw crowds and attention in a fiercely competitive free-trade marketplace. In fact, the presence in the program of some of the more openly promotional events, together with the increasing dependence of the Fringe on corporate sponsorship from the likes of the Bank of Scotland and Becks beer, raises questions about free-market appropriation with brutal directness: where anything goes, could the fringe be taken over completely by corporate publicity ventures "staged" by the MacEwan breweries of the world? Has the line between cultural and other tourism been irrevocably crossed?

But the free-trade fringe is not only a competitive marketplace for audiences as tourists and consumers, it has also come directly to serve national governments as an international trade fair and showcase – indeed, to do so much more directly than does the International Festival, which maintains a veneer of high-cultural superiority to the purely market-driven atmosphere of the fringe. In 1999 delegations of theatre artists and producers from fifty-one nations were brought to Edinburgh by the British Arts Council, with co-sponsorships from the arts councils of the home countries: in Canada the program was called "Theatre International Pilot Program." In addition to breakfasts, receptions, and social occasions, the visiting artists received twenty tickets to a featured showcase series, "the best of British theatre," in hopes that they would "network" with one another and with cultural attachés and agents, plant the seeds of touring, co-production, and collaborative initiatives, and book British companies for their own festivals and theatre seasons.[7]

At both the major Festivals and their fringes, then, the mechanics of "exchange" tend to be modeled more on international diplomacy, intercultural tourism, and transnational trade than on potentially disruptive or genuinely inter-discursive interculturalism. Cultural differences, in these contexts, tend either to be packaged for consumption as exotic or charming – as when the Festival des Amériques featured Vietnamese water puppets in 1995 – or, as in high modernist formalism, to be treated as interesting and energizing but fundamentally incidental local variants on a (therefore more important, or essential) universalist or transcendent humanism – as is arguably the case in such festival successes as Robert Lepage's powerful but orientalist *Seven Streams of the River Ota*, or even the Young Vic's charming and popular production of the *Arabian Nights* at the Edinburgh Fringe in1999. David Graver and Loren Kruger called the two options "mindlessly multicultural" and "hastily universalist" in their 1993 attempt to find "Regionalism and Interculturalism at Edinburgh."[8] It is not accidental that shows brought to the festivals that originate *outside* the Euro-American world upon which such universalism rests its case tend to be based on Western classics, as in the (again charming) Chilean version of Jules Verne's

Journey to the Centre of the Earth that graced the DuMaurier World Stage in 1998, or the powerful Argentinian *Maquina Hamlet* (*Hamletmachine*) at the Festival des Amériques in 1999.

The combined effect of all of this would seem to be that productions mounted in festival contexts are significant primarily as products, and can only "mean" – or be culturally *productive* (rather than *re*productive) – insofar as they are considered to be "about" theatre itself, as a form, or, alternatively, about the promotional public construction of national cultures and identities. It is tempting, then, to consider the constraints and containments of the international marketplace to be virtually all-confining. And there is considerable evidence to support this view in reviews (which tend to focus on formal and aesthetic qualities) and in bar and ticket-line conversations (which tend to be about "the Polish [or German, or Lithuanian] show" as though they were Olympic sports teams). But one of the fissures in the apparently totalizing network of globalization – at least as far as the determined site-specificity of live theatre is concerned – is that there *is no such place* as the international marketplace. Theatre festivals, however international, *take place*, within local markets, and in doing so, as anyone who lives in a Festival city will argue, set up complex tensions between the local and the global that are not always or easily contained or controlled. Moreover as not all international festivals are the same, neither are all sites of origin for productions. And shows from the same local or national site do not all respond to contextual shifts in parallel ways. To what extent, then, do local differences remain, and play themselves out within the festival contexts? In what different ways and to what degrees do productions originating at different national sites create (or exploit) fissures and tensions in the veneer of internationalism as they play against each other in (different) festival settings? By analyzing the reception of the same productions in their original and subsequent festival contexts, and drawing upon a range of performance texts from different points of origin, it may be possible to arrive at a better understanding of the politics of local meaning-making at the point of reception, and of the relationship between the local and the global in the context of the international theatre festival as a local marketplace problematically situated in relation to a late-capitalist theatrical economy.

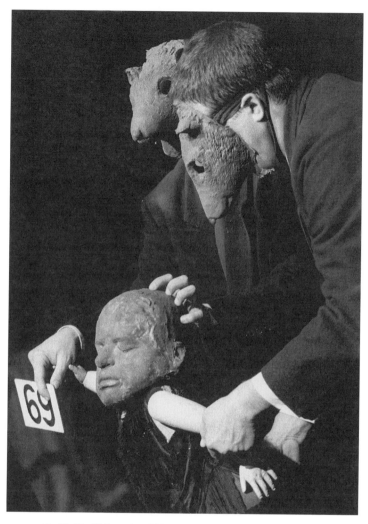

9. El Perférico de Objetos' touring production of *Maquina Hamlet* (Heiner Müller's *Hamletmachine*).

It is possible, of course, to ask the question of a production's political or interventionist efficacy in purely formal terms – to ask, that is, what kinds of interventionist theatre best resist the containments effected by contextual shifts. Thus, for example, El Periférico de Objetos's *Maquina Hamlet* (see illus. 9), the

Argentinian translation and adaptation of Heiner Müller's *Hamletmachine* at the Festival des Amériques in 1999 effectively confronted audience complicity in political tortures and murders through a range of metatheatrical devices, where earlier Robert Wilson and Gilles Maheu versions of *Hamletmachine* had been significantly aestheticized – and therefore comfortably contained. This is the approach taken by David Graver and Loren Kruger when they find "pointedly intercultural and international" productions or those with "judicious borrowings from abroad," such as the Tron Theatre's *The Guid Sisters*, a Glaswegian version of Québécois playwright Michel Tremblay's *Les Belles Soeurs*, to be more effective in challenging chauvinisms and parochialisms than shows which, through generalization or imprecision, "evaporated into bland multicultural mist."[9] I am more interested in this chapter, however, in understanding local meaning-making at the point of *reception*, through tracing the cultural work performed by contextual shifts themselves.

In considering the theatre festival as a marketplace, it is useful to consider the work of Peter Stallybrass and Allon White. The local market, they suggest, is a complex place, "so definite and comforting in its phenomenological presence at the heart of the community," yet "only ever an *intersection* . . . a conjunction of distribution entirely dependent upon remote processes of production and consumption, networks of communication, lines of economic force."

At once a bounded enclosure and a site of open commerce, it [the marketplace] is both the imagined centre of an urban community and its structural interconnection with the network of goods, commodities, markets, sites of commerce and places of production which sustain it. A marketplace is the epitome of local identity . . . and the unsettling of that identity by the trade and traffic of goods from elsewhere. At the market centre of the polis we discover a commingling of categories usually kept separate and opposed: centre and periphery, inside and outside, stranger and local, commerce and festivity, high and low. In the marketplace pure and simple categories of thought find themselves perplexed and one-sided. Only hybrid notions are appropriate to such a hybrid place.[10]

At fair time – or festival – this situation is enhanced by the marketplace's "special status . . . as a popular domain created outside, and beyond, the official sites of authority." But historically,

Stallybrass and White argue, "although the bourgeois classes were frequently frightened by the threat of political subversion and moral licence [at fair time], they were perhaps more scandalized by the deep conceptual confusion entailed by the fair's intermixing of work and pleasure, trade and play." Neither purely festive, disruptive, or carnivalesque nor purely commercial, the festival marketplace, like that of the fair, can potentially function as an agent of transformation because it brings together "the exotic and the familiar, the villager and the townsman, the professional performer and the bourgeois observer," serving as "the point of intersection of different cultures" and promoting "a conjuncture of discourses and objects favourable to innovation" – whether that innovation takes the form of the subversion or advancement of "the progress of capital." But more importantly, the festival, like the fair, can "[juxtapose] both people and objects which [are] normally kept separate" and can therefore *disrupt categories*, and in particular the categories of high and low culture, art and commerce, even ten Cate's "us and them." And there is "never a guarantee that the 'low' spectator [will] not find his or her radical identity in the 'low' spectacle of the fair."[11]

It is interesting in this context to consider briefly the question of performance venue. Most major festivals, of course, are staged in large, permanent, upscale, and purpose-built urban performing venues – theatres, arts centers, and occasionally galleries – and most fringe festivals occur largely in found or variable-purpose spaces (which often gives them their category-defying power). But even relatively innocent work can gain political edge through venue. A perhaps too obvious example is the Australian *Urban Dream Capsule*, mounted as part of the Festival des Amériques in a department-store display window, colorfully furnished and stocked with the latest amenities, at the busy downtown corner of Montreal's Union and St. Catherine Streets. Some 250,000 Montrealers – including a great many reporters, who regularly featured the "show" on front pages and on television news shows – dropped in or passed by during the "run" to watch four men perform the tasks of daily life in full public view, twenty-four hours a day for the two-week duration of the festival. Audiences, often placed unwittingly in the roles of either voyeurs or actors in the street drama, reacted with bemused attention, finding themselves witnessing fully-frontal dining, performative living, and sardonic confrontations with promotional consumer culture: life as a display window, display as life. The efficacy of the show as political commentary relied entirely on its unexpected venue, its disruption of the distinctions between festival visitors and local shoppers, theatre audiences and passersby (there was no admission charge and no "entrance" to the site), and on its blurring of the boundaries between art and commerce.

Venue was at the center of controversy at the 1999 Edinburgh Fringe Festival, in ways that are perhaps illuminated by Stallybrass and White's analysis of bourgeois anxiety around the question of category disruption. One of the great successes of the Fringe over the years has been the annual refitting, revitalizing, and mounting of fringe programming by Assembly Theatre Ltd. at the "Assembly Rooms" on George Street, a multi-venue facility that has otherwise been something of a municipal white elephant. But 1999 threatened to be the last year for the Assembly Rooms as the heart of the Fringe, since Edinburgh City Council came to the decision to charge what it called "fair market rent" for the venues, which Assembly could not afford. One suspects that in part it is the very functioning of the spaces *as* assembly rooms – they do not function as theatres except during the Fringe – that was disturbing to the Council.[12] It is interesting, too, that there were no designs on the other two large Fringe complexes – the distinctly populist Pleasance, on the one hand, or on the other the distinctly respectable Traverse – which physically, aesthetically, and socially serves as a "bridge" between the Fringe and the International main stage:[13] unlike the Assembly Rooms, both venues decorously preserve appropriate category distinctions. Moreover, the actual productions at the Assembly Rooms can themselves be disconcertingly positioned to blur comfortable social, aesthetic, and disciplinary distinctions. One of the most popular shows there in 1999, for example, was Lee Hall's anarchic *Cooking with Elvis*, performed beneath one of three crystal chandeliers which hung next to a disco ball at one end of the Ballroom, a lush old gilded space in some decay at the heart of the Assembly Rooms. The show was by turns camp, comic, horrific, and in-your-face, a tragic farce about child abuse, wife abuse, sex, loss, and cooking. It featured: "Dave," a very good Elvis impersonator, as a quadriplegic in a vegetative state (who nevertheless rises from his wheelchair in fantasy/dream sequences to comment and entertain); his anorexic sex-starved wife; their fat and fourteen-year-old daughter; and Stuart, who "bangs" the mother, "slags" the daughter, and "wanks off" the apparently insentient Elvis/Dave/Dad. The performance was replete with food and drink, and it was subversively leaky in both the categorical (or generic) and literal senses, overflowing as it was with bodily and other fluids – including urine, semen, blood, and marinade. Neither populist nor elitist – or perhaps both – this was a controlled, shocking, funny, and disturbingly hybrid performance of contemporary Scottish life, light years away from that portrayed in the extraordinarily safe and formulaic musical review, *Caledonia Dreaming*, staged across town at the Pleasance by the once formidably alternative 7:84 (Scotland) Theatre company. Interestingly, one critic seemed less upset at the content of *Cooking with Elvis* than at the disruption of social categories it effected at the point of reception, as "two impeccably genteel ladies" beside him, whose pre-show conversation featured "the church fête, support hose and *Countdown*," laughed "uproariously" throughout, and "trotted out at the end professing themselves much amused." "Is it just me," he asked, "or is the country going to the dogs?"[14]

It is important when considering a show's potential for effective cultural intervention to be attentive to shifts in or enlargements of meaning – or even just local emphases – that happen in still more site-specific ways, but that are often dismissed in criticism as incidental. It was impossible, for example, to emerge from RO Theatre's *The Lower Depths* in Edinburgh without heightened awareness of the homeless people on the city streets, and this was so in part because Edinburgh's famous landscape and architecture stand in as stark a contrast to the plight of some of its people as that between the production's bleak set and its lush theatrical setting, as noted earlier. One reviewer commented that watching the opening night audiences was "like watching people walking down Lothian Road deliberately not looking at the people begging on the corners."[15] The resonances were not the result of design decisions or production values – in fact, as reviewer Jeremy Kingston noted, the night shelter that served as the set looked "absurdly spacious on the Lyceum stage" – but of the accidentals of venue and neighborhood.[16] And these types of resonance can emerge from temporal (or occasional) as well as spatial considerations. The Deutches Schauspielhaus production of *Stunde Null oder Die Kunst des Servierens* at the Festival des Amériques in 1997 featured at once hilarious and terrifying deconstructions of political speechmaking, as apparently empty rhetoric, platitudinous bumble, and sentimentality slid seamlessly over into guttural, Dada-esque rant, revealing the incipient, neo-fascist violence beneath the most pacifying of political platitudes. But the show gained much of its power as social critique from its positioning as the opening show of the Festival. The first performance of *Stunde Null* in Montreal followed immediately in the wake of an opening reception that featured a seemingly endless stream of welcoming speeches by sponsors and others, notably senior Canadian politicians engaged in a federal election campaign – speeches that sounded remarkably similar to those in the production itself.

But two productions doing the festival rounds in the late 1990s can perhaps be used to illustrate stark or complex differences in meaning produced at different festival and other venues. The first, De La Guardia's high-energy Argentinian participation piece, *Periodo Villa Villa*, emerged from a company conscious that they had spent their adolescence under a brutally repressive military dictatorship, but the manic, manipulative, and violent energy that informed the show made it hugely popular among young audiences as a kind of celebratory, carnivalesque release at the Festival des Amériques in Montreal in 1997. The same show had been read and understood quite differently the previous winter when it played in Belgrade as part of its European tour. There the small room with black, curtained walls and low ceiling into which the audience was packed tightly at the outset produced more claustrophobic anxiety than the giddy expectancy of the run at the Festival, particularly when, after a terrifying blackout, objects and body parts began to be thrust through the ceiling cloth and at least one audience member was (temporarily) abducted through a slash in the ceiling. As the party erupted with color, swinging acrobatics, audience-drenching blasts of water, and equally abrasive blasts of high-volume, post-punk rock and roll, and as some of the darker and more violently physical images multiplied and gained resonance, the audience in Belgrade experienced something at once more disturbing and more culturally significant as disruption and intervention than did those in

Montreal who chose, were culturally positioned, and were conditioned by the framework of Festival, to experience the show as full-sensory spectacular escapism. The show has since become a major draw in Las Vegas.

The second case-study that I would like to look at in a little more detail is Enda Walsh's club drama, *Disco Pigs*, which was first produced by Corcadorca at the Triskel Arts Centre, its home theatre in Cork, Ireland, in the fall of 1996 before touring intact to (among other places) the Dublin Fringe, the Edinburgh Fringe in 1996 and 97, the main program at the DuMaurier World Stage in 1998, and the Bush and Arts Theatre, London in 1997 and 98 respectively. The production provides the occasion for something of a case-study in itself, particularly because both play and production seem at first to be so overwhelmingly localist. The script is written in what, along with many others, I at first found to be an almost incomprehensible idiolect that combines an extremely thick Cork patois with elements of a kind of Irish teen rap (or dub poetry) and a private language of baby talk shared between the play's two characters, Runt and Pig. Born side by side one second apart (see illus. 10), the two have grown up together in a housing estate and in defiance of everyone else, and they get together to celebrate their shared seventeenth birthday by going out on the town in "Pork Sity," as they call it, beating up bus drivers, playing games of possession at the disco that lead to brutalizing and assaulting their own and one another's dance partners and generally expressing their mutual if deeply troubled love. The play works as a rollercoaster "amphetamine poem"[17] driven by Cormac O'Connor's club score and staged on a ring with two red plastic chairs. The show is punctuated by achingly beautiful monologues by the sexually awakened Pig and his soulmate, Runt, who is finding that she wants something better, but doesn't even know how to imagine it. Visceral, beautiful, violent, and uncompromising, it is both linguistically and, in the specificities of its detail, deeply engaged with the social and material realities of growing up poor in post-industrial urban Ireland.

Not surprisingly, the show was well received in Ireland, and particularly in Cork, where the company takes seriously a responsibility to its home community, and where *Disco Pigs* was first mounted as one in a series of youth projects. "Ultimately," the playwright told Edinburgh journalist Lyn Gardner, "we have

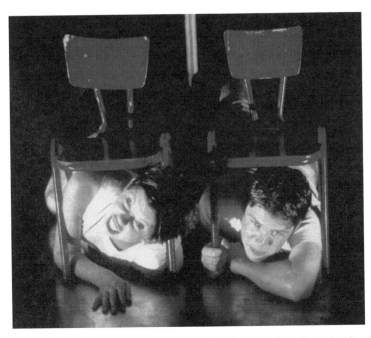

10. The birth scene of Runt and Pig in Corcadorca's production of Enda Walsh's *Disco Pigs*, which opened in Fall 1996 at the Triskel Arts Centre in Cork, Ireland.

to look to our service in Cork."[18] And Irish reviewers noted that the company "relishes the challenge of matching its material to its environment." The review in the *Irish Times* begins, "Midnight: the streets of Cork are alive with the sound of urination, garda sirens, expectoration and the aggressive mating calls of the clannish, cloned young. That's before getting into the theatre at all." Opening a show at midnight is a risky business in more ways than one – the same reviewer marks her "resentment at having to go to work at such an hour." But she also notes that such resentment "fades as the relevance and energy of *Disco Pigs* fists home from the stage of the Triskel Arts Centre."[19] At the Dublin Fringe, where the show was performed in a pub venue, it was hailed most often as "a realistic look at the unreal world of these two teenagers," but where the language was described (only in Ireland) as "a *vulgar* Cork rap dialect."[20]

At the Edinburgh Fringe in 1997 the show was a hit, and was reviewed as fringe hits are, with comments on its high energy and comparisons to Scotland's own earlier downscale hit, *Trainspotting* (or, more often, denials of the comparison). There was also the recognizable tendency – many fringe reviews come in omnibus form – to engage in comparative, competitive assessments of the show's quality, reviews operating at fringe time as consumer guides to the festival marketplace. Unfortunately, in this case the festival context tends to flatten any show's cultural and other specificity, and the imprecision of the comparison to *Trainspotting* was echoed at the 1999 Fringe, when Owen McCafferty's *Mojo-Mickybo*, another high-energy play about young friends growing up, this time, at opposite ends of the bridge in Belfast, was treated promotionally and in reviews as the latest *Disco Pigs*, to the inter-illumination of neither show. Where *Mojo-Mickybo* told a relatively conventional and comfortably familiar story of apparently "normal kids," subjectivities already happily formed, whose innocent childhood friendship is fractured and poisoned by "adult" factions and violence, the strength of *Disco Pigs*, lost in a comparison that privileged high-energy delivery and palatable, consumable "themes," was its complex probing, integral at the structural (versus thematic) level, of the *formation* of adolescent subjectivities in troubled times.

There was also considerable critical commentary in Edinburgh on the language of *Disco Pigs* – "often impenetrable to this English ear," as the reviewer for the *Financial Times* remarked.[21] But there was some tension in the coverage of the show in Scotland, where its origin and setting in contemporary Ireland, it seemed, could neither be entirely ignored nor fully acknowleged. Some journalists, such as Neil Cooper, referring in *Scotland on Sunday* to a scene set in a Provo pub, placed the show squarely in the context of "the troubles," noting, however, that, "whatever" comes of the renewed ceasefire announced by Gerry Adams as the show transferred to Edinburgh, "the Disco Pigs will still be there, sitting in the background, drinking, murmuring, staring people out." A week later in the same paper the same critic treated the play still more directly as metaphor, as did most other reviewers, downplaying the specificities of its social context while granting it "universal relevance": "whether consciously or not," Cooper wrote, the play "sums up a generation in a state of ontological flux, the disaffected youth with no outlet for that overdose of hormonal activity except to party like it's 1999."[22]

Not surprisingly, the further the production moved from Cork, as a general rule, the more it tended to be read in such universalist terms, and the less immediate relevance to local context it seemed to claim. It's a long way from midnight at the Triskel in Cork (or even the International Bar in Dublin) to the elegant brick and glass of the DuMaurier theatre at Toronto's Harbourfront, where *Disco Pigs* was performed as part of the DuMaurier World Stage, and where the actors had aggressively to *seize* a space that was manifestly not their own – which they did with considerable *panache*, drawing considerable praise from audiences and critics there to admire technique. Toronto critics tended to run with the universalizing tendency, few making specific connections to local conditions in Toronto *or* Cork,[23] but many making generalized references to "the world of the violent teenager" or reaching to describe the play generically as "a Romeo and Juliet of the dispossessed."[24] And of all the reviews of the show that I've perused, only in Toronto did I find a critic who felt that the characters "cannot generate any legitimate sympathy":

They deserve none, careering about their urban pigsty, boozing, cheating, bullying, stealing, stuffing down fish and chips, picking fights, screaming and screeching and giggling and generally being a pain in the butt. It climaxes in a two-day birthday 'celebration' that brings a little sense to one of them.[25]

The commentary is not representative, and is ungenerous in the extreme, but it may represent something that the recontextualizing of the production genuinely effected. In Toronto, the combination of the relatively upscale venue, the Festival context, and the generally uncomprehendingly Canadian ears of the audience – one reviewer found it all "pig Latin"[26] – placed considerable, perhaps disproportionate emphasis on the privateness, separateness, and isolation of the world inhabited by Runt and Pig.

It is also a considerable distance from performing as part of a local youth series in Cork (or even from Fringe venues and atmospheres in Dublin and Edinburgh) to taking part in an International Festival that in 1998 featured Irish theatre, notably the Broadway-bound Royal Court production of Conor

MacPherson's *The Wier* and two long-touring, high-culture productions, *Waiting for Godot* and *I'll Go On*, from Dublin's distinguished Gate Theatre. (*I'll Go On* was in no less than its fourteenth year of international touring.) Not surprisingly, again, as Edinburgh Fringe reception had reflected the free-trade market of that festival, the critical discourse in Toronto tended to feature the supposedly representative Irishness of the show and its contribution to "How the Irish Mounted a Theatrical Renaissance."[27] It is not that the topic is wrong, uninteresting, or unexpected at a "World Stage," but in the case of *Disco Pigs*, the show's commonalities with the traditional Irish rural realism of *The Wier* or the high modernism of *Waiting for Godot* would seem to be considerably less striking than its differences – except at festival time.

Not long after its run at the DuMaurier World Stage, *Disco Pigs* emerged from the Festival context for a run in London in the summer of 1998, where, freed from the festival roles of national representation, formalist/technical exemplum, or free-trade commodity, it seemed to regain, if differently, some of its connection to the social that it had resonated with in Cork. Where in Toronto only two months earlier the show had very much seemed to be about the privateness and isolation of the characters' world, at the small Arts Theatre just off Leicester Square in central London the audience was more often and more directly confronted with the characters' violence, their love, and their (social) dilemma as subjectivities in formation. The London audience, however – in spite of there being no mention of England or the English in the production – was also confronted in a way that none of the play's other audiences had been with some of the history and politics around that social dilemma and the social circumstances the play probes. These had to do, of course, with Britain's – or rather England's – complex involvement in and responsibility as colonizer for the social conditions the play probes – and in central London the audience was necessarily constructed as potential victims of IRA bombings. These resonances surfaced most directly in the outrageous Provo karaoke pub scene, where Pig at one point shouts at members of the Sinn Fein army gathered at the bar, "Ere, shouldn't ya be out plantin bombs an beaten up ol ladies, ya fookin weirdos!!"[28] – a moment that had seemed much funnier when I saw the show in Toronto than it did in London, as well as differently (and more locally) resonant than it had been for Neil Cooper in Edinburgh.

Productions that tour or transfer are always, of course, subject to contextually determined shifts in meaning in ways that apply whether the new context is an international festival or not. Festival contexts, as marketplaces for international cultural capital and exchange, however, as I hope to have suggested, introduce particular kinds of constraint and, occasionally, opportunity, to which different productions respond in radically different ways. Producers, artists, and analysts would do well to take such contexts fully into account.

Conclusion

The case-studies of Part Two of *Reading the Material Theatre* have demonstrated some of the potential of the materialist semiotics theorized in Part One. It is my hope that this approach is useful in itself as a flexible tool for the close reading of theatrical performances in all their immediate contextual complexity. But no methodology functions in a vacuum, and within the expanding field of performance analysis it is also my hope that the approach developed here can work with other theoretical approaches towards a richer understanding of the field itself and of the cultural work performed by theatrical productions.

The method I have been articulating and practicing emerges from a conflation of cultural materialism, theatre semiotics, and reception work in the field of cultural studies. As such, it is intended to extend and supplement those approaches. It brings a model of close reading to cultural materialism and theatre semiotics while extending into the world of theatre the cultural studies work of Stuart Hall and others on the reception of popular culture. It also extends Hall's analysis in a way that allows production, performance, and reception to be read, not as operating on a simple, unidirectional line of cause and effect, but as consistently shifting and mutually constitutive. While technologies of production inform performance texts and constitute audiences and their "reading positions," as in Hall, I argue that these technologies of production are themselves similarly constituted, as are performance texts, by the equally determinate technologies of audience reception.

At the same time, the method I have articulated moves semiotics into closer compatibility with phenomenology, on the one hand, and performance studies on the other. It does so by modeling a materialist "reading" practice that understands the performance text to be discursively constructed, but that also takes into account the immanence of the theatrical event *as* event, performance, or phenomenon that occurs and has consequences in the material world, where it is encountered by individual human subjects – or, as phenomenology would have it, human consciousnesses.

Perhaps most importantly, materialist semiotics also reinforces and resonates with a range of diachronic approaches to the study of theatre that are fundamentally concerned with social change. The selection of case studies in *Reading the Material Theatre* has focused synchronically on just over one manageable decade in the English-speaking world at the end of the second millennium. This focus enables analysis of specific productions and performances within their local contexts under controlled conditions. It also minimizes for the moment the impact on the analysis of a set of historical and cultural variables widely discussed in historicist and intercultural scholarship since the 1980s. This book focuses more closely than the broader reach of most new historicist or interculturalist scholarship on theatrical conditions working together at specific sites to produce specific meanings for specific audiences. By modeling some of the ways in which the technologies and relations of theatrical production and reception are specifically implicated in larger social and cultural relations at specific historical moments, I hope to contribute an essential strand of analysis to work that takes a longer historical and broader cultural view than I have taken here. Theatrical productions take place in history and, *as* cultural productions, are inextricably connected to the material, historical, and cultural contexts from which they emerge and to which they speak. Productions mean differently in different geographical, architectural, historical, and cultural contexts. They change meaning as the world in and through which they are produced and received changes. Similarly (and simultaneously), changes in theatrical formations, relations, delivery systems, and modes of reception are themselves both produced by, and productive of, changes in the social formation itself.

Even within the time frame that I have taken as my purview, demonstrable historical change has occurred. To cite a perhaps too obvious example, the same production performed before and after the attacks on the World Trade Center in New York and the

Pentagon in Washington, DC on 11 September 2001 could have radically different meanings. This was recognized in the cancellation of dozens of New York performances and productions that were, in the wake of those attacks, thought to be too sensitive, including such relatively unrelated shows as Robert Lepage's *Zulu Time*, because of its central airport metaphor. Tony Kushner's *Homebody/Kabul* has been the subject of extensive journalistic and critical debate precisely because of a timeliness unanticipated by its author. The play is explicitly concerned with the difficulties of cross-cultural understanding between the west and Afghanistan, part of the Arab world under attack for the purported harboring of terrorists. When the play opened at the New York Theatre Workshop in December, 2001, as written prior to 11 September, the US was at war with Afghanistan, and Kushner was advised to cut several lines "for fear that audiences would think he was taking advantage of the tragedy."[1]

Even in terms of the productions on which I have chosen to focus, it is difficult to imagine that a socialist theatre company such as the English Shakespeare Company, discussed in Chapter Six, with a mandate to take Shakespeare to the English provinces, could be founded, funded, and achieve far-reaching success in the current contexts of New Labour in Britain, the international "war on terror," and the ever-increasing reach of political, military, and economic globalization. The company came into being in the late 1980s as the result of the intersection of a specific set of material and historical circumstances, but those circumstances have changed dramatically, particularly in the United Kingdom, and the company has since folded. Less dramatically, the shifting meanings of the Tron Theatre's production of Sue Glover's *Bondagers*, discussed in Chapter Two in terms of the politics of location, could also be analyzed as issuing from shifts within the discourses of feminism and from an increasing anti-feminist backlash in the early to mid-1990s.

Elsewhere, particularly in countries such as Scotland and Canada living in the shadow of larger economic powers, national governments in recent years have increasingly disinvested in what had been highly successful culturally protectionist funding policies for the development of national artistic and cultural formations, and have turned their attention to the global cultural marketplace that is discussed in Chapter Seven. In this context, the focus of theatres that have implemented fundamentally counterhegemonic nationalist mandates at certain points in their histories, such as the Tron and Traverse Theatres in Scotland (discussed in Chapter Two), or the Tarragon in Toronto (discussed in Chapter Four), has shifted, as these companies increasingly insert themselves into contemporary internationalist political discourse. A company such as Canada's Stratford Festival, discussed in Chapter Three, which once called itself the Stratford National Theatre of Canada and which from its founding in 1953 to the nationalist 1970s concerned itself with performing Shakespeare with Canadian accents and finding peculiarly Canadian ways to interpret the classics, is in the new millennium featuring "mid-Atlantic" accents and a new universalism.[2]

What I hope this book has made available to scholarship, as part of a new materialist semiotics, is a mode of analysis in which careful consideration of the site-specific particularities of production and reception – training, tradition, geography, architecture, organizational structure, funding, marketing, and "the entire theatre experience" – can not only contribute to the fully contextualized performance analysis of particular productions at their moment of reception, but can also complicate, intersect with, and enrich historical and historicized analysis that takes a longer, diachronic view. The site-specific approach that has been articulated here is, moreover, uniquely suited to accommodate the specificities of the increasingly intercultural experience of producers and audiences operating within an increasingly diasporic world. Future theatre histories and performance analyses might take into account, not only the shifting "visions" of artistic directors, repertoires, theatrical movements, or styles, but also determinants of production and reception that are local, technical, intercultural, and, in the most literal of senses, material, addressing the day-to-day, lived realities of producing and attending specific theatrical productions at specific, historically located, and culturally shifting sites. They will, as all theatre histories and performance analyses must increasingly do, take into account the politics of meaning-making at the points both of production and reception.

Notes

INTRODUCTION

1. Michael Billington, *The Guardian* (London), 16 March 1998.
2. Benedict Nightingale, *The Times* (London), 16 March 1998.
3. Peter Charles, *Plays and Players*, June 1998, 7.
4. Harry Haun, "A Pipe Dream Realized," *Playbill* 99, no. 4 (April 1999), 12.
5. J. Cooper Robb, Theatre Reviews Limited, www.theatrereviews.com/pastreviews/icemancometh.htm, 19 April 2000.
6. Michael Feingold, *The Village Voice* online, www.villagevoice.com/arts/9915/feingold.shtml, 22 April 2000.
7. Haun, "A Pipe Dream Realized," 12.

1 THEORY: TOWARDS A MATERIALIST SEMIOTICS

1. Marvin Carlson, *Theatre Semiotics: Signs of Life* (Bloomington: Indiana University Press, 1990), xiii.
2. For histories and analyses of cultural materialism see John Brannigan, *New Historicism and Cultural Materialism* (New York: St. Martin's, 1998); Kiernan Ryan, ed., *New Historicism and Cultural Materialism: A Reader* (London: Arnold, 1996); and Scott Wilson, *Cultural Materialism: Theory and Practice* (Oxford: Blackwell, 1995).
3. See Antonio Gramsci, "The Theatre Industry [i]", "The Theatre Industry [ii]," and "The Theatre Industry [iii]," *Antonio Gramsci: Selections from Cultural Writings*, ed. David Forgacs and Geoffrey Nowell-Smith, trans. William Boelhower (Cambridge, Mass: Harvard University Press, 1985), 56–58, 58–61, and 63–65.
4. Ryan, *New Historicism*, viii.
5. For introductions, histories, applications, and analyses of the semiotics of drama and theatre see Elaine Aston and George Savona, *Theatre as Sign-System: A Semiotics of Text and Performance* (London: Routledge, 1991); Marvin Carlson, *Places of Performance: The Semiotics of Theatre Architecture* (Ithaca: Cornell University Press, 1989) and *Theatre Semiotics*; Keir Elam, *The Semiotics of Drama and Theatre*

(London: Methuen, 1980); Marco de Marinis, *The Semiotics of Performance*, trans. Áine O'Healy (Bloomington: Indiana University Press, 1993); Patrice Pavis *Languages of the Stage: Essays in the Semiology of the Theatre* (New York: Performing Arts Journal, 1982); and Ann Ubersfeld, *Reading Theatre*, ed. Paul Perron and Patrick Debbèche, trans. Frank Collins (Toronto: University of Toronto Press, 1999).

6. See Ien Ang, *Watching Dallas: Soap Opera and the Melodramatic Imagination* (London: Methuen, 1985), *Desperately Seeking the Audience* (London: Routledge, 1991), and *Livingroom Wars: Rethinking Media Audiences for a Postmodern World* (London: Routledge, 1996); Susan Bennett, *Theatre Audiences*, 2nd edn. (London: Routlege, 1997); John Fiske, *Power Plays, Power Works* (London: Verso, 1993); Stuart Hall, "Encoding/Decoding," in Simon During, ed., *The Cultural Studies Reader* (London: Routledge, 1993), 90–103, and "Cultural Studies: Two Paradigms," *Media, Culture and Society* 2 (1980), 57–72; David Morley, *The 'Nationwide' Audience: Structure and Decoding* (London: BFI, 1980), and *Television, Audiences, and Cultural Studies* (London: Routledge, 1992); Virginia Nightingale, *Studying Audiences: The Shock of the Real* (London: Routledge, 1996); and Janice Radway, *Reading the Romance: Women, Patriarchy and Popular Literature* (Chapel Hill: University of North Carolina Press, 1984), and "Reception Study: Ethnography and the Problems of Dispersed Audiences and Nomadic Subjects," *Cultural Studies* 2. no. 3 (1988), 358–76; and John Tulloch, *Performing Culture: Stories of Expertise and the Everyday* (London: Sage, 1999).

7. "Thick description" is a concept introduced by anthropologist Clifford Geertz, *The Interpretation of Cultures: Selected Essays* (New York: Basic Books, 1973), 10–30 and passim. I am drawing on Geertz's "semiotic concept of culture," which reads cultures as texts, conscious of the fact that theatre, like all cultural production and activity, although it phenomenologically transcends mere textuality, enters meaning, as such, only once it is translated into discourse. Thus my title, with apparent logocentrism, constructs the interpretation of theatre as "reading." As Louis Montrose argues in "New Historicisms," in Giles Gunn and Stephen Greenblatt, eds., *Redrawing the Boundaries of Literary Study* (New York: Modern Language Association, 1992), 399:

> Geertz's work offered to literary critics and cultural historians not so much a powerful *theory* of culture as an exemplary and eminently literary *method* for narrating culture in action, culture as lived in the performances and narratives of individual and collective human actors . . . "Thick description" might be more accurately described as "interpretative narration": it seizes upon an event, performance, or other practice and, through the interrogation of its minute particulars, seeks to reveal the collective ethos of an alien culture.

My adaptation of Geertz's approach is to treat the discourses of the contemporary theatre as Geertz does "an alien culture," as my adaptation of cultural materialism, below, involves historicizing, not the past, but the contemporary world.

8. See Jonathan Dollimore and Alan Sinfield, *Political Shakespeare: New Essays in Cultural Materialism* (Manchester: Manchester University Press, 1985). Subsequent references appear parenthetically in the text. See also the second, revised, and expanded edition, 1994).

9. Alan Sinfield, "Give an account of Shakespeare and education, showing why you think they are effective and what you have appreciated about them. Support your comments with precise references," in Dollimore and Sinfield, *Political Shakespeare*, 141.

10. Wilson, *Cultural Materialism*, ix; Dollimore and Sinfield, *Political Shakespeare*, vii; my emphases.

11. Brannigan, *New Historicism*, 9, 10.

12. Wilson, *Cultural Materialism*, 19.

13. Tony Bennett, "Texts in History: The Determinations of Readings and Their Texts," in *Post-Structuralism and the Question of History*, ed. Derek Attridge, Geoffrey Bennington, and Robert Young (Cambridge: Cambridge University Press, 1987), 72, quoted in Bruce McConachie, "Reading Context Into Performance: Theatrical Formations and Social History," *Journal of Dramatic Theory and Criticism* 3, no. 2 (1989), 231.

14. Ian Watson, "'Reading' the Actor: Performance, Presence, and the Synesthetic," *New Theatre Quarterly* 11, no. 42 (1995), 135.

15. Elam, *Semiotics of Drama and Theatre*, 1.

16. Aston and Savona, *Theatre as Sign-System*, 6.

17. Ibid., Elam, *Semiotics of Drama and Theatre*, 21–27.

18. Roland Barthes, "Literature and Signification," *Critical Essays*, trans. R. Howard (Evanston: Northwestern University Press), 261–79; Watson, "'Reading' the Actor," 136.

19. De Marinis, *Semiotics of Performance*, 48, emphasis in original.

20. See Kier Elam, "The Wars of the Texts," *Shakespeare Studies* 24 (1996), 90.

21. See Mark Fortier, *Theory/Theatre: An Introduction* (London: Routledge, 1997), 27.

22. Carlson, *Theatre Semiotics*, viii.

23. Nightingale, *Studying Audiences*, x, and see 126–44.

24. For practical and financial reasons I have been unable, unfortunately, to take into account productions in Australia and New Zealand, including those that I do discuss by Robert Lepage, whose work is an exception in several senses: the work is multilingual and in any case oddly positioned within "English-language theatre" (though most of his productions now open in Toronto). It does,

however, extend the range of my explorations here, and problematize them, as the best example of the "globalization" of theatrical production. It is for this reason, too, that I include discussion of productions in Montreal, Japan, and Madrid. Although I did not see the performances in Australia, New Zealand, Spain, or Japan, I did consult reviews of them extensively, and did see each of the shows in at least three national locations. The failure to consider Australian and New Zealand theatrical cultures, however, can only be redressed on another occasion.

2 PRACTICE: CONDITIONS OF PRODUCTION AND RECEPTION

1. I am adapting the idea of the "political unconscious" from Marxist critic and cultural theorist Frederic Jameson's *The Political Unconscious: Narrative and a Social Symbolic Act* (Ithaca: Cornell University Press, 1981).
2. Hugh Morrison, *Directing in the Theatre*, 2nd edn. (London: Black, 1989), 15; Louis E. Catron, *The Director's Vision: Play Direction from Analysis to Production* (Mountain View, CA: Mayfield, 1989), 25, 27–29, and passim. Subsequent references to Morrison and Catron will appear parenthetically in the text.
3. Maurice Good, *Every Inch a King: A Rehearsal Journal of "King Lear" with Peter Ustinov and the Stratford Festival Company Directed by Robin Phillips* (Victoria: Sono Nis, 1982), 3–4.
4. See Peter Brook, *The Empty Space* (Harmondsworth: Penguin, 1976).
5. See Herbert Marcuse, "The Affirmative Character of Culture," in Marcuse, *Negations: Essays in Critical Theory*, trans. J. Shapiro (Boston: Beacon, 1968), 88–133.
6. J. Michael Gillette, *Theatrical Design and Production*, 3rd edn., (Mountain View, CA: Mayfield, 1997), 6–16.
7. W. Oren Parker and R. Craig Wolf, *Scene Design and Stage Lighting*, 6th edn. (Fort Worth: Holt, Rinehart, and Winston, 1990), 15.
8. Rebecca Cunningham, *The Magic Garment: Principles of Costume Design* (New York: Longman, 1989), 3–12.
9. "*To-be-looked-at-ness*" is a coinage of feminist film theorist Laura Mulvey, "Visual Pleasure and Narrative Cinema," in *Visual and Other Pleasures* (Bloomington: Indiana University Press, 1989), 19, where she uses it to describe the construction of the female actor in classic Hollywood narrative films.
10. See, for example, Francis Reid, *The ABC of Stage Lighting* (London: A. & C. Black, 1992), a glossary of technical terminology in use in the United Kingdom; and Robert C. Mumm, *Photometrics Handbook* (Shelter Island, NY: Broadway, 1992), which provides

technical specifications for theatrical lighting instruments available in the United States.

11. A perhaps extreme, but otherwise representative English example of this tendency is Scott Palmer's *Essential Guide to Stage Management, Lighting, and Sound* (Oxonford: Hodder & Stoughton, 2000), but see also Francis Reid, *The Stage Lighting Handbook*, 4th edn. (London: A. & C. Black, 1992), Gillette, *Theatrical Design*, and Mumm, *Photometrics Handbook*.

12. See Christopher J. McCullough, "The Cambridge Connection: Towards a Materialist Theatrical Practice," in Graham Holderness, ed., *The Shakespeare Myth* (Manchester: Manchester University Press, 1988),112–21; Ellen J. O'Brien, "Mapping the Role: A Means to Performable Feminist Critiques," paper presented to the Feminist Theatrical Practice seminar at the Shakespeare Association of America conference, Philadelphia, 12 August 1990; and Elin Diamond, "Brechtian Theory/Feminist Theory: Towards a Gestic Feminist Criticism," in Diamond, *Unmaking Mimesis: Essays on Feminism and Theater* (London: Routledge, 1997), 43–55.

13. Sonia Moore, *The Stanislavski System: The Professional Training of an Actor*, new rev. edn. (Harmondsworth: Penguin, 1976). Subsequent references will appear parenthetically in the text.

14. The use of "perspective" here draws attention to the mutually reinforcing relationships within the naturalistic theatre between (naturalized) characterological/psychological understandings of depth and perspective and those of depth perspective on the proscenium stage, all of which reinforce Newtonian notions of the neutral and scientific "objectivity" of the spectator as observer.

15. Notice the significant slippage here from "character" to "person," a slippage that is at the heart of the naturalistic/method acting understanding of mimesis, which conflates dramatic and "human" understandings of "character," and thereby willfully "forgets" "character" as a dramatic device. *Do* dramatic characters "have" character?

16. Susan Swan, "Taking Hype to Hollywood," *Toronto Life* (Sept. 1984), 64, 67.

17. For accounts and analyses of these methods, see Alison Hodge, ed., *Twentieth Century Actor Training* (London: Routledge, 2000); and Phillip B. Zarrilli, ed., *Acting (Re)Considered: Theories and Practices* (London: Routledge, 1995).

18. Brook's most direct and documented connection is with Artaud's "Theatre of Cruelty," by way of Brook's 1964 five-week "Theatre of Cruelty" Royal Shakespeare Company season in collaboration with Charles Marowitz at the London Academy of Musical and Dramatic Arts, but his explorations throughout his career since have run parallel to those of experimental theatre pioneers Jerzy Grotowski and Eugenio Barba.

19. The voice work of Berry, Linklater, Rodenberg, and their disciples was first developed by Berry in her collaboration with Brook on his 1970 *A Midsummer Night's Dream* and formulated in her 1973 book, *Voice and the Actor* (London: Harrap), for which Brook wrote an introduction. For an analysis of the six most widely influential voice texts, two by each of Berry, Linklater, and Rodenberg (Kristin Linklater, *Freeing the Natural Voice* [New York: Drama Book Publishers, 1976] and *Freeing Shakespeare's Voice: The Actor's Guide to Talking the Text* [New York: Theatre Communications Group, 1992]; Cicely Berry, *Voice and the Actor* and *The Actor and His Text* [London: Virgin, 1987]; and Patsy Rodenberg, *The Right to Speak: Working with the Voice* [London: Methuen, 1992], and *The Need for Words: Voice and the Text* [London: Methuen, 1993]), see Richard Paul Knowles, "Shakespeare, Voice, and Ideology: Interrogating the Natural Voice," in James Bulman, ed., *Shakespeare, Theory, and Performance* (London: Routledge, 1996), 92–112.

20. See Paul Connerton, *How Societies Remember* (Cambridge: Cambridge University Press, 1989).

21. Richard Paul Knowles, "Voices Off: Deconstructing the Modern English-Canadian Dramatic Canon," in Robert Lecker, ed., *Canadian Canons: Essays in Literary Value* (Toronto: University of Toronto Press, 1991), 103–04.

22. Margaret Hollingsworth, interviewed by Judith Rudakoff, in Rudakoff and Rita Much, *Fair Play: 12 Women Speak: Conversations with Canadian Playwrights* (Toronto: Simon & Pierre), 157–58.

23. Walter Benjamin, *The Origin of German Tragic Drama*, trans. John Osborne (London: NLB, 1977), 175–218.

24. Information on the director and actors is derived from the published script that served as program for the production: Zinnie Harris, *Further than the Furthest Thing* (London: Faber and Faber, 2000).

25. Joyce MacMillan, "The Spirit of Islands," *The Scotsman*, 9 August 2000. See Harris, *Further than the Furthest Thing*.

26. See Simon Reade, *Cheek by Jowl: Ten Years of Celebration* (Bath: Absolute Classics, 1991), 16.

27. Declan Donnellan, interviewed in Gabriella Giannachi and Mary Luckhurst, eds., *On Directing: Interviews with Directors* (London: Faber and Faber, 1999), 21.

28. See especially Katie Laris's review of the 1994 remount of the production in *Theatre Journal* 47 (1995), 300–02; and Alisa Solomon, "Much Virtue in If: Shakespeare's Cross-dressed Boy-actresses and the Non-illusory Stage," in Solomon, *Redressing the Canon: Essays on Theater and Gender* (London: Routledge, 1997), 21–45.

29. Judith Greenwood, *Cheek by Jowl*, ed. Susanna Harding, co-ord. Mark Slaughter (London: Cheek by Jowl, 1998), W1. (The pack is paginated by individual section. I use "W" to indicate the section

"Working with Shakespeare," "S" to indicate "The Cheek by Jowl Story," and "I" to indicate the interviews section. Subsequent references will appear parenthetically in the text. For more information on the company and its first decade of productions see Reade, *Cheek by Jowl.*)

30. Declan Donnellan, quoted in Simon Reade, "Fringe," *Plays International* 4, no. 4 (1988), 6.

31. See Donnellan, interviewed in Giannachi and Luckhurst, *On Directing*, 22.

32. Introduction to "Declan Donnellan and Nick Ormerod," 81, and "Declan Donnellan and Nick Ormerod in Conversation with Paul Heritage at the Coliseum, London, 30 May 1995," in Maria Delgado and Paul Heritage, eds., *In Contact with the Gods? Directors Talk Theatre* (Manchester: Manchester University Press, 1996), 84.

33. Gwyn Morgan, "The Britches Parts," *Plays and Players* (Feb. 1992), 16; Ian Christensen, "As They Liked It," *Plays International* 7, no. 5 (1991), 7; Jonathan Bate and Russell Jackson, *Shakespeare: An Illustrated Stage History* (Oxford: Oxford University Press, 1996), 7; and Carol Chillington Rutter, *Enter the Body: Women and Representation on Shakespeare's Stage* (London: Routledge, 2001), xiv. Rutter is citing Anthony Dawson, "Performance and Participation: Desdemona, Foucault, and the Actor's Body," in James C. Bulman, ed. *Shakespeare, Theory, and Performance* (London: Routledge, 1996), 40; and Peter Holland, *English Shakespeares: Shakespeare on the English Stage in the 1990s* (Cambridge: Cambridge University Press, 1997), 91.

34. Lyn Gardner, "Fringe," *Plays International* 5, no. 6 (1990), 6.

35. Robert Lepage, quoted in Alison McAlpine, "Robert Lepage in Conversation with Alison McAlpine, at Le Café du Monde, Québec City, 17 February 1995," in Delgado and Heritage, *In Contact with the Gods?*, 154.

36. See Rémy Charest, *Robert Lepage: Connecting Flights*, trans. Wanda Romer Taylor (London: Methuen, 1997), 66.

37. Lepage in McAlpine, "Robert Lepage in Conversation," 139, 135.

38. Jacques Lessard, "Les Cycles Repère," *L'Annuare théâtral* 8 (Fall 1990), 133. My account of the Repère cycles is indebted to this article, as well as to Hélène Beauchamp, "The Repère Cycles from Basic to Continuous Education," *Canadian Theatre Review* 78 (Spring 1994), 26–31, and James Bunzli, "The Geography of Creation: Déclage as Impluse, Process, and Outcome in the Theatre of Robert Lepage," *The Drama Review* 43, no. 1 (Spring 1999), 88–89. Subsequent references to Bunzli will appear parenthetically in the text.

39. See Barbara Hodgdon, "Looking for Mr. Shakespeare After 'the Revolution': Robert Lepages Intercultural *Dream* Machine," in

Bulman, 68–91. For an extended discussion of Lepage's continuities with the modernist tradition see Richard Paul Knowles, "From Dream to Machine: Peter Brook, Robert Lepage, and the Contemporary Shakespearean Director as (Post)Modernist," *Theatre Journal* 50 (1998), 189–206.

40. Kate Valk, quoted in Ben Dowell, "Giving Classics a Soapy Feel," *The Stage* (London), 8 June 2000. The Wooster Group has since developed *Phaedre* into a theatrical production, the first working version of which opened at the Performing Garage in June 2001 as *To You, The Birdie! (Phèdre)*, and has since toured internationally.

41. Roy Faudree, quoted in Eddie Harrison, "House/Lights," *Metro Life* (Glasgow), 6 June 2000.

42. Joyce MacMillan, "Tonight's Highlights: House/Lights," *The Scotsman* (Edinburgh), 7 June 2000.

43. Philip Auslander, "Task and Vision: Willem Dafoe in LSD," in Zarrilli, 307 reprinted from the *Drama Review* 29, no. 2 [1985]: 94–98.

44. "House/Lights," "Rencontres avec les artistes" at Le Festival du Théâtre des Amériques, Montreal, 28 May 1999.

45. Neil Cooper, "Scottish Theatre," *The Times* (London), 16 June 2000.

46. Faudree, in Harrison, "Tonight's Highlights."

47. Deborah Cottreau, "Homage to a Master," *Canadian Theatre Review* 105 (Winter 2001), 38.

48. Lecoq-trained performer and teacher Jim Calder at the Tish School of the Arts, New York University, quoted in Sara Brady, "Looking for Lecoq: A Master's Legacy Lives On," *American Theatre*, July 2000, 33.

49. Sears A. Eldredge and Hollis W. Huston, "Actor Training in the Neutral Mask," in Zarrilli, *Acting (Re)considered*, 128. Eldredge and Huston provide no source for their quotation of Frisch.

50. Rush Rehm, "Lives of Resistance: Theatre de Complicite, An Appreciation," *Theatre Forum* 6 (Winter/Spring 1995), 88.

51. Ibid., 92.

52. Lyn Gardner, "The Face of the Future," *The Guardian*, 19 November 1997, 12.

53. Rehm, *Lives of Resistance*, 92.

54. Ibid.

55. Simon McBurney, quoted in Vit Wagner, "Earthy Sage of Past and Peasant," *The Toronto Star*, 12 September 1998. G3.

56. Benedict Nightingale, review of *The Three Lives of Lucy Cabrol*, *The Times* (London), 25 January 1995.

57. Rehm, *Lives of Resistance*, 91.

58. Matt Wolf, "Death Becalms Her," *American Theatre* (May/June 1996), 28.

59. Mark McKenna, Lecoq-trained artistic director of Pennsylvania's Touchstone Theatre, quoted in Brady, "Looking for Lecoq," 33.

60. McBurney, quoted in Wagner, "Earthly Sage."

61. Irving Wardle, review of *Street of Crocodiles, The Independent* (London), 16 August 1992.

62. Tom Morris, review of *Street of Crocodiles, Time Out* (London), 17 August 1994.

63. John Peter, review of *Street of Crocodiles, The Sunday Times* (London), 16 August 1992.

64. Ben Brantley, "A Haunting Vision Untainted by Order or Logic," *The New York Times*, 18 July 1998.

65. See Nicolas de Jongh, review of *Street of Crocodiles, Evening Standard* (London), 14 August 1992.

66. Rehm, *Lives of Resistance*, 95.

67. See Michael Billington, "The Three Lives of John Berger," *The Guardian*, 1 February 1995.

68. Billington, and John Berger quoted in ibid.

69. John Berger, historical afterword to *Pig Earth*, quoted in *The Three Lives of Lucy Cabrol*, Theatre de Complicite, Dancehouse Theatre, Manchester, 1994, program.

70. John Berger and Jean Mohr, *Another Way of Telling* (New York: Pantheon, 1989), 100.

71. Gardner, "The Face of the Future."

72. Michael Ratcliffe, "Collusion between Celebrants, *The Three Lives of Lucy Cabrol* program.

73. Simon McBurney quoted in Matt Wolfe, "Complicite Spreads Far and Fast," *The Globe and Mail* (Toronto), 12 September 1996: C5.

74. Wolfe, "Complicite Spreads." 28.

75. Rehm, *Lives of Resistance*, 90.

76. Ibid., 92–93.

77. Larson died of an aortic aneurysm after leaving the final dress rehearsal for the East Village first production on 25 January 1996 at age thirty-five, and publicity for the show has made (perhaps too) much of this. All quotations from *Rent* publicity and reviews are from the official Broadway website at <http://www.siteforrent.com>.

78. Jeffrey Seller, quoted in *Newsweek*, "Rent Strikes," 13 May 1996.

79. Bernard Dolland, "Flaws Aside, Rent Lives and Breathes," *New York Times*, 17 March 1996.

80. See Ann Wilson's critique of the normalizing effect of peer review in "A Jury of Her Peers," *Canadian Theatre Review* 51 (Summer 1987), 4–8.

81. Alan Read, *Theatre and Everyday Life: An Ethics of Performance* (London: Routledge, 1993), 234.

82. Bert Gruver, *The Stage Manager's Handbook* (New York: The Drama Book Shop, 1952). Gruver's book is now somewhat out of date,

more recent texts tending to give up before the proliferation of
unions and including only short sections on "Getting to Know
the Unions," with sample situations (see what is currently the
most widely used stage management text, Lawrence Stern's *Stage
Management: A Guidebok of Practical Techniques*, 3rd edn. (Boston:
Allyn and Bacon, 1987), 220–24.

83. The complexities of the stage manager's job increase in a repertory
system, in which more than one show is in rehearsal and production
at one time – often at more than one theatre. In this event a Production Stage Manager is usually appointed, usually from among
the stage managers working on individual productions, to oversee
scheduling. The complications and implications of a repertory system are immense, and are explored in more detail in Chapter Three.

84. Scott Duchesne and Jennifer Fletcher, "*Sled*: A Workshop Diary,"
Canadian Theatre Review 89 (Winter 1996), 35.

85. In an informal talk to students at Toronto's Glendon College,
12 April 2001.

86. Ann Ubersfeld, *Reading Theatre*, ed. Paul Perron and Patrick
Debbèche, trans. Frank Collins (Toronto: University of Toronto
Press, 1999), 96.

87. Marvin Carlson provides a brief survey of the mutually reinforc-
ing "symbolic" relationship between perspective and social order in
Places of Performance: The Semiotics of Theatre Architecture (Ithaca:
Cornell University Press, 1989), 135–40.

88. Although the scientific method achieved widespread prominence
and practice in the Enlightenment and was most fully articulated
in late nineteenth-century empiricism, it was arguably first posited
and theorized by writers such as Francis Bacon in the Renaissance.

89. Gwen Orel, "The Proscenium Arch: A Room of His Own," paper
delivered to the American Society for Theatre Research, Pasadena,
California, November 1996.

90. See my essay, "Shakespeare at Stratford: The Legacy of the Festival
Stage," *Canadian Theatre Review* 75 (Spring 1988), 29–33.

91. I am directly indebted here to Michael McKinnie, "Urban National,
Suburban Transnational: Civic Theatres and the Urban Development of Toronto's Downtowns," *Theatre Journal* 53 (2001), 258,
and to Carlson, *Places of Performance*, 14–37, whom McKinnie cites.

92. Carlson, *Places of Performance*, 2.

93. Iain Mackintosh, *Architecture, Actor, and Audience*. London:
Routledge, 1993.

94. Gay McAuley, *Space in Performance: Making Meaning in the Theatre*
(Ann Arbor: University of Michigan Press, 2000), 9.

95. McAuley, *Space in Performance*, 71, quoting Henri Lefebvre,
The Production of Space, trans. Donald Nicholson-Smith (Oxford:
Blackwell, 1991), 26.

96. McAuley *Space in Performance*, 74.

97. Ibid., 73.

98. Baz Kershaw, *The Politics of Performance: Radical Theatre as Cultural Intervention* (London: Routledge, 1992), 24, 257. See also Marvin Carlson, *Theatre Semiotics: Signs of Life* (Bloomington: Indiana University Press, 1990), 44; and Susan Bennett, *Theatre Audiences: A Theory of Production and Reception*, 2nd edn. (London: Routledge, 1997), 125–39, 163–65.

99. See Carlson, *Places of Performance*, 92–97 and passim.

100. Kier Elam, *The Semiotics of Drama and Theatre* (London: Methuen, 1980), 63.

101. Bennett, *Theatre Audiences*, 129.

102. McAuley, *Space in Performance*, 62.

103. Steve Gooch, *All Together Now: An Alternative View of Theatre and Community* (London: Methuen, 1984), 16, cited in Bennett, *Theatre Audiences*, 130.

104. McAuley, *Space in Performance*, 63.

105. Ibid., 62.

106. Ray Conlogue, "Measure for Measure Astonishing," *Globe and Mail* (Toronto), 31 May 1985.

107. For an excellent discussion of curtain calls and other elements of audience participation see Baz Kershaw, "Oh for Unruly Audiences! Patterns of Participation in Twentieth-Century Theatre," *Modern Drama* 44, no. 2 (2001), 133–54.

108. Carlson, *Places of Performance*, 142.

109. Catherine Locherbie, "Working Bonds at a Premium," review of *Bondagers, The Scotsman*, 6 May 1991.

110. Michael Tumelty, "Earthly Sound of Toil, Soil, and Trouble," review of *Bondagers, The Glasgow Herald*, 8 May 1991.

111. Joyce McMillan, review of *Bondagers, The Guardian*, 7 May 1991.

112. Terry Brotherstone, "Triumph of the Oppressed," review of *Bondagers, Workers Press*, 18 May 1991, 7.

113. Julie Morrice, "Bonds with the earth," review of *Bondagers, Scotland on Sunday*, 5 May 1991.

114. McMillan, *The Guardian*, 7 May 1991.

115. Alasdair Cameron, "In Touch with the Local Tongues of Yore," review of *Bondagers, The Times* (London), 14 May 1991.

116. Mark Fisher, "Field Day," review of *Bondagers, The List* (Glasgow and Edinburgh), 17–30 May 1991.

117. Peter Whitebrook, review of *Bondagers, The Scotsman*, 14 August 1995.

118. Carlson, *Theatre Semiotics*, 47–53; *Places of Performance*, 10–12 and *passim*, especially 14–127. Carlson is drawing upon Kenneth Lynch's book, *The Image of the City* (Cambridge: Harvard University Press, 1960) and on Roland Barthes, *Eiffel Tower, and other Mythologies*, trans. Richard Howard (New York: Hill and Wang, 1979), 9–13.

119. McAuley, *Space in Performance*, 248.
120. See, for the last three, the excellent May 2001 volume of *Theatre Journal*, devoted to "Theatre and the City."
121. Bennett, *Theatre Audiences*, 126.
122. Ibid., 125–26.
123. Cordelia Oliver, "25 Years of the Traverse," *Plays International* 3, no. 7 (Feb. 1988), 28.
124. Scottish actor Duncan Moore, quoted in Joyce McMillan, *The Traverse Theatre Story* (London: Methuen, 1988), 50.
125. McMillan, *Traverse*, 9.
126. Sarah Hemming, "25 Years On," *Plays and Players* 413 (Feb. 1988), 8, 9.
127. Oliver, "25 Years of the Traverse," 29.
128. Ibid., 28.
129. Michael Rudman, quoted in Vera Lustig, "Brown Rice and High Ambition: Twenty-Five Years at the Traverse," *New Theatre Quarterly* 4, no. 6 (Nov. 1988), 380–81.
130. McMillan, *Traverse*, 57.
131. Ibid., 57.
132. Ibid., 62.
133. Ibid., 63.
134. Jenny Killick, in Hemming, "25 Years On," 9. The Traverse in fact first accepted Arts Council funding as early as 1964, but it amounted then to a total of only £350. By the time the theatre moved to the Grassmarket location this had increased to £12,000. (These figures are from Lustig, *Brown Rice and High Ambition*, 373–74.)
135. Killick, in Hemming, "25 Years On." 10.
136. The positioning of the Traverse among the major "mainstream" theatres in Edinburgh is indicated by the publicity statement at the opening of the newly renovated Edinburgh Festival Theatre in 1998: "The Theatre aims to complement the work of Edinburgh's receiving theatres (the 1,300 seat King's Theatre, Edinburgh City Council managed, and 3,000 seat Playhouse, Apollo managed), producing theatres (principally Royal Lyceum Theatre, Traverse Theatre and Brunton Theatre, Musselburgh), and concert halls (Usher Hall and Queen's Hall)." <http://www.eft.co.uk/about/index.html>, consulted 27 May 1998.
137. Quoted by Steve Cramer in *The List* (Glasgow and Edinburgh), 12–19 August 1999.
138. Cramer, *The List*.
139. Gabe Stewart, *The List* (Glasgow and Edinburgh), 19–26 August 1999.
140. Thom Diblin, *Edinburgh Evening News*, 26 August 1999.
141. Neil Cooper, *Sunday Herald*, 22 August 1999.

142. Sophie Constanti, review of *The Trick is to Keep Breathing*, *The Financial Times* (London), 13 June 1996.

143. Kate Taylor, "Harrowing Story is Great Theatre," *The Globe and Mail* (Toronto), 26 April 1996.

144. Constanti review, *Financial Times*.

145. Ian Brown, quoted in Kevin Prokosh, "Sonsies howking taties [sic] at PTE," *Winnipeg Free Press*, 27 January 1994.

146. Reg Skene, review of *The Bondagers*, CBC (Canadian Broadcasting Corporation) Information Radio, 28 January 1994.

147. Kevin Prokosh, "Hard Lives Translate to Gripping Drama," review of *Bondagers*, *Winnipeg Free Press*, 29 January 1994.

148. Andrea Geary, "Play depicts lives of Scots laborers," *The Manitoba Co-operator*, 3 February 1994.

149. Prokosh, "Hard Lives;" Skene, review, CBC.

150. All COC advertising is quoted from copies provided by the company's publicist, Susan Harrington. I am deeply indebted throughout this section to Harrington, Jeremy Elbourne, the company's marketing director, and Richard Bradshaw (the company's artistic director since 1994 and General Director since 1998).

151. Robert Everett-Green, *The Globe and Mail* (Toronto), 21 September 1996.

152. Everett-Green, *Globe and Mail*; Gary Michael Dault, "Cut! Cut!" *The Financial Post Magazine*, November 1996, 146, 148.

153. Urjo Kareda, *The Globe and Mail*, 30 September 1996.

154. Carole Corbeil, *The Toronto Star*, 5 October 1996.

155. Corbeil, *Toronto Star*.

156. Richard Bradshaw, interview with the author, 1 May 1998.

157. Jeremy Elbourne, interview with the author, 1 May 1998.

158. William Littler, "Spirit, Magic, Wonderfully Alive in Vixen," *The Toronto Star*, 29 January 1998.

159. Alan Horgan, "Sophisticated tragicomedy a triumph," *The Globe and Mail*, 29 January 1998.

160. Jon Kaplan, "Spectacular Stravinsky," *Now* (Toronto), 2–8 October 1997.

3 THE STRATFORD FESTIVAL

1. Eric Bentley, "Stark Young," in Stark Young, *The Theatre* (New York: Limelight, 1986), 138.

2. "Textbook orientalism" refers to Edward Said's classic study, *Orientalism* (New York: Random House/Vintage, 1979) concerning the scholarly construction of the idea of "the Orient" as mysterious, exotic, feminine, unchanging, and ultimately inferior to "the Occident."

3. Lorne Kennedy, interview, *The Beacon Herald*, Stratford Festival Edition (Stratford, Ontario, 1993).

4. Elliott Hayes, Stratford Festival 1993 season brochure.

5. Ibid.

6. David William, "Welcome to the 1993 Season," in ibid.

7. Stratford Festival 1993 Souvenir Program.

8. "The Stratford Story," Stratford Festival Publication, 1993.

9. See Richard Paul Knowles, "Shakespeare, Voice, and Ideology: Interrogating the Natural Voice," *Shakespeare, Theory, Performance*, ed. James C. Bulman (London: Routledge, 1996), 92–112.

10. "To-be-looked-at-ness" is a coinage of feminist film theorist Laura Mulvey, in her seminal 1975 article, "Visual Pleasure and Narrative Cinema," reprinted in *Visual and Other Pleasures* (Bloomington: Indiana University Press, 1989), 14–26.

11. See J. L. Styan, *The Shakespeare Revolution: Criticism and Performance in the Twentieth Century* (Cambridge: Cambridge University Press, 1977).

12. *Antony and Cleopatra*, program for the 1993 Stratford Festival, Ontario production.

13. Richard Monette, interview, *The Beacon Herald*, Stratford Festival Edition, 1993.

14. "*Antony and Cleopatra*," *The Beacon Herald*, Stratford Festival Edition, 1993.

15. Ibid.

16. For a discussion of representations and casting of Cleopatra's attendants as women of color, but rarely, in spite of historical evidence and critical argument, Cleopatra herself, see Carol Chillington Rutter, "Shadowing Cleopatra: Making Whiteness Strange," in *Enter the Body: Women and Representation on Shakespeare's Stage* (London: Routledge, 2001), 57–103.

17. "*Antony and Cleopatra*," *The Beacon Herald*, Stratford Festival Edition, 1993.

18. "*A Midsummer Night's Dream*," *The Beacon Herald*, Stratford Festival Edition, 1993.

19. Ibid.

20. Ibid.

21. Alan Sinfield, "Royal Shakespeare: Theatre and the Making of Ideology," *Political Shakespeare: New Essays in Cultural Materialism* (Ithaca: Cornell University Press, 1985), 176.

22. "Ideological State Apparatuses" is a term used by the Algerian philosopher Louis Althusser to refer, in contradistinction to "Repressive State Apparatuses" (the army, the police, the prisons system, and so on) to institutions such as the church, the school system, the family, the political system, the media through which dominant ideology is disseminated and reproduced. See "Ideology and Ideological State Apparatuses (Notes Towards an Investigation)," in *Lenin and Philosophy and other essays*, trans. Ben Brewster (New York: Monthly Review, 1971), 127–86.

4 TARRAGON THEATRE

1. I am deeply indebted throughout this chapter to my former graduate student Jennifer Fletcher. Although she played no direct part in the writing, I have drawn directly on her research on Tarragon Theatre, on her interview with its general manager, Mallory Gilbert, on her unpublished essay on *The Retreat* written for a graduate course that I taught at the University of Guelph in fall 1996, and on her paper, "Show, Don't Tell: Judith Thompson's *Sled* and The Tarragon Theatre's Public Workshop Program," co–authored with Scott Duchesne as part of an Independent Study graduate course at Guelph in the spring of 1996.

2. See Mark Czarnecki, "The Regional Theatre System," in Anton Wagner, ed., *Contemporary Canadian Theatre: New World Visions* (Toronto: Simon and Pierre, 1985).

3. See Denis Johnston, *Up the Mainstream: The Rise of Toronto's Alternative Theatres* (Toronto: University of Toronto Press, 1991).

4. I am quoting this from the "Tarragon 96 97," its season brochure, which in is in turn quoting from what it cites as the "CBC, November, 1995." The phrase suggests that Tarragon aspires more to be *avant-garde* than alternative; that is, it presents itself as doing work that is in advance of, and poised to take its place within, an evolving canon rather than work that is consciously oppositional.

5. See Johnston, *Up the Mainstream*, passim.

6. See Barbara Ehrenreich and John Ehrenreich, "The Professional-Managerial Class," *Between Labour and Capital*, ed. Pat Walker (Montreal: Black Rose, 1979), 5–45.

7. Mallory Gilbert. Interview with Jennifer Fletcher (unpublished), 8 March 1996; "Tarragon Subscriber Households/Tarragon Single Ticket Buyers by Address," 30 January 1995, Tarragon Theatre files.

8. Johnston, *Up the Mainstream*, 147.

9. The capacity can vary according to the audience–stage configuration. The capacity listed in "Coming on Strong: Tarragon Facts and Figures," a brochure used for fundraising purposes housed in the Tarragon Theatre files, is 205, while 100 is the capacity listed for the Extra Space. The capacity for the March–April 1997 production of *The Glass Menagerie* was 218.

10. Jennifer Fletcher, "*The Retreat*: A Quest for Peace, Balance, and Stability Within the Context of the Tarragon Theatre." Unpublished essay, University of Guelph, April 1996.

11. Urjo Kareda, "Director Needs Time to Restore His Creative Energy," *Toronto Star*, 15 March 1975 (Tarragon Theatre Archives, McLaughlin Library, University of Guelph).

12. In significant contrast to Tarragon's policies, Factory Theatre has consciously differentiated between lower ticket prices for weekday performances, when audiences tend to arrive at the theatre by

public transit from addresses in city neighborhoods with significant working-class, "ethnic," student, or artist populations, and higher prices for suburban and better-off weekend audiences that tend to come by car from the suburbs and are able to pay higher prices. According to George F. Walker (in conversation), who was for a time artistic director at Factory and who has premiered most of his work there, this decision was a conscious political choice, and it has resulted in the constitution of two distinct interpretative communities for the theatre's shows. But Tarragon, like Factory and other theatres in the city, does have a pay-what-you-can matinée performance on Sundays (a certain minimum is expected).

13. Johnston, *Up the Mainstream*, 146, 149.
14. Urjo Kareda, "Tarragon's Short History Buoyant With Success," *The Toronto Star*, 15 March 1975 (Tarragon Theatre Archives, McLaughlin Library, University of Guelph).
15. DuBary Campau, "Home for Irish, Canadian Drama." *The Toronto Telegram*, 17 September 1971 (Tarragon Theatre Archives, McLaughlin Library, University of Guelph).
16. Johnston, *Up the Mainstream*, 149.
17. Ibid., 144.
18. Ibid., 144, 148.
19. The third, Richard Rose, appointed to take over the theatre for the 2003–04 season, also has a record of serving a long term as artistic director of Toronto's Necessary Angel Theatre, in this case twenty years. Like Tarragon, Necessary Angel specializes in new play development and in fundamentally literary plays.
20. Urjo Kareda, "Director Needs Time."
21. Johnston, *Up the Mainstream*, 153.
22. Urjo Kareda, quoted in Vit Wagner, "Gilbert Makes a Little Tarragon go a Long Way." *Toronto Star*, 9 April 1995.
23. Ibid.
24. Robert Nunn, "Tarragon Theatre," in *The Oxford Companion to Canadian Theatre*, ed. Eugene Benson and L. W. Conolly (Toronto: Oxford University Press, 1989), 518.
25. Urjo Kareda, introduction to David French, *Leaving Home* (Toronto: New Press, 1972), viii, ix.
26. Tarragon Theatre, "Tarragon Theatre 96 97," season brochure.
27. This applies directly to *The Retreat* as well as to *The Glass Menagerie*: Joe Zeigler, playing the central role, is, like Henry and Leblanc, a graduate of NTS and a rightly respected actor in the naturalist tradition.
28. Denis Salter, "Body Politics: English-Canadian Acting at NTS," *Canadian Theatre Review* 71 (Summer 1992), 4–14.
29. Bill Glassco, "Why Tarragon?" (Tarragon Theatre Archives, McLaughlin Library, University of Guelph, [2]).

30. Tennessee Williams, *The Glass Menagerie* (New York: New Directions, 1966), 5. All parenthetical references to the play are to this edition.

31. Kate Taylor, "Popular Play Needs Balancing Act," *The Globe and Mail* (Toronto), 26 March 1997.

32. Scott Duchesne and Jennifer Fletcher, "Show, Don't Tell: Judith Thompson's *Sled* and the Tarragon Theatre's Public Workshop Program," paper presented to the Association for Canadian Theatre Research, Brock University, May 1996, 5–6. "Complete freedom" is Mallory Gilbert's phrase, in her interview with Jennifer Fletcher. See also Kathleen Flaherty's account of the typical play-development workshop in Canada, "Where's the Thrust? Putting Your Finger on the Conceptual Framework," *Theatrum* 14 (June/July/August 1989), 21–24.

33. Michael Devine, "Tarragon: Playwrights Talk Back," *Theatrum* 9 (Spring 1988), 14, 15, 14.

34. Quoted on the back cover of Jason Sherman, *The Retreat* (Toronto: Playwrights Canada, 1996). All parenthetical references to the play are to this edition.

35. Jonathan Dollimore, "Shakespeare, Cultural Materialism, and the New Historicism," in *Political Shakespeare: New Essays in Cultural Materialism*, ed. Jonathan Dollimore and Alan Sinfield (Ithaca: Cornell University Press, 1985), 13.

36. Ian Prinsloo, quoted in Jill Lawless, "Failed Messiah Visits Writers in The Retreat," *Now* (Toronto), 22 February 1996.

5 THE WOOSTER GROUP

1. The group of artists who began working under the direction of Elizabeth LeCompte as a splinter group of Richard Schechner's Performance Group in 1975 was officially constituted as The Wooster Group in 1980. Since then, working out of the tiny Performing Garage on Wooster Street in New York's SoHo district, the group's core members have included Jim Clayburgh, Willem Dafoe, Spalding Gray, Elizabeth LeCompte, Peyton Smith, Kate Valk, and the late Ron Vawter. Of these, only Kate Valk, as actor and dramaturg, and Elizabeth LeCompte, as director, were involved in the final versions of *House/Lights*, though Peyton Smith worked on its development.

2. Elinor Fuchs, "Another Version of Pastoral," *The Death of Character: Perspectives on Theater After Modernism* (Bloomington and Indianapolis: Indiana University Press, 1996), 92–107.

3. Susan Bennett, *Performing Nostalgia: Shifting Shakespeare and the Contemporary Past* (London: Routledge, 1996), 5. Bennett acknowledges, quoting David Lowenthal, that "the left no less than the

right espouses nostalgia" (Lowenthall, "Nostalgia Tells It Like It Wasn't," in Malcolm Chase and Christopher Shaw, eds., *The Imagined Past: History and Nostalgia* [Manchester: Manchester University Press, 1989], 27), but she argues convincingly that even in its left-wing manifestations, the cultural work nostalgia performs is, in both her senses, conservative. She also cites Fred Davis, *Yearning for Yesterday: A Sociology of Nostalgia* (New York: The Free Press, 1979), 112.

4. For neo-cubist see Ben Brantley, "A Case for Cubism and Deals with Devils," *New York Times*, late edn., 3 February 1999; for interrogative see Hervé Guay, "Les plaisirs des choses complexes," *Le Devoir* (Montreal), 29–30 May 1999; for incomprehensible see David Kaufman, "'House/Lights' not a Shining Hour: Meanings are Dim in Wooster Group's Offbeat Faust Tale," *Daily News* (New York), 3 February 1999; and for "explosive multimedia deconstructions" see Jonathan Kalb, review of *House/Lights*, *New York Press*, 10–16 February 1999.

5. Brantley, "A Case for Cubism."

6. David Savran, *The Wooster Group, 1975–1985: Breaking the Rules* (Ann Arbor: UMI Research, 1986), 170.

7. *Doctor Faustus Lights the Lights* has since been staged by, among others, the Judson Poet's Theatre in 1978, Richard Foreman in 1982, and Robert Wilson in 1992. See Betsy Alayne Ryan, *Gertrude Stein's Theatre of the Absolute* (Ann Arbor: UMI Research, 1984), 165–89 for a chronological listing, and 191 for reviews of productions.

8. Richard Kostelanetz, ed., *Gertrude Stein Advanced: An Anthology of Criticism* (Jefferson, NC: McFarland, 1990), xi.

9. See Philip Auslander, *From Acting to Performance* (London: Routledge, 1997), 59.

10. Bonnie Marranca, "Introduction: Presence of Mind," in Gertrude Stein, *Last Operas and Plays*, ed. Carl Van Vechten (Baltimore: Johns Hopkins University Press, 1995), xxi.

11. On the distinction between the avant garde and the alternative see Renate Usmiani, *Second Stage: The Alternative Theatre Movement in Canada* (Vancouver: University of British Columbia Press, 1983), 1–2.

12. Kate Valk, quoted in Chris Conti, "Double Talk: The Wooster Group's Kate Valk," *Columbus Alive* (Columbus, OH), 8–14 October 1997, 12.

13. William Carlos Williams, "The Work of Gertrude Stein," in Kostelanetz, *Gertrude Stein Advanced*, 20.

14. Quoted in Auslander, *From Acting*, 71–72, citing Savran, *Wooster Group*, 39.

15. It must be acknowledged that *Doctor Faustus Lights the Lights* is not normally considered to be one of Stein's "landscape plays" (which

Ryan considers to be the plays of her "second period of playwriting" [51]; she groups *Doctor Faustus* . . . with other plays written after
1932 as her "last period," comprising "plays as narratives" [55]).
The play nevertheless evolves out of the earlier work and shares
many dramaturgical features with it. It may be worth noting that,
whether consciously invoking Stein or not, LeCompte explains the
appeal to her of a famous acid-assisted rehearsal for *LSD (. . . Just
the High Points)* . . . by saying "I just knew there was something about
landscapes" (quoted in Savran, *Wooster Group*, 196).

16. Fuchs, "Another Version of Pastoral," 92.
17. Stein, quoted in Ryan, *Gertrude Stein's Theatre*, 22–23 ("a definitely
    American thing"), 1 ("Nothing really moves in a landscape but
    things are there"), and xlvii ("always in relation)."
18. Marranca, "Introduction: Presence of Mind," xxvi–xxvii.
19. LeCompte, quoted in Savran, *Wooster Group*, 53.
20. Savran, *Wooster Group*, 54.
21. Stein, quoted in Ryan, *Gertrude Stein's Theatre*, 25.
22. William C. Demastes, *Theatre of Chaos: Beyond Absurdism into
    Orderly Disorder* (Cambridge: Cambridge University Press, 1998);
    Tom Stoppard, *Arcadia* (London: Faber and Faber, 1993).
23. Fuchs, "Another Version of Pastoral," 95.
24. Peter Sellars, Foreword to Savran, *Wooster Group*, xv.
25. Fuchs, "Another Version of Pastoral," 95.
26. Ibid., 103.
27. Jane Palatini Bowers, *"They Watch Me as They Watch This": Gertrude
    Stein's Metadrama* (Philadelphia: University of Pennsylvania Press,
    1991), 102.
28. Baz Kershaw, "The Politics of Performance in a Postmodern Age,"
    in *Analyzing Performance: A Critical Reader*, ed. Patrick Campbell
    (Manchester: Manchester University Press, 1996), 133–52.
29. Charles R. Simpson, *SoHo: The Artists in the City* (Chicago: Uni-
    versity of Chicago Press, 1981), 1–5.
30. Sharon Zutkin, *Loft Living: Culture and Capital in Urban Change*
    (Baltimore: Johns Hopkins University Press, 1982); Barbara
    Ehrenreich and John Ehrenreich, "The Professional-Managerial
    Class," in *Between Labour and Capital*, ed. Pat Walker (Montreal:
    Black Rose Books, 1979), 5–45.
31. Zutkin, *Loft Living*, 16.
32. Ibid., 4.
33. Ibid., 17.
34. Jim Stratton, *Pioneering in the Urban Wilderness* (New York: Urizon,
    1977).
35. Simpson, *SoHo*, 1.
36. Quoted in Savran, *Wooster Group*, 50.
37. LeCompte, quoted in Robert Coe, "Making Two Lives and a
    Trilogy," *The Village Voice*, 11 December 1978.

38. Mindy Levine, *New York's Other Theatre: A Guide to Off Off Broadway* (New York: Avon, 1981), 5.

39. Ruth Leon, *Applause: New York's Guide to the Performing Arts* (New York: Applause, 1991), 92.

40. Chuck Lawliss, *New York's Other Theatre Guide* (New York: Rutledge [sic], 1991), 246.

41. Mike Steele, "Combination of Stein, Soft Porn is Beguiling," *Star Tribune*, 22 November 1997.

42. Brantley, "A Case for Cubism."

43. David Savran, "Revolution…History…Theatre: The Politics of the Wooster Group's Second Trilogy," in *The Performance of Power: Theatrical Discourses and Politics*, ed. Sue-Ellen Case and Janelle Reinelt (Iowa City: University of Iowa Press, 1991), 53.

44. Thornton Wilder was a friend of Gertrude Stein, and acknowledged her influence in the composition for *Our Town*, a play that was also subject early on to Wooster Group deconstruction in *Route 1 & 9*.

45. Nietzche, quoted in Savran, *Wooster Group*, vii.

46. Kate Valk, at the "Café des artistes du Monument-National," Theatre Festival of the Americas," 28 May 1999.

47. Mark Fisher, "Funny Peculiar," *The List* (Glasgow and Edinburgh), 25 May–8 June 1999.

48. Richard Ades, "Stimulating," *The Other Paper* (Columbus, Ohio), 16–22 October 1997.

49. Achy Obejas, "Wooster Group stuns the crowd with 'HOUSE/LIGHTS'," *Chicago Tribune*, 14 November 1997.

50. Obejas, "Wooster Group."

51. Fisher, "Funny Peculiar."

52. Jean-Louis Perrier, "De New York à la Bastille, les feux de la rampe enflamment le théâtre," *Le Monde*, 14 December 1999.

53. Jean-Pierre Bourcier, "Docteur Faust, vidéos et petites pépées," *La Tribune*, 13 December 1999.

54. Elisabeth Mahoney, "A World Apart," *The Guardian*, 5 June 2000.

55. Molly Grogan, "'House/Lights' A Postmodern Dance with Technology," *Paris Free Voice*, December 1999–January 2000.

56. R.S., "Culture et la lumière Faust: La pièce du Wooster Group de New York jette sur le mythe un élaifage désaxé," *Liberation*, 10 December 1999.

57. Bourcier, "Docteur Faust."

58. See Robert Thomson, "Way Back: Following a 2-Year Lottery-Funded Redevelopment. Tramway Relaunches with an International Programme," *City Live*, 6 June–5 August 2000; and Neil Cameron, "Design: Tramway," *The Scotsman*, 12 June 2000.

59. Jackie McGlone, "Back on track: The Tramway Celebrates its Face-lift with a Programme as Eclectic and Exciting as Those Which Put it on the Map," *Scotland on Sunday*, 28 May 2000.

60. Thomson, "Way Back."
61. Joyce McMillan, "Lights, Camera, Interaction: The Wooster Group are in Exhilarating Tune with their Times," *The Scotsman*, 12 June 2000.
62. See Mark Brown, "Theatre: House/Lights," *Scotland on Sunday*, 18 June 2000. Contradicting "a willingly enraptured press corps" who welcomed the Wooster Group as the ideal way of reopening the Tramway, Brown wrote: "I'm sorry to rain on a long and eagerly awaited parade, but I just don't buy the promotion of sexy technology over theatrical purpose which characterizes this work from intriguing beginning to exasperatingly unfulfilling end."
63. Nicky Agate, "Stage proves a Valk in the Park," *Sunday Herald*, 11 June 2000; Eddie Gibb, "Power Struggle," *Sunday Herald*, 4 June 2000.
64. Agate "Stage"; Brown, "Theatre: House/Lights."
65. Neil Cooper, "Scottish Theatre: House/Lights," *The Times*, 16 June 2000.
66. Elisabeth Mahoney, "Devil and the Detail," *The Guardian*, 10 June 2000; McMillan, "Lights, Camera, Interaction."
67. LeCompte, quoted in Fisher, "Funny Peculiar."

6 THE ENGLISH SHAKESPEARE COMPANY

1. Bill Taylor, "Revival of Absurdist Farce Exhilarating, *The Toronto Star*, 2 March 1988; Ray Conlogue, "Pendulum's Daft Swings Deft but Mostly Dated," *The Globe and Mail* (Toronto), 3 March 1988.
2. See, for example, Michael Billington, *The Guardian*, 4 May 1988; Sheridan Morley, *Punch*, 20 May 1988; and Christopher Edwards, *The Spectator*, 14 May 1988.
3. Peter Roberts, *Plays International* 6, no. 2 (Sep. 1990), 21.
4. Ray Conlogue, "Much Smoke, Little Fire," *The Globe and Mail* (Toronto), 10 January 1991.
5. Kenneth Hurren, *Mail on Sunday*, 9 December 1990; Jane Edwardes, *Time Out*, 12 December 1990; Jeremy Kingston, *The Times*, 6 December 1990; Lynne Truss, *The Independent on Sunday*, 9 December 1990.
6. Rod Currie, "Pedigrees Can't Save a Tired Play," *Vancouver Sun*, 9 March 1991; Geoff Chapman, "Time and the Conways Saved by its Skilful Cast," *The Toronto Star*, 27 February 1991; Currie; Ray Conlogue, "Time and the Oliviers," *The Globe and Mail* (Toronto), 28 February 1991.
7. Philip C. McGuire, review of Barbara Hodgdon, *Shakespeare in Performance. Henry IV, Part Two. Essays in Theatre/etudes théâtrales* 16, no. 1 (Nov. 1997), 103, quoting Barbara Hodgdon, *Shakespeare*

in Performance. Henry IV, Part Two (Manchester: Manchester University Press, 1993), 123.

8. Michael Bogdanov and Michael Pennington, *The English Shakespeare Company. The Story of 'The Wars of the Roses' 1986–1989* (London: Nick Hern, 1990), xi–xiv; Bogdanov and Pennington, *English Shakespeare Company*, 23; Michael Bogdanov, quoted in Ralph Berry, *On Directing Shakespeare: Interviews with Contemporary Directors* (London: Hamish Hamilton, 1989), 221.

9. Bogdanov and Pennington, *English Shakespeare Company*, xiv.

10. Ibid., 3, 4; Bogdanov quoted in Marianne Ackerman, "Mirvish, Marx, and Shakespeare," *Canadian Theatre Review* (Spring 1987), 63.

11. Bogdanov in Berry, *On Directing Shakespeare*, 217.

12. Bodganov and Pennington, *English Shakespeare Company*, 21, 6.

13. Ibid., 4, 6.

14. Ibid., 7, 75, 21, 65.

15. John C. Lindsay, *Royal Alexandra: The Finest Theatre on the Continent/The Old Vic: The Most Famous Theatre in the World* (Erin, Ontario: Boston Mills, 1986), 3. See also D. F. Cheshire, Sean McCarthy, and Hilary Norris, *The Old Vic Refurbished* (London: The Old Vic, 1983).

16. Honest Ed Mirvish, *How to Build an Empire on an Orange Crate or 121 Lessons I Never Learned in School* (Toronto: Key Porter, 1993), 92.

17. Ibid., 179.

18. Ibid., 179–80, emphasis in original.

19. Bogdanov, in Berry, *On Directing Shakespeare*, 221.

20. Ibid., 221.

21. Cheshire et al., *The Old Vic Refurbished*, 34; Marvin Carlson, *Theatre Semiotics: Signs of Life* (Bloomington: Indiana University Press, 1990), 70. I am drawing on Carlson's detailed semiotic analysis of the Old Vic, pages 56–74, throughout this paragraph.

22. Carlson, *Theatre Semiotics*, 72.

23. Francis X. Clines, "Updating the Bard with Falstaff in Pin Stripes at the Old Vic," *The New York Times*, 26 April 1987, 35; Giles Gordon *London Daily News*, 23 March 1987; Michael Coveney, *Financial Times*, 23 March 1987.

24. Bogdanov in Berry, *On Directing Shakespeare*, 218.

25. Christopher Edwards, *The Spectator*, 28 March 1987.

26. Mirvish, *How to Build on Empire*, 175.

27. Andrew Rissik, "The Henry Trilogy," *Plays and Players*, March 1987, 11.

28. Ackerman, *Mirvish, Marx, and Shakespeare*, 64.

29. Jon Kaplan, *Now* (Toronto), 21–27 May 1987.

30. Robert Crew, "The Henrys Marathon an Enriching Event," *The Toronto Star*, 25 May 1987; David Prosser, "The Henrys: Staircase to Power," *The Whig-Standard* (Kingston, ON), 30 May 1987; Kaplan, *Now*.

31. *Royal Alexandra Theatre Backstage* (April–May 1987), 3.

32. Ibid., 3.

33. Ray Conlogue, "Henrys Shun Elizabethan Nostalgia," *The Globe and Mail* (Toronto), 25 May 1987. Bob Pennington, "O Henry, How You Do Go On!" *The Toronto Sun*, 25 May 1987; Prosser, "The Henrys,"; *Royal Alexandra Theatre*, 3.

34. Bogdanov, quoted in Ray Conlogue,"The Cheerful Iconoclast who Shakes up Shakespeare," *The Globe and Mail* (Toronto), 19 May 1987; Bogdanov in Berry, *On Directing Shakespeare*, 218.

35. Bogdanov and Pennington, *English Shakespeare Company*, 48.

36. Ibid., 31.

37. See Daniel Statt, "The Case of the Mohocks: Rake Violence in Augustan London," *Social History* 20.2 (May 1995), 179–200.

38. Bogdanov and Pennington, *English Shakespeare Company*, 89.

39. Ibid., 90, ellipses in original.

40. Ibid., 91, 92.

41. John Bemrose, "Turned on Shakespeare," *Macleans* 100, no. 22 (1 June 1987), 54.

42. Pennington, "O Henry."

7 INTERNATIONAL FESTIVALS

1. Ritsaert ten Cate, "Festivals: Who Needs 'Em?", *Theatre Forum* 1, (1992), 86–87.

2. Dennis Kennedy, "The Language of the Spectator," *Shakespeare Survey* 50 (1997), 29–40; and "Shakespeare and Cultural Tourism," *Theatre Journal* 50, no. 2 (1998), 175–88.

3. Anthony Thorncroft, "Rewards in a Cultural Maelstrom," *Financial Times*, 14 August 1999.

4. John Coulbourn, "Christ on the Quay," *Toronto Sun*, 25 April 1998.

5. Thorncroft.

6. Ger Fitzgibbon, review of the Edinburgh Festival 1990, *Theatre Ireland* 23 (Fall 1990), 54.

7. I am grateful to Jacquie P. A. Thomas, the Artistic Director of Toronto's theatre gargantua and a member of the Canadian delegation, for the information in this paragraph.

8. David Graver and Loren Kruger, "Locating Theatre: Regionalism and Interculturalism at Edinburgh," *Performing Arts Journal* 15, no. 2 (1993), 84.

9. Ibid., 84, 71, 71.

10. Peter Stallybrass and Allon White, *The Poetics and Politics of Transgression* (Ithaca: Cornell University Press, 1986), 27.

11. Stallybrass and White, *Poetics and Politics*, 28, 30, 36, 30, 37, 43.

12. The information in this paragraph is drawn from Guy Masterson, "Assembly in Jeopardy," *The Stage* (Edinburgh), 5 August 1999, 11.

13. Alex Thomson, "Bridging the Festivals," *Three Weeks* (Edinburgh), 11 August 1999.

14. Rupert Christiansen, "Older and Much Wiser," *The Daily Telegraph*, 30 August 1999.

15. Thom Dibdin, "Lower Depths Scales Stunning New Heights," *Evening News* (Edinburgh), 25 August 1999.

16. Jeremy Kingston, review of Maxim Gorky's *The Lower Depths*, *The Scotsman*, 26 August 1999.

17. Jocelyn Clark, "How the Irish Mounted a Theatrical Renaissance," *The Toronto Star*, 18 April 1998, M16.

18. Lyn Gardner, "Bring on the Dancing Pigs," review of Enda Walsh's *Disco Pigs*, August 1997, included without attribution in the DuMaurier World Stage press kit, April 1998.

19. Mary Leland, rev. of Enda Walsh's *Disco Pigs*, *Irish Times*, 1 October 1996.

20. Seán Conolly, "Tough Task has been Set for Judges," *Examiner* (Dublin), 11 October 1996; Siobhan Cronin, "Tearaway Trip that Needs to be Taken," *Irish Independent*, 9 October 1996, my emphasis.

21. Alastair Macauley, "All Smiles 'n Tears," *Financial Times*, 16 August 1997.

22. Neil Cooper, "Love's First Dance," *Scotland on Sunday*, 3 August 1997; Cooper, "Take a Taxi Ride to the Traverse and Catch Some of the Most Exciting Theatre Premieres of the Fringe," *Scotland on Sunday*, 10 August 1997.

23. One oddity in Toronto – or for Canadian audiences anywhere – was the disconcerting familiarity of the pre-show music, by Canadian singer-songwriter Ron Sexsmith, music which I would have assumed had been used to generate local resonances in Toronto had the same music not been used elsewhere.

24. Kate Taylor, "Teen Rancour Ends Up Hogging All the Intensity," *The Globe and Mail* (Toronto), 20 April 1998; John Coulbourn, "It's All Pig Latin to this Reviewer," *Toronto Sun*, 20 April 1998.

25. Geoff Chapman, "Urban Piggies Root Out a Pain-filled Life," *The Toronto Star*, 19 April 1999.

26. Coulbourn, "It's all Pig Latin."

27. Clark, "How the Irish Mounted a Theatrical Renaissance."

28. Enda Walsh, *Disco Pigs* & *Sucking Dublin* (London: Nick Hern, 1997), 22.

CONCLUSION

1. Peter Marks, "For Tony Kushner, an Eerily Prescient Return," *New York Times*, 25 November 2001.
2. See Richard Paul Knowles, "From Nationalist to Multinational: The Stratford Festival, Free Trade, and the Discourses of Intercultural Tourism," *Theatre Journal* 47, no. 1 (March 1995), 19–41. Reprinted as Chapter I of Ric Knowles, *Shakespeare and Canada: Essays in Production, Translation, and Adaptation* (Brussels: P. I. E. Peter Lang, 2003).

Index